Flaming Floorboards and

By St

GH01454463

Steve@rand

First Print Edition 2013

This book is dedicated to my father,

who taught me a love of all things mechanical.

And to my wife,

who has patiently endured the results.

Table of Contents

Introduction

Over the years, I've met a great many full-fledged car nuts. These are the guys (and for some reason they are almost always guys) who can tell you the compression ratio of every engine Ferrari/Chevy/Ford/Chrysler (pick one) ever built. They spend hours every weekend polishing their own car, and they devour every issue of every car magazine, lusting over photos of the newest Ferrari, Chevy, Ford, or Chrysler. I am not one of these people. On my best day, I could maybe qualify as a semi-fledged car nut. I can tell you the compression ratio of a Model A Ford, and I wash my own car at least once a year. Or at least, that's my goal. I'm afraid I don't lust after new cars, though. Never have. I did buy my wife a new car once, but that was because the numbers made sense. When I estimated the satisfaction she would get from a new car compared to the satisfaction promised by a used car, integrated the satisfaction over the expected life of the vehicle, divided it by the purchase price, and took into account the dealer financing incentives, the new car won. Besides, my wife wanted the new car.

It's not that I don't like new cars. It's just that I'm an engineer. A gearhead. I look at a car and see a very clever device designed to transport people from Point A to Point B. Shiny paint, built-in DVD players, and rich Corinthian leather do not affect its practicality. Unlike a pure gearhead, however, I do appreciate the fact that it can be a lot of fun to drive from Point A to Point B. And in a travesty of logic that would cause Spock to raise his eyebrows so high his nose turned up, I pay lip service to reliability while secretly regarding anything that breaks as an engineering challenge. This assumes that whatever breaks is something I can fix, which means it must be something mechanical. I'm a mechanical engineer. I can't look at a microchip and see clever engineering, and I certainly can't fix it if it goes bad. I can, however, appreciate the unique, some would say bizarre design of an MGB choke linkage, and if that breaks (which is more than likely) I can fix it by the side of the road and be on my way again in a jiffy! And when I look at the cotter pin which Henry Ford put in the drain hole of the Model A clutch housing, I shudder because I'm in the presence of genius. Anyone can drill a drain hole, but drain holes tend to clog with dirt. By putting a cotter pin through the hole, and by leaving it loose so it would rattle around as the car shook (and believe me, a Model A will shake), Henry invented the self-cleaning drain hole! So what if the thing drips oil all over your driveway. The owner's manual says you should count your blessings if you get more than 500 miles to the quart. That hole isn't just a leak, it's an elegant engineering solution! New cars employ very sophisticated technology and are marvels of engineering, but they don't have the elegant simplicity of that Model A cotter pin. So when I look at a brand new car and see shiny paint, a top that won't come off, and a lot of electronics which probably aren't going to break but which couldn't be repaired if they did, I don't see fun and I don't see elegance. Cup holders, air conditioning, surround sound, digital satellite navigation system – these might be nice to have if it's pouring down rain and driving is no fun anyway, but why would you want a car like that on a sunny day? But show me a nice, clapped out MG TC and wow! Cut down doors, fold down windscreen, worm and peg steering, chronometric gauges – the opportunities for fun and breakdowns are almost limitless! Not only that, it's got an emergency hand crank! I can start that sucker even if the battery is dead!

Even when I was a kid in high school my taste in automobiles was a bit off the beaten track. The teen years are the age when a young man's fancy is supposed to turn to bellowing exhausts and squealing tires. Since I was a teenager in the 60s, the golden age of muscle cars, there was no shortage of potential dream cars. My classmates were literally foaming at the mouth in automotive ecstasy. They spent hours debating the relative merits of Mustangs, Camaros, Corvettes, Super Birds, and GTO's. Somehow, those cars always looked a bit silly to me. Like a Hollywood starlet who's had so many breast implants she looks more like a parody than a paramour, I'd look at the hood scoops, racing decals, and jacked up rear ends on muscle cars and I just couldn't take them seriously. My fantasy was a Stanley Steamer. Any Stanley would do, but what I really lusted after was a 1906 Gentleman's Speedy Roadster. Looking back, it may not have been a coincidence that I didn't get many dates.

In the years since then I've owned a fair variety of cars from almost every decade of the 20'th century. Fords, Chevys, MGs, Jaguars, and many other contrivances have graced my garage. I've also had at least a passing acquaintance with Ferraris, Bentleys, Shelbys, Renaults, Peugeots, Fiats, Triumphs, and more. I've worked as a professional mechanic, pitted for some of the least successful racing teams in history, and owned the only running MGA on the island of Guam. I'm not a car collector, carefully restoring vintage automobiles to gem-like perfection and trailering them to elegant car shows. I'm a gearhead who has a masochistic obsession with patching up junk cars and relying on them for daily transportation. If the junk car happens to be 50 or 60 years old, so much the better. I've had a lot of fun with these cars. I've also sat by the side of the road with broken pistons, blown engines, and dysfunctional differentials. I've told my family and friends about these adventures so often they shouted "For God's sake! Go bore someone else with these stories!" And so I wrote this book.

I'd like to make it clear that this book is not a memoir. Jack Benny opened his long running radio career with the words "This is Jack Benny talking. There will now be a slight pause while you say 'Who Cares?'" Obviously, Jack knew his audience. I'm no Jack Benny, but I know that no one wants to read a memoir written by someone they've never heard of. This book is not about me. It parallels one portion of my life, but I've done many things that aren't in this book, a few of which might actually count in my favor. This book is about the motley assortment of cars that have covered my hands with grease, and about the extraordinary cast of characters I've met while fooling with these junkers. Sadly, one car that is missing from this collection is a Stanley Steamer. I've seen them in museums, looked longingly at ads in antique car magazines, and gasped when I learned the price, but I've never owned one. Of course, the story isn't over yet. Who knows? Maybe if enough people buy this book . . .

Stanley Gentleman's Speedy Roadster

A brief comment on truthfulness. The vehicles and events in this book are true, at least as I remember them. Someone else might remember them differently or, more to the point, wish that I'd remembered them differently. Some might simply wish I'd had the good sense to keep my mouth shut. I realize some people might not want their friends or family to know they were ever associated with the cars and events described in this book, and some authors (me, for one) might not want to spend years in court defending themselves against lawsuits. For that reason I have altered the names of all the people and some of the locations in this book. Since I was already fibbing about the names, I occasionally took the liberty of fibbing about a few more things, such as emphasizing a personality quirk, shuffling time sequences, or making up dialog that is probably pretty close to what was said at the time. The stories are true. The cars are true. The people are, mostly true. So, if you think you recognize someone in this book and you're shocked by what you read, it probably isn't true.

Note: The illustrations in this printed book are black and white. Full color illustrations may be seen at www.random-writings.com.

Chapter 1 – My Father's Cars

A small, Amish town in northern Indiana is probably the last place you'd expect to find a honky-tonk pool shark serving as the Episcopal parish priest, but that's exactly what we had in Father Dupree. He got the calling late in life. Before that he kicked around depression-era Chicago for a number of years, playing ragtime piano in speakeasies. He supplemented this erratic income by hustling pool in the dives that surrounded the speakeasies. Later he worked as a newspaper reporter, another profession whose ranks are not known for their strict observance of the Ten Commandments. Then, as if to prove that there were no depths to which he would not stoop, he tried his hand at being a writer. These forays into the shadows made his sermons a little more interesting than those given by ministers who only knew about sin from book learning. His background also allowed him to spice up the choir practice every now and then by playing "Sugar Blues" and other ragtime hits. He kept a pool table in the parish hall basement, much to the delight of the acolytes. Whenever we got to thinking we were getting good at the game he'd pick up a cue and run the table. "Always leave yourself a good setup, and never give your opponent an opportunity to shoot" were his words of pastoral advice as he taught us these lessons in humility. I have no idea how he hid that table from the bishop during his annual visits. Maybe he didn't even try. It was no great secret that Fr. Dupree wasn't impressed by authority figures. Once, during his annual visit, the bishop whispered something in Fr. Dupree's ear just as the processional was about to begin. Fr. Dupree whispered a reply and the bishop disappeared. The acolytes looked at each other in stunned silence. We always started the service exactly on time. A delay like this was unthinkable. Fr. Dupree turned to face us, his hands pressed together in the prayer position, and the most pious look imaginable on his face. Then he solemnly announced "His Eminence desires to urinate."

Despite his disregard for authority, and despite the fact that he had his own ideas about how to run things, he had enough street smarts to recognize the real power of the parish - the Ladies of the Church. The Ladies were a group of elderly widows and spinsters whose donations of time, talent, and money were essential to keeping the church going. I suspect it was their idea to celebrate the first day of Epiphany with a high tea, an event which demanded fine china, formal attire, and excruciatingly correct behavior. In my mother's words, everything had to be "nice." My mother dreaded this pompous event but she knew it was important to Fr. Dupree so she dutifully attended every year. This led to the infamous Epiphany Tea Incident.

At the time, my mother was driving a 1941 Buick Sport Coupe. She had inherited this car from my grandfather, and it's one of the first cars I can remember. It was beautiful. Long, sleek, with a tiny back seat and an enormous steering wheel. The hood seemed to stretch to the horizon, and it had to because it covered a straight-eight engine. The one vice that this car had, besides the fact that every kid in town wanted to race it at stop lights, was that once you shut it off it would refuse to restart until it had cooled down. There was only one way to start the car when it got into one of these moods, and that was to open the hood and squirt some gas into the carburetor. Ever resourceful and always the good husband, my dad gave my mother an oil can full of gas just for this purpose.

1941 Buick Coupe

One sunny January afternoon my mom dressed in her 50's finest – white dress, pillbox hat, high heels, and long white gloves – and set out for the Epiphany Tea. In the middle of town she somehow stalled the car at the intersection of Main and Lincoln. A cold dread came over her as she tried to restart the car. I think everyone who has ever driven an old car knows the feeling. You know instinctively that the car is not going to start. It's let you down this way time and time again, but somehow you keep hoping that this time it's going to be different. This time the car will start.

"Ruh-Ruh-Ruh-Ruh-Rurrrrrr. Ruh-Ruh-Ruh-Ruh-Rurrrrrr." The Buick cranked over without even a cough to indicate it might start. Traffic was beginning to back up. Shoppers walking on the sidewalk stopped to watch the drama unfold. A police car stopped and the officer asked if he could help.

"I can call for a tow truck" the officer volunteered.

"I just need to squirt some gas in the carburetor" my mother explained.

"Oh, you're out of gas?" Either the officer didn't understand my mother's explanation or he didn't believe she knew what she was talking about. He walked back toward his patrol car. With a disgusted sigh my mother got out of the car and threw open the hood. In her white gloves and pillbox hat she used her little oil can to squirt gas into the carburetor. Then she slammed the hood and got back into the car. The policeman was just pulling a can of gas out of his trunk when she started the car and drove off.

The next weekend my dad installed a thin copper tube from the carburetor to the dashboard so she could squirt gas into the carb without leaving her seat. She appreciated the effort, but it wasn't enough. Somehow she regarded it as his fault that her car broke down on Main Street. He didn't get out of the doghouse until he disassembled the entire fuel system, cleaning and examining every piece, and found the problem. There was a kink in the fuel line, hidden behind a mounting clamp,. He replaced that line and the problem went away.

To me, disassembling the fuel system seemed like an awful lot of work for only a marginal improvement. It always started if you squirted gas in it, and running the pipe to the dashboard meant you didn't even have to get out of the car to do that! It is only now that I realize how this incident foreshadowed hundreds of similar incidents in my life. I should have learned back then that to some people, wives especially, reliability means something more than the fact that a car is easy to fix after it breaks. Some people don't place the same value on resourcefulness that I do, and sometimes even trivial events can land you in the doghouse. I'm tempted to offer a sweeping generalization and say this represents a difference between men and women, but I've met some men who were finicky that way, too. Maybe my father and I just saw things differently because we were engineers.

The Epiphany Tea incident did have a postscript. Several years after Mom sold the Buick, two of the Ladies of the Church were involved in an episode which partially made up for the high teas they inflicted on my mother and Father Dupree. Every year they took a trip to New York City, where they enjoyed staying in a fine hotel, eating at proper restaurants, and taking in a Broadway show. In the late 1960's they bought tickets to a musical based solely on its reputation as a smash hit. It was called "Hair." Dressed in their finest evening clothes, these two Midwestern Grand Dames headed to the theater. They forgot to bring their opera glasses that year, and seated in the balcony, they couldn't see the stage very well. They also couldn't understand much of the dialog, as the actors were using slang terms that were unfamiliar to them, but they gamely sat through the performance. Well into the second half of the musical, one of them leaned forward, squinted at the stage, and then gasped in horror. "Why they aren't wearing any clothes!!" I suspect that to this day the actors wonder why the balcony erupted in laughter that night.

I know from family lore that when I was born my dad owned a 1932 Ford Coupe, the model immortalized by the Beach Boys as a "Little Deuce Coupe." Today I would love to have that car, but at the time I was too young to appreciate it. My parents named this car "Elmer." (I suspect that Mom was the one who named it. Dad wasn't the type to give names to mechanical contrivances.) Mom always remembered Elmer as a fun car; the car they drove when they were impoverished but deliriously happy newlyweds struggling to make ends meet while dad worked his way through college on the GI bill. After scraping through the depression Mom and Dad graduated from high school just in time for World War 2. My dad flew combat missions in a B-24, so Mom worried her way through the war. When the war ended they were safe, they were together, and they had a car. My dad wasn't quite as romantic about Elmer. He remembered it as the car that would sometimes shift into two gears at once. From an engineering standpoint, the concurrent engagement of two distinct gear ratios created a set of simultaneous equations that could only be satisfied if the rotational speed was zero. From a practical standpoint, when it shifted into two gears at once the rear wheels locked up and the car skidded off the road, amid much swearing. Dad would then have to take the cover off the transmission and beat on the shifting forks until he could force it back into a single gear. This done, he could resume his drive, always keeping his eyes peeled for a safe place to land should the rear wheels lock up again. I don't believe my father remembered that car as fondly as my mother did.

I'm not certain how my dad wound up with Elmer. I suspect he may have gotten it before the war. By the time he got out of the service it was not in running condition, but cars were hard to come by so he and his father rebuilt it. While they were working on it Mom decided it was time to go to the hospital and have a baby. Dad went with her, and although back then there wasn't much for a father to do in a maternity ward he had the good sense to hang around until my older brother was born. Maternity wards had even less use for grandfathers, so my grandfather stayed home and worked on the Ford. He got it running that evening, so it passed into family lore that Elmer and my older brother were born on the same day.

The first car I remember well was my dad's green Pontiac sedan, probably of 1940s vintage. The thing I remember most about it was the hood ornament, a beautiful stylized chrome and orange plastic bust of an Indian chief. I also remember a family trip out west when we tried to drive it up a mountain to a park called Cloud Croft. Time after time we would make it half-way up the mountain, only to have the radiator boil over. We'd coast back downhill to a gas station, refill the radiator, and try again. Eventually my dad bought a canvas water bag so he could refill the radiator when it boiled over and we made it to the top of the mountain. (I suspect I remember more trips up and down the mountain than actually occurred, as my father wasn't one to make mistakes. He probably bought the water bag after the first trip.)

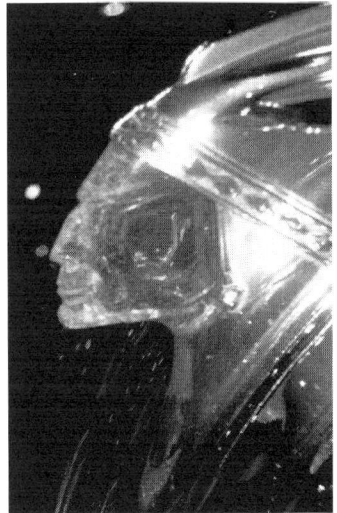

Chief Pontiac Hood Ornament

1957 was a watershed year for my father. After years of driving used cars, "other people's problems," barking his knuckles on recalcitrant transmissions and clogged fuel lines, he finally reached the point in life where he was ready to buy a new car: a two-tone gray and white Plymouth station wagon! It was, by all accounts, the worst car he ever owned. Mechanically it was sound, and the only drivability problem was the fact that Mom was constantly breaking fingernails on the push button transmission. The body, however, was a different story. You could hear the rust gnawing away at the coachwork as it sat in the driveway. The first rust holes appeared while it was still under warranty. Those were fixed by the dealer, but after 12 months or 12,000 miles, it was all ours. Within a few years the floorboards had decayed to the point where my brother and I were in danger of falling through to the pavement. Always the handyman, Dad cured the safety issue by fabricating plywood floorboards, but it was clear that this car was not destined to live a long and happy life. Ironically, when he bought that car the dealer gave him a free barbecue grill, and that was the best grill we ever owned. We were still using that grill twenty years later, long after the Plymouth had been consigned to the boneyard. When the grill finally gave up the ghost my dad seriously considered going back to the Plymouth dealer and saying "I'll never buy another car from you as long as I live, but where did you get that barbecue grill?"

My dad never bought another used car, but he never bought another Plymouth either. In 1962 he bought another new car, a two-door Ford Falcon. This model was Robert McNamara's parting gift to the Ford Motor Company. Later, Lee Iacocca would add fake cooling scoops and turn it into the wildly popular Ford Mustang, but in 1962 the Falcon was pretty prosaic. A car designed by a bean counter for bean counters and other practical persons. Strictly utilitarian, it lacked such frills as a radio, a cigarette lighter, or even a switch to turn on the dome light when you opened the door. My dad was a no-frills kind of guy himself, and an engineer to boot, so this car appealed to him. Working for Bendix he had helped develop power brakes and had the patents to prove it, but it was years before he would allow them on his car. "Just something else to go wrong" was the way he described them. The Falcon had standard brakes and a "three on the tree" 3-speed manual transmission. It transported him to and from work with no problems, and that's all he wanted. He could light his cigarettes with a Zippo and, on the rare occasions when he felt like listening to music, a transistor radio on the passenger seat suited him just fine. He liked this car so well that a few years later he bought my mom a 1964 Falcon station wagon. His one concession to creature comfort on that car was a Ford-O-Matic two-speed automatic transmission.

As a kid, I was pretty much oblivious to these cars. They were exciting for a day or two when we first bought them, and after that they were just something my parents used to drive me to scout meetings and piano lessons. I only vaguely remember the day my dad bought his Falcon, and then I remember the salesman's car better than my father's car. The salesman had a Falcon Sprint – a sport model with a V-8 engine. My older brother thought this was the coolest thing imaginable, but my father was unimpressed. He couldn't imagine why anyone would put a V-8 engine in an economy car. Not only were there four more cylinders to go bad, it drank more gas in the process. I didn't care much one way or the other about the cylinders, but I was fascinated by the fact that the salesman was missing his right hand. He still managed to steer and shift gears with the stump. Did he lose it in the war? Was it bitten off by sharks? I was dying to ask, but I knew that would be impolite so I kept quiet and pondered that question for the next 50 years.

I did have one fleeting interest in a car, but that car was owned by a neighbor. When I was eight my folks bought a summer cottage on a small lake in Michigan. "Cottage" is perhaps too grand a word for this place. It had been built as a hunting cabin in the 1920's, and although the previous owner had turned it into a year-round house by installing an oil heater and indoor plumbing, it still lacked such amenities as hot water, a roof that kept out all of the rain, and a foundation. When we bought it an abandoned outhouse graced the front yard and a giant galvanized wash tub was hanging beside the front door. Rust marks on top of the oil stove made it clear he used to heat water on the stove and pour it into the wash tub for his weekly bath. My dad, however, was able to see past these minor quirks and picture the gem that lurked within, resting on the stacked concrete blocks that substituted for a foundation. He had built our home from scratch, and in a remarkably short time he transformed this shack into a snug little paradise for the endless summer days of my childhood.

Two houses down the dirt road from our cottage was a slightly newer cottage owned by an Air Force pilot. These were the years when SAC, the Strategic Air Command, was on the front lines of the cold war. Our neighbor was a B-52 pilot, back in the days when B-52s were brand new. He was stationed in Kansas, but every June he drove his wife and kids to Michigan where they spent the summer. Near the end of the summer he would drive up to join them for a few weeks leave, and then they would all drive back to Kansas together. He had a son named Chris who was just my age and we quickly became best friends. All summer long we'd swim, fish, shoot B-B guns, and generally have a great time. In the summer of 1961 Chris's dad surprised us when he showed up for his annual vacation driving a brand new Jaguar E-Type coupe.

1961 Jaguar E-Type Coupe & E-Type Engine

8

My parents were incredulous, and I remember hushed conversations at the dinner table when they discussed rumors that he had spent nearly $6,000 for that car. Later I would learn that was more than they had paid for our cottage, but I didn't care. To me it was money well spent. That Jaguar was the most beautiful car in the world, and the fact that it would see 150 mph just added to its allure.

Like most Americans I thought it was called an "XKE," but Chris soon set me straight on that account. It was, according to the factory literature, an "E-Type," not an "XKE." More specifically, it was an "E-Type Fixed Head Coupe." (According to purists, Jaguar never made a car called an "XKE." Jaguar developed the E-Type from their legendary C-Type and D-Type race cars and not from their XK series of street cars. The name "E-Type" never caught on in the US, though, and eventually American advertising companies ignored what the factory called the car and ran ads that called it an XKE.) I knew nothing about engines, but when his dad opened the hood even I could tell that powerplant was a work of art. The exhaust note was pure music, even to my untrained ear, and the jet black bodywork gave my pre-pubescent brain its first inkling of what was meant by sex appeal. I can still hear its snarling exhaust echoing across the corn fields as Chris's dad headed back to Kansas. Sadly, his dad was killed in a midair collision a few months later, a casualty of a cold war that was anything but cold to those who fought its battles.

Chapter 2 – First Love

My twelfth birthday turned out to be a life-changing event, although it did not seem so at the time. It was on that day that I got an Aurora "Old Timers" plastic model of a 1909 Stanley Steamer. I enjoyed building the model, but what really fascinated me was the brief history of the car that was printed on the instruction sheet. I learned that Stanley Steamers were built by the Stanley Brothers, identical twins who were remarkable entrepreneurs. After making a small fortune in the photography business – they invented a dry plate process which they sold to Eastman Kodak – they became interested in horseless carriages. Not finding anything on the market that suited them, they built their own car and immediately began winning competitions with it. Soon people were begging to buy their car, so in 1897 they went into business building steam cars. By the turn of the century, they were the largest manufacturer of automobiles in the country.

To me, the car was even more remarkable than its inventors. I had never before heard of a car that ran on steam, and here was a spindly-looking two-cylinder steam car that could reach 70 mph! I wasn't sure my dad's brand new Falcon could go 70 mph. Not only that, in 1906 a Stanley race car had set the land speed record at 126 mph! I was almost certain Dad's Falcon couldn't keep up with that! According to the instructions, in 1907 the Stanleys made another attempt at the land speed record and the driver claimed the speedometer stood at 197 mph when the car hit a rough patch of sand, became airborne, and crashed. What a car! On top of everything else, steam cars were silent, required neither a starter nor a transmission, and had only 37 moving parts -- 13 of which were in the engine. Why didn't modern cars run on steam? I was hooked.

Every Wednesday night I had a Boy Scout meeting. It was held in the basement of a church next door to the Yodersburg Public Library. I wore my scout uniform to the meetings, of course. Shirt, neckerchief, shorts, knee socks, sock garters, and those strange green tufts called "flags" than hung off the garters. As soon as the meeting was over I would scoot next door to the library. It was the first Carnegie library built in Indiana, and even as a boy I was impressed by the grand staircase, marble floors, and wrought iron windows. You entered the library through a rotunda, where the ornately painted ceiling provided a Midwestern version of the Sistine

Chapel. In the center of the rotunda was the checkout desk. That's where The Librarian sat. She was a severe looking woman, with a jet black stripe in her gray hair (pulled back in a bun, of course) and ornate spectacles hanging on a gold neck chain. Nothing got past The Librarian. Once, when my scout meeting ran late, she called my parents to see if I was sick. People looked after each other in a small town. Or maybe she was just a sucker for a man in uniform. Of course, it could be that I attracted her attention because my taste in books followed the road less traveled. I was interested in World War One at the time (I still am) and after reading every WW1 book in the main library I learned how to fill out a form to get a book from the house next door where they stored their less popular books. I would pore through the index cards in the dark oak drawers of the card catalog, write down a list of the books I wanted, and when I came in the following week the books would be waiting for me. Those were the days when they stamped your library card number and the due date in the back of the book. When I got a book out of storage, it wasn't unusual to see that "30859" was the first person to check out the book since the 1930's. If it was a particularly good book there might be a whole string of "30859's" in the back. (OK. I memorized my library card number. Maybe I was just a little bit geeky back then.)

One night when I couldn't find any WW1 books that caught my interest, it occurred to me that they might have books about Stanley Steamers. They had one book, and it turned out to be one of the best books I ever read. It was a thin volume by George Woodbury called *The Story of A Stanley Steamer*. Woodbury was a wonderful storyteller who bought an abandoned Stanley in the late 1940s, years before collecting antique cars became fashionable, and restored it to roadworthy condition. His tales of driving behind steam convinced me I had to have a Stanley. Unfortunately, I had neither the money to buy a Stanley nor the license to drive one. I convinced my dad to read Woodbury's book and he became mildly interested. He wasn't obsessed with steam cars like I was, but he promised if I could find one for under $1,000 he'd buy it. Excitedly, I turned to the classified section of The Yodersburg News. I searched that paper every day, but there didn't seem to be any Stanleys for sale. None of the kids at school knew where I could buy one, even the kids who took Auto Shop and knew a lot about cars. My older brother was clueless, and even my grandfather had no suggestions as to where I could buy a Stanley. I finally decided I would have to bite the bullet and go to Knofsky's. They wouldn't have one in running condition, but I was convinced my dad could fix anything.

Officially known as "Yodersburg Auto Salvage," the local junkyard was more commonly called Knofsky's after the family that owned it. I'd never been there before. At school, it had the reputation of being the last resort for kids who were desperate to own a car but who had no money. You could buy a complete car for under $50 at Knofsky's, but you had to drag it home. With a lot of work you could sometimes get it to run, but it was never going to be "cherry." (I wasn't sure what "cherry" meant when kids talked about cars, but based on how the word was used I knew it was something good.) "Man, that car is cherry!" they would say as a particularly hot car thundered into the school parking lot. On the other hand, they'd whisper "It's a Knofsky Special" when a derelict clattered its way into a parking spot.

Actually, I had wanted to see the inside of Knofsky's for a long time. I used to scour antique shops and Army/Navy surplus stores looking for World War 1 gear, and an older gentleman in one store told me about a WW1 rotary aircraft engine that was on display in Knofsky's. Or at least it had been when he was in high school. Judging by his appearance that couldn't have been too long after the war, but if they'd had it once I couldn't imagine them ever getting rid of it. Think of the crowds it would draw! On a Saturday morning I mounted my trusty Schwinn Hornet and pedaled my way to Knofsky's.

Saturday morning turned out to be a bad time to go to a junkyard. There was a line of men waiting for their turn at the counter, most of them carrying mysterious greasy objects. The walls were lined with shelves of car parts. At least, I assumed they were car parts. I didn't know much about cars at the time. I pretended to look at them while waiting for the crowd to thin out. There was something vaguely unsettling about these objects, vital bits of car innards that had been ripped from the bodies of automobiles that had once motored serenely down Main Street. Some of them were still oozing oil onto the shelving or, worse yet, a mysterious red fluid. I didn't want to know what that was.

"Can I help you, kid?" A voice called out from behind the counter, and I suddenly realize all the other customers had left.

"You got any Stanleys out back?" I asked, as nonchalantly as possible. I'd learned not to appear too anxious while looking at World War 1 stuff in antique stores. If they knew you really wanted something, they wouldn't negotiate the price.

"Any WHAT?" He almost shouted this question.

"Stanleys. Stanley Steamers" I said, still trying to act uninterested.

He stared at me for a long time. "Kid, we ain't never had any Stanley Steamers in our lot."

"Oh. OK. Just thought I'd ask." He was still staring at me and I was trying desperately to think of something to say to show him I wasn't a complete idiot. Something to show I knew my way around junkyards. Especially this junkyard.

"I see you got rid of your rotary engine" I said casually.

"My what?" He was staring at me again.

"Your rotary aircraft engine. A friend told me you had a French LeRhone rotary engine from World War 1 on display, but I don't see it."

Once again he stared at me for a long time. "Kid, I worked here over 20 years, and we never had a World War 1 engine in here."

Fortunately a customer came in, and I was able to slip out the door unnoticed. Evidently, finding a Stanley was going to be tougher than I thought. (In fact, it has turned out to be a lifelong quest.)

As the years went by and I learned more about steam cars I gradually learned that not everything I'd read about Stanleys was the Gospel truth, and even Woodbury himself was not above telling a few "stretchers" if it made a better story. Steam cars definitely had some interesting virtues, but they had their vices as well. By 1920 Ford made more cars in an afternoon than the Stanley brothers made in a year. Even the fabulous tale of the 1907 land speed attempt didn't stand up to careful scrutiny. The car was certainly moving very fast when it left the ground, but stopwatches indicated the speed was close to 150 mph. The driver's claim that the speedometer stood at 197 mph would seem to be at odds with the fact that the car didn't have a speedometer. No matter. Even if steam cars were not quite the miracle I first imagined, they were still fascinating, and my quest for steam eventually led me into the world of antique cars, swap meets, Hemming's Motor News, and more than enough characters to keep life interesting. This obsession also helped fan my interest in all things mechanical and played not an insignificant role in my eventual decision to become an engineer.

As I slogged my way through High School I never lost my passion for Stanleys, but I gradually came to terms with the idea that I wasn't going to find one any time soon. Along the way I learned to drive in my parents' Falcons and earned my driver's license, with a little help from a Driver's Ed class taught by the high school basketball coach. To this day I often hear his voice when I drive.

"When you're making a left hand turn, pull up to the manhole cover and wait for the traffic to clear, but don't cut your wheels until you're ready to move."

I was a bit confused the first time I tried to turn at an intersection that didn't have a manhole cover, but I soon learned to estimate where the middle of the intersection was.

"If you're turning onto a street with more than one lane, always turn into the near lane. That way cars coming from the other direction can turn into the other lane. He can turn, and you can turn."

I hear those words replayed every time I have to slam on the brakes to avoid hitting some idiot who swings wide into my lane.

Initially, it seemed like there was an impossible list of driving rules to memorize. Then one Sunday morning it all came together. I was kneeling at the front of the church while Father Dupree prepared communion. There's not much for an acolyte to do at that point in the service so I had a lot of time to think. Father Dupree wanted us to think about God, but He's really not on the top ten daydream list for most teenage boys. On this particular Sunday I was thinking about the number two item on that list - cars. It was a warm summer morning and the stained glass windows were pivoted open in the vain hope that they might direct a slight breeze into the church. There was no air conditioning, of course. For one thing, this was Indiana and during the 1960's most Hoosiers viewed air conditioning as a sinful luxury. Father Dupree occasionally made disparaging comments about the "padded pew priests" at other churches, implying there was something decadent about sitting on anything softer than the black walnut pews that had served our church for over 100 years. I couldn't imagine what he'd say about the idea of air conditioning a church! We simply opened the windows and thanked the Lord for whatever breeze He provided. In the spring He sometimes provided wasps as well, and they would buzz menacingly around the acolytes while searching for a place to build a nest. Sometimes the younger, more skittish acolytes would bolt for the other side of the altar, away from the windows. Even when fleeing the wasps, however, they remembered the rules. Fr. Dupree had taught them well. They always paused to genuflect as they dashed in front of the cross.

By the time summer arrived the wasps had long since found homes elsewhere, so we had no distractions as we daydreamed our way into semi-consciousness. I was thinking about cars and Driver's Ed while half-listening to Fr. Dupree. Suddenly everything blended together! All the rules I learned in Driver's Ed could be summarized in two commandments. Father Dupree was reading from the Book of Common Prayer (the 1928 edition, of course) but I could swear his words were about driving:

"Thou shalt not endanger thy neighbor.

This is the first and greatest commandment, and the second is like onto it:

Thou shalt not impede thy neighbor's progress.

On these two commandments hang all the laws and the statutes."

Now the rules made sense! Turn into the correct lane? Rule number one. Keep right except to pass? Rule number two. Speeding? Rule number one. Driving too slow? Rule number two. Turning on your turn signal before you hit your brakes and make the guy behind you wonder what in the hell you're doing? Rules number one and two. I began to relax and enjoy driving, at least when things went right. My mom's station wagon was a breeze to drive because it had an automatic transmission, but I must confess the manual gearbox on my dad's Falcon gave me problems. I lurched that car around town in a series of fits and stalls, with much grinding of teeth – both mine and the car's.

As time went by some of my friends picked up their own cars, everything from an Opel Kadett to a Chevy Camaro. I had no interest in any of those cars, of course. Just as Don Quixote remained faithful to his unattainable Dulcinea, I remained faithful to my Stanley. Muscle cars had no appeal for me. Sports cars were foreigners' playthings. My parents, like virtually every other parent on the planet, drove mere cars, generic transportation devices unworthy of the name "automobile." Only a Stanley could satisfy my desires. That is, until a kid with the unlikely nickname of "The Bump" introduced me to the pleasures of the here and now.

I don't know how Bump got his nickname. I never asked. There is something about adolescent boys that just seems to attract nicknames, names that stick like glue through college and then fade into obscurity, except for the occasional awkward revival during class reunions. Over the coming years I would get to know The Bear, Squirrel, Buddha, Guttergums, Howdy Doody, Fuzzy, The Lone Eagle, The Phantom, Lunchbox, Baby Huey, Tarzan, and a host of other characters with interesting names, but Bump was the first. No matter where his name came from, his dad owned a 1930 Model A Tudor Sedan which Bump occasionally drove to school. It was an interesting car, but no Stanley. Then one fall weekend in 1968, my senior year in high school, The Bump and I drove to a neighboring town to look at a fully restored Model A roadster. His dad was looking for a roadster, and this one was advertised in the paper. It was a beautiful car, but the owner wanted the outrageous sum of $2800 for it. We politely examined it, but we both knew his dad would never pay that much for an old car. Then, for reasons known only to himself, the owner pulled the tarp off a project car he had sitting in his driveway. I was stuck by the thunderbolt. It was love at first sight. There in the driveway, dazzling in its brilliance was a 1928 Model A Fordor Sedan. The sun glinted off its nickel-plated bright-work, drawing a sharp contrast to the inky depths of the sinuous curves of its jet black body.

OK. So maybe the only things that glinted were my eyes as they imagined what it could look like, and the only inky depths were my ignorance of what it would take to restore the car. In truth there was more rust than nickel on its bright-work, and what remained of its black paint was buried under a thick accumulation of greasy dust. It had obviously spent several years in a barn, possibly in the company of chickens. The rubberized cloth roof was peeling back, revealing the wood framework, brown padding and, appropriately enough, chicken wire which had supported the roof when it left the factory many years ago. The back of the car showed unmistakable evidence of bodywork done with the wrong end of a ball peen hammer, the rear window was sitting in the back seat amid shards of rotten wood that had once held it in place, and the wheels were shedding the Chinese red paint that had been thickly applied with a brush several decades ago. The car would not start due to a serious accumulation of rust in the gas tank, but the owner assured us this would be easy to fix. He explained that he had bought this car to restore with his son, but his son was only interested in building a hot rod so he would be willing to part with it for about $500. I had $500 in the bank, but what would my dad say?

During the drive home I carefully rehearsed my sales pitch. Mom and Dad were sitting in the living room when I got home, and I immediately began describing our trip. The Model A roadster was beautiful, but way too much money. But this man also had a 1928 Sedan that he only wanted $500 for. I described the car in exquisite detail, with particular emphasis on the fact that it only needed the rust cleaned out of the gas tank to be in perfect running condition. I finished my glowing description of this gem and waited expectantly.

"So" my dad asked. "Is Bump's father going to buy that car?"

I stood in the middle of a room filled with an awkward silence. I wasn't quite sure how to proceed. I had come to the end of my rehearsed speech and had fallen flat. Fortunately, Mom was a little more perceptive than Dad.

"I think maybe Steve wants to buy the car" she said. This caught my dad by surprise. He thought about it for a while and then said "We'll see."

The next day Dad and I drove out to look at the car. He didn't seem as enthused about it as I was, especially when the owner expressed surprise at the fact that I thought the price was $500. "Oh no," he protested. "I said I had at least $500 in the car already. I'd have to get more than that for it." My heart sank. My dad talked to him a little while longer, but I wasn't really paying attention. Then, much to my surprise, I suddenly realized my dad had talked him into selling the car plus all the materials needed to replace the roof for $500. Both men were now looking at me for the final decision. I didn't quite know what to do. I'd never had two grown-ups depend on me to make such an important decision, and I'd certainly never spent such a huge sum of money. After spending all night dreaming about this car, I was suddenly faced with the reality that I could have it, but it would take almost all my savings. In a state of shock I replied that the price sounded reasonable.

Two days later a truck pulled into our driveway, towing the object of my affection on a trailer. I gave the owner $500. He gave me the title, unloaded the car, and drove off. I was now the proud owner of a forty year old Ford.

First Love – My 1928 Model A Ford

Chapter 3 – High School Heaven

As soon as the truck left the excitement over owning a Model A Ford faded and I began to feel a mixture of helplessness and panic. I felt like the proverbial dog that finally caught a car and didn't know what to do with it. I supposed I could drive it. After all, that was why I bought it. On the other hand, I didn't know anything at all about this car, and I'd always heard it was a good idea to "check out" a car before you drove it. I didn't have a clue what it was I was supposed to check, so maybe driving it wasn't such a good idea. I knew the roof needed replacing, but I didn't know how to do that. The rear window didn't belong in the back seat. I needed to put it back where it belonged, but I didn't know how to do that either. There was one thing I did know, however. Dad would know what to do.

I decided to simply wash the car and play it safe until Dad came home from work. I couldn't wash the top because of the gaping holes in it, but I could at least get the worst of the grime off the body and fenders. It was then that I discovered one of the unpleasant truths about washing your own car. Every dent, every scratch, and every blemish stands out in stark relief when you run a sponge over the car. In this case, blemishes were the least of my worries. For the first time I really noticed the rust holes, rotten wood, slapdash body repairs, and other major flaws in my most prized possession. Fortunately it was about that time that Cory showed up.

Cory was a good friend from high school. I have no idea how he knew that I had bought the Model A, let alone that it was being delivered that day. I guess word spreads quickly in a small town like Yodersburg. All thoughts of simply marking time until my Dad got home disappeared the moment Cory arrived. It was time to take a drive. We dumped a can of lawn mower gas into the Model A tank and I climbed into the driver's seat. Cory climbed into the passenger seat beside me. Once again, I was filled with doubt. You sit bolt upright in a Model A, high off the ground, with a massive steering wheel in front of you, two mysterious levers called "spark advance" and "hand throttle" on the steering column, and four pedals on the floor. You stare out through a narrow windshield in the front and a ridiculously small window in the back. Or in my case, a ridiculously small hole where the rear window was supposed to be.

I desperately tried to remember what the previous owner had told me about starting the car. A Model A is a wonderfully simple piece of machinery – so simple it's complicated. None of the automatic systems we take for granted on modern cars are present in a Model A. No automatic choke. No automatic spark advance. The starter isn't even connected to the ignition switch. Everything is manual. Mentally reviewing the instructions I'd received, I opened the petcock at the base of the gas tank to let fuel flow to the carburetor. (On a Model A the gas tank is thoughtfully located just over your knees, where the dashboard is on modern cars. Gravity pulls fuel to the carburetor, whether the engine is running or not, so there's a gas shut-off petcock conveniently located between the passenger's knees. Next to that is a mixture control, which lets you fine tune the ratio of gasoline to air as the engine warms up.) I opened the mixture control a couple of turns and pulled out the choke. I adjusted the two levers on the steering column to the "ten minutes to two o'clock" position like I'd been told, not really knowing which was the throttle and which was the spark. I remembered that one of the pedals was the starter switch so I stepped on each one in turn until the engine groaned through a couple of revolutions. It didn't even cough. Then I remembered to take the key out of my pocket and turn on the ignition. I stepped on the starter pedal again and, miraculously, the engine caught. After a few tentative sputters, the long dead machinery roared to life. The entire car seemed to shake with excitement. To be honest, I was more frightened than excited. I had gone through the motions of starting the car, but somehow I never really thought that it would run – let alone that it would shake so much and make so much noise. This wasn't anything at all like my parents' Falcons! Nervously, I pressed down on the clutch, ground the gearshift into reverse, and backed out of our driveway. OK, I lurched out of the driveway. The clutch sounded like someone had dropped a bowling ball into a clothes dryer when I let it up and the car was shuddering even more than I was as we backed into the street, but we were actually moving! A bit more grinding of the gears and we were in first, lurching through the neighborhood.

It's hard to describe my feelings as we rattled down the street. I was tremendously excited that after years of idle slumber the ancient mechanicals actually worked, and there was an exhilarating sense of freedom at being in command of my very own car. We had the windows rolled down and the windshield swung open, and the warm fall air stirred up a heady aroma of decaying wool, gasoline, and fine aged grease inside the car. Even after 40 years the memory of that intoxicating scent makes me smile. On the other hand, I was terrified by the fact that I knew almost nothing about this car, including how to drive it, and it seemed as though I was hurtling down the road perched atop a massive collection of antique scrap metal. I could turn the big red steering wheel a long ways in either direction with no appreciable effect, and then suddenly the car would dart to one side, swaying alarmingly on its ancient leaf springs. A block or two later I decided discretion was the better part of valor and stepped on the brakes. The brakes shuddered and ground even louder than my shifts, but eventually they slowed the car to a stop. I turned around in Ellen Cripe's driveway so we could head for home. (Ellen and I had been friends since we were toddlers. She once caused a minor stir in our neighborhood baseball team when she came back from a Catechism class and announced that it was a sin to use signals in baseball.)

We'd barely gotten turned around when the engine died with a series of dry "chuffs." In the years to come, I'd learn to recognize that sound all too well. The gas line had clogged with rust. That afternoon I didn't know what the sound meant, so we opened the hood and stared helplessly at the machinery. We tried to identify key components we'd learned about in Science class, major items like the carburetor and the distributor. We didn't see anything obviously wrong, but fortunately we also did no harm and while we were impotently poking at the engine enough gas seeped past the rust to fill the carburetor again. When we climbed back in and I pressed the starter pedal the engine caught once again and carried us almost all the way back home. It died as I was turning into our driveway, but we were able to push it the rest of the way into its parking spot. We spent the rest of the afternoon poking around under the hood and even managed to get the carburetor off the car to clean the rust out. I hadn't yet learned to pay close attention to how things were put together as I took them apart, so after we scraped a thick layer of reddish-brown goo out of the carburetor we just sort of guessed at how to put it back together again. Not surprisingly, we guessed wrong. There was no hope of starting the car again that day, but we didn't break anything my dad couldn't set right. We did discover the horn made a most satisfying "Ahoooooooga!" sound when we pressed the button in the center of the steering wheel. Dinner time came, Cory went home, and after dinner my Dad started showing me the correct way to work on a car. It wasn't until much later that my Mom told me Dad had actually come home early from work that day, something he almost never did, to help me get the car running. When he saw that Cory and I already had the carburetor on the workbench he sat down to read the paper while we floundered, wisely figuring I'd be more open to the less exciting process of doing things right when it was just he and I in the garage.

In the following weeks my Dad helped me rebuild the carburetor correctly, rebuild the brakes, replace the rotten wood around the back window, install the new top, repair the generator, and otherwise get the car in more or less roadworthy condition. He also helped me blow the rust out of the tank, at least all we could reach. For years afterward the line would clog with rust at the most inopportune times and I'd have to coast off to the side of the road, take off the fuel line, and blow out the rust. I could then motor on until the next time it plugged.

Now that the car was drivable, I experienced a new found sense of freedom. In the morning I'd fire up the Model A and proudly drive to school – at least, on the mornings when it would start. I was always careful to try starting the car before the school bus came, just in case. After school I'd go out to parking lot with my best friend Don and we'd set off on an adventure. I'd known Don since junior high school, and it was a minor miracle that such a small town would be home to two kids with such, uh, unusual interests. We'd spend hours discussing airships, 78 RPM records, Sherlock Holmes, gangsters from the 1920's, and other topics not generally associated with the Age of Aquarius. We avoided politics (Don was a big fan of FDR while I thought Hoover got a raw deal) and while Don liked Stanleys he was a bigger fan of Rolls Royce. (Particularly the 1906 Silver Ghost.) In all other matters we pretty much saw eye to eye.

For sheer aimless pleasure, there are few things that can compare with having the school day behind you, the afternoon ahead of you, your best friend beside you, and a Model A Ford to drive you wherever your fancy took you. Our fancy never took us very far, of course, but it was grand just being able to cruise to Stark & Weaver's drug store for a green river and a quarter pound of cashews. Sometimes we just went for a drive. The standard cruising route for all the other high school kids was to take Main Street to the Lincoln Highway, and take that east to Bower's Drive In. We, of course, disdained that route. We were more likely to drive to Wilson's

Army/Navy Surplus, or Kintigh's Hobby Shop, or maybe we'd drive all the way to Wakarusa to peer through the dusty windows of the Citizen's Bank. (The Citizen's Bank had closed in December of 1936. You could still see the Christmas tinsel twisted around the wrought iron teller's cages, and a 1936 calendar hung forlornly on one wall.) Gas was 25¢ a gallon so we could fill the tank, add a quart of oil, and get change back from a $5.00 bill. Or at least we could if we went to the Hudson gas station on the north side of town. The Hudson station was distinguished primarily by its cheap prices and perplexing billboards. Rumor had it the prices were cheap because they bought refinery dregs and sold it as gasoline, but that didn't bother the Model A. With a 4.24:1 compression ratio it would run fine on almost anything. The billboards were a little harder to explain. Mostly they consisted of odd analogies, such as a picture of a fisherman holding a giant salmon beneath the words "From Coast To Coast Hudson Is The Big Catch." I had never before considered the similarities between fish and gasoline, but that didn't perplex me as much as the picture of a camel beneath the words "First It Was Camels In The West, Now Hudson Serves You Best." My knowledge of cavalry history was rather sketchy, but I thought the US Army's experiment with using camels in the west had been a dismal failure. Still, for 25¢ a gallon I was willing to take a chance that maybe Hudson would turn out to be more successful than camels, and Hudson gasoline propelled Don and me on many a trip. Along the way we experienced blowouts, loose wires, dead generators, and a host of other minor problems, but those just added spice to the trips.

Starting the car was always a challenge. The battery was marginal at best, and I didn't want to squander my limited cash reserves on a new one, so we'd cross our fingers every time I stepped on the starter pedal. If it didn't cough on the first few revolutions we'd initiate our emergency troubleshooting routine. We'd flip a coin, and the loser would get out of the car, open the hood, and place one finger on each spark plug. The winner would then step on the starter pedal and turn the engine through one revolution. If the loser got shocked, the electrical system was OK. If there was no shock, something was wrong. The next step was to isolate the problem. The loser would pull the coil wire off the distributor, hold it in his hand, grit his teeth, and say "Hit it!" If the points and coil were OK you could feel the jolt all the way up to your elbow. This generally meant the rotor or the distributor cap weren't on correctly. If there was no jolt, or if the jolt was weaker than usual, the points were dirty or there was a loose wire. Once we'd isolated the problem, it usually took only a minute or two to fix it and be on our way. Sometimes the battery was too weak to turn the engine through even one revolution and we had to push start it. We'd both get out and push it until it was rolling at a fair clip, then I'd jump into the driver's seat and throw it into gear to spin the engine. Eventually I found a hand crank at an antique car swap meet and we no longer had to depend on the battery. (Electric starters were new when the Model A was built and people weren't sure they could be trusted, so the car left the factory with an emergency hand crank under the seat "just in case.") Cranking the car by hand was not only easier than pushing it, it often drew a crowd of admirers. Or at least, it often drew a crowd. We chose to believe the pointing, smiles, and occasional laughter were evidence that they admired our technique.

Winter brought a new sensation to driving the Model A. Cold. My car had the optional Autolite manifold heater, a cast iron funnel that bolted onto the exhaust manifold and supposedly blew hot air through a hole on the floor of the passenger side. It actually did keep the passenger's left foot moderately warm and it kept the driver's right leg from freezing. Passengers in the back seat had to fend for themselves. Henry Ford had thoughtfully put a rack in the back that held a woolen lap robe to help the back seat passengers fight off hypothermia. Don and I had to be judicious about who we allowed to use this lap robe, because in my car its main function was to hide the wooden mock-up of a Thompson submachine gun we'd built. We'd watched enough reruns of The Untouchables to know that no black sedan from the 20s was complete without a Tommy gun, and the lap robe provided a perfect hiding place. Many of my high school classmates rode for miles in the back seat without ever suspecting there was a Thompson just inches in front of their knees. It came in handy for parades, gag photos, and just fooling around.

Don with the Thompson

Surprisingly, starting the Model A in cold weather was never a problem. The electric starter was pretty much worthless when it got cold, but I never relied on it anyway. I'd turn on the gas, pull the choke all the way out, and prime the engine with a couple turns of the hand crank. When it made a wet, slushy sound as I cranked I knew it was primed. Then I'd push the choke half-way in, turn on the ignition, and crank it for real. One or two pulls on the crank was usually all it took to start it. (You pull up on the crank when starting the car, though half a turn only. That way if it backfires your hand pulls away from the crank. You don't spin the crank around in a full circle, regardless of what you see in the movies. If it backfires when you're doing that the crank will spin around and break your arm.)

I had a part-time job over Christmas vacation, and one day I parked next to my boss's Cadillac. After work, I had just finished priming the Model A when my boss came out of the office and climbed into his car. He took one look at the hand crank and said "You ought to get yourself one of these new-fangled cars with electric start!" I gave the crank one flip and the engine caught instantly. He was still grinding away with his starter as I backed out. I thoughtfully gave him a short "Ahooga!" and tipped my hat as I drove away.

Chapter 4 – Trouble in Paradise

It's just another winter. . .

"You've got a problem." My father's voice was deadly serious. This voice usually meant I was in trouble. This time it was worse. This time it was my car that was in trouble. The problem began just a few minutes earlier, when I was starting the Model A. My dad happened to be in the garage at the time. He immediately waved his hand and told me to shut it off.

"What's that pounding noise?" he asked.

I hadn't heard anything unusual. The Model A always made a lot of noise, and I never paid much attention much attention to it. "It always sounds like that." I suggested.

"Not like that." he replied. We checked the oil and looked at the engine, but didn't see anything unusual. "Try it again." he said. I started the car, and he stared at the engine grimly. "Hear that deep thumping noise?" he asked. This time I heard it. "That's a bearing." he announced. "That's not good."

My parents had given me a workshop manual for Christmas, and we looked up the procedure for rebuilding the engine. We also looked up the price of a rebuilt Model A engine in the J. C. Whitney catalog. Ford sold so many Model A's and they lasted so long that 40 years later you could still buy a surprisingly wide assortment of parts through J. C. Whitney, Sears, Montgomery Wards, and other mail order merchants. The price was well beyond my pocketbook but the catalog did list the shipping weight. It wasn't as heavy as Dad expected, and he calculated that with proper reinforcement and bracing we could hook a block and tackle to the garage door track and use that to pull the engine. (This was not as hare-brained as it sounds. Dad had built the house himself and it was a bit sturdier than most houses as a result.) We had a few dicey moments when the engine was half-way out and the garage door track started to bow alarmingly, but we managed to shore it up with some 2 x 4's and finish pulling the engine. Later we discovered that J. C. Whitney shipped the engines without the flywheel (75 pounds) and other weighty accessories. Dicey or not, the engine was out of the car and we proceeded to disassemble it. OK, Dad proceeded to disassemble it. I watched and handed him wrenches. Dad did compliment my uncanny ability to always stand in his light, plunging whatever part he was working on into darkness. Unfortunately, even with my shadow the problem was all too obvious. The center main bearing had melted. Somehow a piece of string had gotten into my engine (probably from some former owner's futile attempt to make an oil seal) and had clogged the oil line to the center main bearing.

Modern cars have replaceable bearings – thin, semi-circular pieces of metal that are machined to exact tolerances. When you rebuild an engine you buy a new set of bearings from an auto parts store, throw away the old ones, and slip the new ones into your engine. The Model A is different. In a Model A the bearings are made of a soft metal called babbit that was poured into the block at the factory and then machined to the correct size using a special tool called a line bore. I talked to several local machine shops and learned the nearest shop with a line bore and the ability to pour new babbit bearings was in Rochester Indiana, about 100 miles away. Worse still, they charged $350 to replace a set of Model A bearings. If I cleaned out my bank account, I could just barely afford to have this done, but I was saving that money for college.

Once again, Dad came to my rescue. I was already convinced my dad could do anything, but even I was surprised when he came home from work one day with a giant ladle and a hunk of babbit and announced we were going to pour the new bearing ourselves. Using a grinding wheel, an old piece of plumbing pipe, and some modeling clay we swiped from my baby brother, Dad made a form for the new bearing. We then melted the babbit on the kitchen stove and I carried it into the garage, being very careful not to spill any on the linoleum. (Mom freaked out if we spilled jelly on the floor. I couldn't imagine how she'd react if I spilled molten metal on it.) Meanwhile Dad was heating the block and the form with a blow torch, so when I got to the garage we poured the molten babbit into the block. Dad then spent hours scraping the bearing with a small knife, measuring it to find the high spots, and then scraping some more. When he finally got the bearing to exactly the right size and shape, we reassembled the motor. It ran perfectly, and that homemade bearing has performed flawlessly for over 40 years now.

Spring was in full bloom when we got the car back on the road, and Don and I continued our aimless after school wanderings. Driving the Model A in the spring was pure joy. We could swing open the windshield and experience the same unbridled ecstasy a dog feels when it sticks its head out of a car window and lets the wind ram a cornucopia of scents up its nostrils. Unfortunately, the wind also left our hair looking like a well-used Brillo pad. One sunny April afternoon Don commented that we really needed straw hats to go with the Model A.

"Where in the world are we going to get straw hats?" I asked.

"At the Adams Store" was his reply. The Adams Store was a men's clothing store that didn't appear to have changed since the 1920s. It was a long, narrow store with wooden counters on each side, behind which were innumerable bins containing shirts, trousers, hats, and (no kidding) celluloid shirt collars. It was run by Mr. Adams, who looked to be as old as the store itself, and his elderly daughter Polly. The only reason I ever shopped there was because they were the only store in town that was authorized to sell Boy Scout supplies. Uniforms, backpacks, canteens, and other scouting items – all with the official BSA logo – occupied one small corner of the building. The rest of the store was filled with merchandise from a bygone era.

Customers were few, even with the Boy Scout franchise, so the Adams kept expenses low by only turning on the lights when they actually had a customer. Even then, they didn't turn on all the lights at once. When you walked in, they turned on the lights in the front of the store. If you walked to the back, they turned off the lights in the front and turned on the lights in the back. Scattered here and there were small motorized displays, such as a small cardboard man tipping his hat to Stetson quality. If you stopped to look at the display, they turned on the motor. When you looked away they turned it off again. When Don and I walked in they turned on the front lights and Mr. Adams asked if he could help us.

"We'd like to look at your straw hats" Don announced.

Mr. Adams blinked in surprise at this request. I was beginning to suspect this was a fool's errand. Straw hats were so out of date that even the Adams store didn't carry them. Then Mr. Adams spoke. "Bit early in the season, aren't you boys? I usually don't get them out until May or June."

We convinced him that we were indeed willing to push the boundaries of fashion, and after looking around the store he rolled a wooden ladder to the correct position and pulled a couple of round pasteboard hatboxes off a high shelf. Inside were brand new "boaters," the type of straw hat that was popular when the Model A was new. Unfortunately, he only had one in our size.

"I didn't realize I was getting so low" he said, almost to himself. "I'll have to reorder." I have no idea where he ordered them from, but he was as good as his word and in a few weeks Don and I each had proper headgear for cruising in the Model A.

They say that in the spring a young man's fancy turns to love. I have no idea how they came to that conclusion, as it's been my experience that a young man's fancy is pretty much focused on love, or at least some aspects of it, 24 hours a day, 7 days a week, for all 12 months of the year. The Model A didn't prove to be quite the chick magnet I hoped it would be, but it was certainly serviceable in this regard and I had my first dating experiences in that car. It was small enough to be cozy, could generally be relied upon to get us to a movie and a pizza parlor, and it had a window shade in the back seat that could be pulled down for privacy. Not that I was lucky enough to spend any time in the back seat, mind you. Maybe it was because the sexual revolution hadn't yet spread to Indiana. Maybe it was because I was a bit behind the culture of the day, or maybe it was because I occasionally had to stop and blow rust out of the gas line, but my dates consisted primarily of driving and talking, with an occasional hug. I did have my first real kiss on a Model A date, or rather I made my first futile attempt to kiss a girl on one of these dates. At the end of the evening I walked my date to the front of her house, opened the screen door for her, and then paused to look deeply into her eyes. The time seemed right, so I put my arms around her waist and bent forward for a kiss. She looked up expectantly and pursed her lips. Unfortunately, our lips never quite met. I forgot I was wearing my straw hat, and the brim of my hat slammed into her forehead. If you've never examined the brim of a straw boater, it's about as stiff as a sheet of plywood but with a serrated edge. She jerked backwards, sporting an ugly gash above her eyebrows. I leaped backward and managed to catch my belt loop on the screen door handle. I stood there on tiptoes, half-suspended by my belt, while I frantically tried to unhook myself from the handle before I ripped the door off its hinges and woke her parents. When I finally untangled myself from the door I took off my hat and we more or less pecked each other on the lips, but the moment had passed.

One day as I was driving through the country I had an unusual experience. I was held up by a slower car! That had never happened to me in the Model A. Even an Amish buggy could give the "A" a good run. Actually, on a good day the Model A could go 60 mph, assuming I had a long straight road with no headwind. It wasn't happy at that speed, though. It was much more comfortable cruising at 45 or 50 mph. I usually drove with one eye on my rear view mirror, and when a car came up behind me I'd pull over to let them pass. So I was a bit surprised when I came up behind a slower car, particularly since the car was a late model Camaro with wide tires, a loud exhaust, and other signs of youthful indiscretion. For some reason, the driver was choosing to drive 35 mph in a 50 mph zone. Looking closer, I could see that "some reason" was sitting next to him. Perhaps it would be more accurate to say she was as close to sitting on his lap as she possibly could be without blocking his view of the road ahead. Not that he was spending much time looking at the road ahead, mind you. It was obvious they only had eyes for each other, and they were so close they probably only had breath for each other as well. With a sigh of resignation I settled down to follow them to the next town. Suddenly I was seized with a radical idea. I could pass this guy! I'd never before passed anyone in the Model A, but this was a long straight road with no traffic in sight. I checked my mirror the way they taught us in Driver's Ed, signaled my lane change, pulled into the other lane, and stepped on the gas. I wasn't exactly beside him in a flash, it was more like a quick sunrise, but in any event I did make it past the Camaro. As I passed, I gave him a friendly little "Ahh-Oooh-Ga!" with the horn and tipped my straw hat to show I appreciated his letting me pass. I didn't stay in front of him for long, of course. I heard the roar of a big block V-8 behind me and in an instant the Camaro was disappearing from view in front of me. The driver was hunched over the steering wheel and his date was leaning against the passenger door with her arms folded over her chest, as far away from him as she could get. Apparently I'd spoiled the magic of the moment.

As the end of the school year approached I began to realize that the mother of all dating events was looming on the horizon – the Senior Class Prom. I'm not certain why I felt obligated to get a date for the prom. I had successfully avoided the Junior Class Prom with no apparent ill effects, I didn't know how to dance, and I didn't like the music that was popular with my fellow classmates. (Not surprisingly, I preferred 1920s jazz.) Maybe it was because my mom was constantly telling me that if I didn't go to the prom I'd regret it to my dying day. In any event, as the weeks slipped by I began to feel my entire life would be a failure if I didn't go to the prom. The only thing I dreaded even more than missing the prom was asking a girl to go with me. I didn't have a steady girlfriend, and all the girls I'd dated before already had a date for the prom. (Or at least, that's what they said when I called.) It usually took me several weeks to get up the courage to ask a girl to a movie, and this was a much bigger event. Finally, about a week before the prom, a girl I knew from Speech Club subtly mentioned that she had just finished her prom dress but didn't yet have a date. OK. Maybe it wasn't so subtle. In any event it only took me a day or two to realize this was the opportunity I'd been looking for. I finally screwed my courage to the sticking-place and called her house to invite her to the prom.

When I say "called her house" I'm talking about a process that took the better part of an afternoon. My usual routine when asking a girl for a date was to think about it for several hours. Then I'd get

31

out the phone book and look up her number, secretly hoping it wouldn't be in the book. It would be disappointing that we couldn't go on the date of course, but at least I had a valid excuse to avoid the agony of the invitation. In this case I found her number all too quickly. I started to dial it, and then hung up when I realized I hadn't figured out what to say. I couldn't just call and say "Wanna go to the prom?" That was way too blunt, and it almost forced her to give a yes or no answer. I tried to think of some other reason for the call, something we could talk about while I subtly steered the conversation around to the prom. Then I could "sound her out," listening to her inflection while trying to decide if she'd be flattered or insulted if I asked her out. After several more aborted attempts to dial her number, sometimes getting as far as the final digit before losing my courage and hanging up, I placed the call. When she answered I completely forgot everything I'd planned to say. I stammered through a few questions about the Speech Club, the weather, and last week's math homework before finally asking if maybe she wouldn't mind going to the prom with me. To my surprise, she said yes. I breathed a sigh of relief, thinking my troubles were over. How little I knew.

Fortunately, although I was clueless about proms, my Mom seemed to be an expert on them. She informed me I'd need to rent a tuxedo, something that had never occurred to me. She even knew where I could rent one, and in no time at all I picked out a white dinner jacket that looked (to me) like something James Bond would wear to a casino in Monte Carlo. I was still reeling from the cost of the tuxedo when my Mom informed me that it was customary to take your date to dinner before the prom. She helped me pick out a restaurant and make dinner reservations. She then came up with a suggestion which I regarded as pure genius – she suggested I buy a corsage for my date! I'd only seen one corsage before in my life, and that was one Dad had bought for Mom on their 25th anniversary. Mom had been ecstatic when he gave it to her, and I could only imagine how surprised and pleased my date would be if I gave her a corsage for the prom. Just when things seemed perfect, Mom said I'd have to find out what color her prom dress was so we could get a corsage that complimented it.

How the deuce was I supposed to find out what color her dress was without tipping my hand about the corsage? This was supposed to be the big surprise of the night, maybe the biggest surprise of her life. I didn't want to spoil it by asking her what color her dress was. Fortunately we had a Speech Club meeting the next day, so I had a good excuse to talk to her. Somehow I managed to steer the conversation around to her dress. I was suddenly overwhelmed with details about hems, beltlines, necklines, lace, and something called a bodice, but I did catch the word "purple." Or maybe it was "lavender." I wasn't exactly sure of the color, but it would have to be close enough. I'd never get away with asking her a second time. With Mom's help I ordered a corsage from a local florist, and for the first time I actually started to look forward to the prom.

On the day of the prom I washed and polished the Model A until it gleamed. My Mom came home from the grocery as I was finishing, but she didn't seem as pleased with its appearance as I was. I realize now that her view of the Model A wasn't filtered through love the way mine was, but she had the good sense not to criticize my car. Instead she tried an indirect approach, a strategy which has been favored by mothers for centuries. She asked a few subtle questions which were intended to guide me to her way of thinking. "Do you think the generator will make it to the restaurant and back?" she asked. Doubts began to cloud my mind. The restaurant was in Elkhart, almost 20 miles away. The chances of the generator working reliably for such an extended journey were slim at best. Then she asked the killer question: "What if the gas line clogs?" My vision of James Bond strolling into a casino dissolved into a nightmare that featured James Bond covered in grease, standing in the rain beside a disassembled car on a dark country road, blowing into a gas line. Reluctantly I accepted her suggestion and began polishing the Falcon station wagon for my prom date.

Hours later the car was clean, and I'd mastered the mysteries of studs, suspenders, and a cummerbund. (Actually, I hadn't quite mastered the cummerbund, as years later I discovered I had worn it upside down. Fortunately no one else in Yodersburg knew how to wear a cummerbund either, so my faux pas went unnoticed.) The Falcon provided reliable, if uninspiring, transportation and in no time at all I was standing at my date's door holding the corsage behind my back. Her mother invited me into the parlor, and a few minutes later my date appeared. She looked absolutely stunning – nothing at all like the gangly girl from the Speech Club. I presented her with the corsage and she thanked me, but the effect wasn't as dramatic as I'd hoped. It was almost as though she'd expected it. Then she

33

did something that totally stunned me – she presented me with a flower to wear on my tux! James Bond didn't wear flowers. In fact, the only man I'd ever seen wear a flower was Captain Kangaroo, and I certainly didn't want to look like him! Realizing there was no way out, I thanked her and pinned it to my lapel. What would the other guys at the prom think? The shock of wearing a posy was soon forgotten, however. When my date left the room to get her coat her mother casually asked me what car I was driving. When I told her I had my parent's car she said "Oh good. Kelly was so worried that you'd drive that old car and she'd get her dress dirty."

The rest of the night was an anticlimax. I drove the girl who thought my Model A was dirty to dinner, and then we went to the prom. The prom was being held in my high school gym, which was decorated with balloons and streamers in a fashion that was supposed to represent Camelot. If you don't know how to dance there's not much to do at a prom. Mostly we walked around, taking note of the dresses every other girl was wearing. I was relieved to see that lots of other guys had flowers on their tuxes too, but I was disappointed to see that all the other girls were wearing corsages. I guess my Mom wasn't the only one who thought of that. When the prom was finally over I drove my date home, and then drove the Falcon back to our house. I parked it next to the Model A, thinking that maybe I should have driven the A after all. Blowing rust out of a gas line couldn't have been any worse than walking around that damn gym talking about girls' dresses.

Chapter 5 – The Endless Summer

Don and Andy with the "A"

After the prom, the last few weeks of school passed quickly. Don and I were frequently joined in our aimless wanderings by our friend Andy, whom we'd known since grade school. Andy had a 1963 Dodge Dart with a slant six engine, a car that was almost as slow as the Model A. Not surprisingly, we usually chose the Model A for our after-school adventures. Graduation came and went, and we began driving the "A" to the lake for canoeing, skiing parties, and other summertime activities. Of course, that summer we didn't spend all our time playing. Like all high school graduates we found ourselves face to face with the curse of adulthood – a job.

We were all college bound, so we didn't have real jobs. We had summer jobs. I was lucky to find a meaningful job as an engineering trainee with an HVAC (Heating, Ventilating, and Air Conditioning) controls manufacturer. Don ran an injection molding machine, making pressure-cooker gaskets at a rubber plant. Andy had the most interesting job of all. He worked in the concession stand of a drive-in theater. He used his influence to get Don and me part-time jobs, working in the concession stand on Friday and Saturday nights.

Drive-in theaters are a piece of our automotive heritage that has sadly all but disappeared from the American landscape. The concept was simple – a large outdoor movie screen in front of a parking lot

35

dotted with posts that held portable speakers on short wires so you could hang the speaker on your car window while you watched the movie. They specialized in "B" movies, the type where teenagers at a beach party are suddenly attacked by giant potato bugs that have escaped from a neighborhood radiation lab. Before each movie there was a cartoon showing dancing popcorn boxes extolling the virtues of the concession stand located at the back of the parking lot. This triggered a rush to the concession stand, where Andy, Don, and I dispensed sodas, popcorn, and pizza in a frenzy of activity.

The owner/manager of the theater was a no-nonsense man named Bill. He had his hands full just trying to keep everything running smoothly so the business would generate some semblance of a profit. He had an assistant manager named Lenny who specialized in creating confusion. I suspect Bill kept Lenny around because he secretly enjoyed straightening out the things Lenny messed up. Bill wanted to keep the theater a respectable family place, so one of Lenny's primary responsibilities was walking between the cars, rapping his flashlight on the windows and demanding "two heads above the window" as required. The admission charge was based on the number of people in the car, so Lenny also kept an eye out for drivers who tried to sneak into the theater with unpaid passengers hiding in the trunk. Another one of Lenny's responsibilities was to post the names of the movies we were showing on the marquee out front. I'm not quite sure why Bill chose Lenny for this job, as Lenny had to be the world's worst speller. Even with the name of the movie written on a piece of paper in front of him he invariable got it wrong. This was perhaps understandable when the title was something tricky, like "Counterpoint." Lenny proudly displayed this as "Counterpiont." It was a little harder to understand how "Fire Creek" could become "Fir Crick."

Harvey was our projectionist. When the equipment was working properly his job was pretty straightforward. There were two projectors in the projection booth. One would be showing the current reel, and Harvey would load the next reel into the other projector. When the current reel ended the second projector would start automatically, and Harvey would then load the next reel into the first projector. This didn't take long, so he had plenty of time to wander down to the concession stand and sip coffee between reels. Sometimes he spent a little too much time sipping coffee, and both projectors would run out of film. The screen would go blank, and the parking lot would erupt in a cacophony of car horns while Harvey ran back to the projection booth to load the next reel. Sometimes he got confused and loaded a reel the audience had already seen, resulting in another outbreak of car horns. Either way, we'd get a flood of ill-tempered customers in the concession stand, loading up on popcorn and soda while Harvey got the reels straightened out.

I found the customers even more fascinating than the people who worked at the theater. The majority of them were good, honest, salt-of-the-earth Midwesterners, but there were more than a fair share of characters among them. Maybe I'd led a sheltered life, but I encountered a few individuals at the theater who were unlike anyone I'd met anywhere else, before or since. I got my first inkling of the diversity among our customers my first day on the job, when I made a trip to the rest room. Scratched on the wall, amid the usual assortment of misspelled sexual insults (people who write on bathroom walls seldom win spelling bees) was a quote by the 18th century French philosopher Diderot. True, the quotation "Man will never be free until the last king is strangled with the entrails of the last priest" had a definite anti-social bent, but it did indicate a decidedly higher level of pervert than you encounter in most public facilities. If the person who scratched that quote on the wall ever visited the concession stand I didn't know it, but perhaps that is because he would have blended in nicely with the rest of the crowd. One gentleman wore a full head Frankenstein mask while he bought his refreshments. On another occasion a lady purchased popcorn and a soda while wearing only a negligee. I was surprised to discover that many of our patrons apparently couldn't count money. They'd place an order, and when we told them how much it would cost they'd place a wad of bills and coins on the counter. We'd count out the correct amount, and they'd scoop up whatever was left and shove it back into their pocket. We sold the usual assortment of popcorn, hot dogs, miniature pizzas, and soda, so it was a bit of a surprise when one customer ordered pancakes.

"Pancakes?" Don asked in disbelief.

"Blueberry, if you have them" the customer replied hopefully.

Of course, the customers weren't the only ones who sometimes acted irrationally. In the rush to serve as many customers as quickly as possible we sometimes made mistakes ourselves. I once served a gentleman who spoke so softly he was hard to understand amid the din, but I was pretty sure he just asked for a cup of coffee. When I gave it to him he looked at it oddly and then asked "Did you ever hear of iced coffee?"

"Oh yes, I've heard of it." I replied. I then turned to the next customer, but I was vaguely aware that the coffee buyer had given me an odd stare as he left. It wasn't until much later that it occurred to me that perhaps he actually wanted iced coffee. Don had a similar experience when a customer asked for peaches.

"I'm very sorry, sir, but we don't serve fresh fruit here" Don replied. The customer gave him a long, perplexed stare before leaving. Later, when the rush was over, Don told me about the weirdo who asked for peaches.

"Are you sure he wasn't asking for pizzas?" I asked.

The smile slowly faded from Don's face. "Oh" was all he said.

Business at the concession stand definitely came in spurts. During intermissions, or when the movie plot slowed down, we would be overwhelmed by a crush of customers. We'd work frantically to fill everyone's order, and then we wouldn't see another customer for an hour or so. During these slack periods we'd mop the floor, assemble pizzas, and fold popcorn boxes. The boxes were shipped to us in flattened bundles, and we had to pop them back into a box shape, fold in the flaps on the bottom, and lock a tab into a slot so they'd be ready to fill with fresh popcorn when the next rush of customers arrived. Andy, Don, and I were sitting in a circle one night, swapping lies and folding boxes. We finished one bundle so Andy opened a new bundle, folded one box, and then tossed it down in disgust. "Shoot," he said. "They sent us the wrong size boxes." He called Bill over and showed him the box. Bill looked at the box with disdain.

"They know we don't use this size." He fumed. "I told them that when we placed the order. They sent us a bunch of these boxes last summer, and it took me weeks to get it straightened out. Now I've got to do it all over again. I hope we've got enough of the right boxes to tide us over until they send us replacements." Just then Lenny walked into the concession stand.

"Hey, Lenny!" Bill called out. "Take a look at the boxes those clowns sent us again this year." Lenny walked over to the place where Bill, Andy, Don, and I were all standing in a circle, glaring at a solitary popcorn box. Bill handed him the box and Lenny studied it intently. Suddenly he jerked upright, with a shocked look on his face.

"Wait a minute!" Lenny shouted. "This is the wrong size!" He turned to Andy. "Don't fold any more of these" he ordered. "This is the wrong size box!" Then he turned to Bill. "We don't sell this size" he explained. "They sent us the wrong boxes." He then repeated this message to Don and me in turn, in case we'd missed it. Pleased with himself for having discovered this potentially catastrophic mistake he hurried off to tell Harvey about it, on the off chance that our projectionist would get a sudden urge to fold popcorn boxes. Lenny may not have been especially quick, but he was thorough.

When we weren't screwing things up at the theater or slaving away at our factory jobs we had plenty of time to enjoy the summer. Andy's parents had built a cottage on a small lake in Indiana, and we often went there to go swimming, canoeing, skiing, or to just hang out and play cards. Usually Andy, Don, and I just decided on the spot what we felt like doing, but every once in a while we'd invite a gang over for a cookout. These affairs usually ran more smoothly if Don or I planned them. Andy was a terrific guy and as true a friend as you could ask for, but he did tend to be a bit absent minded. Don once said that Andy would give you the shirt off his back if he'd remembered to put it on that morning. Planning was not Andy's strong suit.

One particularly memorable skiing party began gestating on a Tuesday, when Andy first suggested inviting a gang out to his folk's place for a cookout on Saturday. All week long he vacillated, worrying about the weather, someone who might have to go to Indianapolis on Saturday, and a dozen other factors that might interfere with the party. Finally on Friday afternoon he decided to press ahead, invited everyone for Saturday, and began stocking up on boat gas and other necessary supplies. I drove the Model A to his cottage early Saturday afternoon to help him set up. I immediately noticed a crowd of people I didn't recognize. It turned out Andy's brother had also planned a party for that Saturday, and neither of them had bothered to mention their plans to the other. Fortunately there was plenty of room for both parties and we took turns using the boat to go skiing. When Andy's guests began to arrive, Andy took me aside.

"I forgot to get pop" he said. (In Indiana, sodas are called pop.) "Can you run me over to Bill & Casey's to get some?" Bill & Casey's was a small grocery store on the far side of the lake. We piled into the Model A and made a quick run for pop. A little while later Don asked Andy "You got any munchies?" Andy hadn't thought of munchies either, so we made another trip to Bill & Casey's to load up on chips and pretzels.

After an afternoon of skiing Andy asked me to start the charcoal while he made the hamburgers. I asked where the charcoal was, and it turned out Andy hadn't thought to buy charcoal. At this point Don and I began to question Andy about what he did have, and we made a list of things we needed to buy at Bill & Casey's. He had the hamburger, but no buns. His parents had some ketchup and mustard in the fridge, but we needed to buy paper plates, napkins, coleslaw, and a host of other sundries. When we returned from our third trip to Bill & Casey's we quickly discovered that none of us had thought to buy charcoal lighter, but Andy was able to borrow some from a neighbor and save us from making a fourth trip. In a little while I had a good hot bed of coals, and I told Andy I was ready to put on the hamburgers.

"Here it is!" Andy announced proudly. He opened the freezer and hauled out a five pound block of frozen hamburger. Andy was too embarrassed to go inside Bill & Casey's a fourth time, so he sat in the car while I bought unfrozen hamburger.

That summer was also when I first discovered that there is a special brotherhood of people who drive old cars, and as in any other family, sometimes you'd rather not admit that you're related to a few individuals. When a local car parts store didn't have the dome light switch I needed for my Model A the man behind the counter suggested I go see a man named Otis Swinehart. "Otis has a lot of Model A stuff" he assured me as he gave me directions to Otis's house.

As I drove up to Otis's house I could see that he did indeed have a lot of Model A stuff. A dilapidated Model A pickup truck was parked next to a shed behind his house, and the remains of another Model A truck were quietly decomposing in his back yard. A rusty engine block was leaning against the cracked steps that led up to his front door, and a familiar "Ahh-Ooooh-Ga" split the air when I pressed on the doorbell. A nervous looking woman opened the door and stared at me without saying a word. Something in her eyes told me she'd heard one too many "Ahh-Ooooh-Ga's" in her life. I asked if Otis was there and she silently backed away from the door. A minute later Otis appeared.

Otis was a short, heavyset man in a grimy white T-shirt and tattered blue jeans. He had a two-day stubble on his chin, but his face lit up in a smile when he saw my Model A in the driveway. "Ya got an A!" he said as he walked past me to get a better look at my car. Otis was a man of few words and fewer teeth. Actually he made a lot of sounds, but my Hoosier ears weren't attuned to his thick Appalachian accent so very few of his sounds were recognizable as words. I wound up smiling and nodding my head a lot that afternoon as I tried to decipher his conversation. Eventually he asked what had brought me to his house and I told him I was looking for a dome light switch. "Ah got one in t'other barn" he said and he motioned me to follow him to the pickup truck.

The pickup truck started on the second crank and we lurched off across his yard, taking a shortcut to the dirt road beside the house. As soon as we were on the road he reached down by his feet and lifted a warm six-pack of beer onto the seat. "Hep yerself" he said as he popped one open.

"No thanks." I replied. Then, worrying that he might take this as an insult I quickly added "I'm not 21 yet." He looked at me in confusion as if he had no idea why I was mentioning my age, but he shrugged it off and continued to guzzle his own beer.

It only took a few minutes to get to the barn on the back side of his property, but that was more than enough time for him to finish his beer and show me how he could throw the empty can up through the hole were the truck's top used to be and have it land in the pickup bed behind us. The barn was jammed with old farm tools, furniture, saddles, and more than a few Model A parts. He dug through several dusty piles of effluvia, occasionally handing me pieces of an old distributor, wires, and other odds and ends that he thought I should carry in my car "just in case." Eventually he found the dome light switch, but when he looked at it he frowned and said "tain't the raht one." He gave it to me anyway, saying I might be able to make it fit, and we climbed back into his truck. A few minutes and another beer later and we were back at his house.

He insisted I come into the house for a glass of water, and we spent the next hour or two sitting at the kitchen table talking about Model A's. Actually, he did most of the talking, as I found it hard to get a word in edgewise. Eventually I was able to excuse myself, saying my mom was expecting me home for dinner. When I got home I piled the parts he'd given me in the garage, and at dinner I told my folks all about my visit with Otis.

A few weeks later I came home from work and found my mother looking a bit dazed. "Otis was here" she said as I walked in the door. I don't know how he found out where I lived, but that afternoon he had suddenly appeared at the door. "Ah need mah call whar" he said. "Steve's got mah call whar." My mother had no idea what he was talking about, but based on my description and the Model A pickup truck sitting in the driveway she guessed this was Otis. She showed him the pile of parts in the garage and he immediately grabbed a coil wire from the pile. Saying "this is mahn too" he picked up the rest of the parts he'd given me, thanked my mother, and drove off with his treasures. I never saw him again, but I never forgot him either. I was beginning to discover that owning a Model A was broadening my horizons.

If people who drive old cars belong to a brotherhood, their meeting hall is the Parts Store. Over the years that I've been fooling with cars parts stores have become a commodity. Now they are almost universally clean, friendly, and incredibly efficient. Thanks to computers and overnight shipping they can look up virtually any part in seconds, and if they haven't got it in stock they can get it for you by the following afternoon. That's not the way it used to be. There used to be clean parts stores, but those were the stores that specialized in big fuzzy dice and miracle engine elixirs. You could seldom find real parts in those stores, at least not if you drove a 40 year old Ford. Car dealers had everything you needed to fix a new car, at mind-boggling prices, but by the time a car got old enough to actually need replacement parts the dealer wasn't interested in it. If you needed parts for an older car you looked for an old dilapidated parts store that had been in business since your car was new. They were seldom found on Main Street but could usually be found just a block or two off the main thoroughfare. Their dusty showroom windows displayed car jacks, wrench sets, and genuine "glass pack" mufflers. The walls were adorned with calendars and posters from parts suppliers, urging you to use Hastings piston rings and always add Bardahl to your oil.

Inside there might be a few tables with bargain tools and other items for self-service shopping, but a wooden counter divided the customer area from the bulk of the store. Often there were bar stools bolted to the floor in front of this counter, with rust stains on the pedestals and tears in the red plastic upholstery. These stools were a blessing, as you often had to wait a long time until it was your turn to be served. Invariably the guy ahead of you would spend an eternity studying whatever part had been presented to him, pointing out the differences between that part and the one he'd removed from his car, and debating with the parts guy as to whether or not this new part could be made to fit his car. When it was finally your turn to be served you told the parts guy what you wanted and he began to search for the correct catalog. (They were always called parts guys, never store clerks. They were at least 40 years old, and they had a wealth of knowledge about every kind of car except the one you were working on.) In the days before computers, every parts supplier had its own catalog and every parts store kept hundreds of catalogs behind the counter. If you needed a fan belt, they got out the Gates catalog. If you needed a spark plug, they got out the Champion catalog. If you needed a muffler, they had to remember which company made mufflers for your car, as there would be a dozen or more muffler catalogs behind the counter. The latest catalog from each vendor only listed parts for cars made within the last few years, so the parts stores kept back issues of all their catalogs. Thus, if you drove a 40 year old car, they not only needed to figure out which vendor had once made parts for that car, they had to find a suitably aged copy of that vendor's catalog to find the correct part number for your car. Once they found the part number, they would spend an hour or two wandering through the endless rows of shelving behind the counter, squinting into boxes at random, and peering at the hundreds of fan belts, mufflers, and other parts that were hanging from the ceiling. Finding the part you needed had become their personal quest, and they wouldn't rest until they succeeded. In rare cases of extreme frustration they would ask Joe for help. Joe had spent at least 50 years behind the counter and he knew where everything was, but he was a crusty old coot so nobody asked him for help unless they had to.

One of my more memorable trips to a car parts store involved a search for headlight bulbs. As I was driving home one evening a loose wire had suddenly let my generator voltage jump from 6 volts to around 30 volts. Needless to say, this over stimulated most of the electrical components in the car. My headlights had been loafing along, projecting their customary weak yellow dimness, when suddenly they were goosed into producing a brilliant, blue white glare that illuminated the street like a thousand flashbulbs. Sadly, this brilliance only lasted an instant as both bulbs immediately burned themselves out. In a panic I switched on my brights, a move which blinded all oncoming traffic within a 5 mile range with another explosion of brilliance. This lasted almost as long as the first flash. Fortunately I was within a few blocks of my house and there was enough daylight left for me to limp home. It only took my dad a few minutes to find and fix the loose wire, but I was left with the need for two new headlight bulbs.

By this time I had learned which car parts stores were most likely to have each kind of part (a store which had a good selection of fan belts could almost never be counted upon to have the distributor cap you needed) so I went to the store with the best selection of electrical parts. To my surprise, I was waited upon by a parts guy I had never met before. (I suspect all the guys who knew what I drove kept a low profile whenever I walked into the store.) He smiled and asked how he could help me.

"Do you carry headlamp supplies?" I asked, as innocently as possible.

"We sure do" he replied, still smiling.

I pulled one of the burned out headlight bulbs from my shirt pocket. "I'd like two of these, please."

He held the bulb lightly between his fingers and squinted at it, the smile slowly fading from his face. "You sure know how to hit a guy below the belt" he muttered. Holding the bulb away from him like a dead rat, he walked to the bookshelf where they kept their mustiest catalogs. After leafing through a half-dozen catalogs he began wandering through the shelves, muttering to himself. After a long search, he came back to the counter, proudly holding out a flat cardboard box. With exaggerated effort he blew a cloud of dust off the top of the box, then opened the lid to display a dozen brand new bulbs, each in its own cardboard divider. "How many bulbs did you say you needed?" he asked in triumph. Clearly I had made his day.

A close cousin to the Car Parts store was the Machine Shop. Some machine shops were located in back rooms behind a parts store, and some machine shops were their own independent business. Wherever they were located they were dark, cluttered, and filled with a wide arrangement of expensive machine tools. This was where you took your engine to get the cylinders bored or the crank reground. They could press bearings in and out of differential cases, turn your brake drums, and balance your driveshaft. The walls were lined with lathes, drill presses, boring machines, hydraulic presses, and mysterious machines with a bewildering array of cranks and knobs. Pieces of customers' cars were stacked everywhere, the hardwood flooring was covered with oil stains, old coffee cans were strategically placed to serve as spittoons, and everything was covered with a peculiar oily gray dust. The machines were usually painted gray-green, but because of the dust, the wooden workbenches, the hardwood floors, and the dark stains around the coffee can spittoons the dominant color was brown. The only colorful item in the room was the Ridgid tool calendar. Only hard-core mechanics ventured into a machine shop so the shop was freed from the requirement to maintain a "respectable" customer service area. Inside the machine shop, everyone was free to admire the curvaceous, bikini-clad models who lovingly caressed pipe wrenches and conduit benders on the Ridgid Tools calendar. There was usually only one machinist in each shop. Small, frail looking men of indeterminate age prevailed. Their skinny arms and coke bottle glasses belied a surprising ability to effortlessly hoist an engine block onto a workbench. I made my first ventures into machine shops when the bearing burned out in my Model A. Before my dad decided we could fix it ourselves I was vainly trying to find a machine shop that could pour babbit bearings at a price I could afford. I quickly discovered there was no such thing as an inexpensive machine shop. I found some very talented machinists, but you paid for that talent. One shop was particularly fascinating. In a back corner of the shop, half-buried beneath other customer's projects, was an object I recognized from books and photographs which I had studied for years.

"Is that a Stanley engine?" I asked incredulously.

"Yep" the machinist replied, punctuating his reply by shooting a stream of tobacco juice into the nearest coffee can. "Busted all to hell." That was the extent of his conversation. He turned back to the project he had been working on when I entered the shop. He had already told me the price to pour new bearings in a Model A engine and it was clear from my expression that I couldn't afford it, so he saw no reason to continue the conversation. Clearly he saw nothing unusual about the fact that there was an engine from a 70 year old steam car sitting in his shop, nor in the fact that an 18 year old kid could even recognize such an artifact.

In August of that year my father and I were sitting in the kitchen, eating peanut butter and mayonnaise sandwiches. (My father introduced me to the simple pleasure of peanut butter and mayonnaise sandwiches, a delicacy which for some reason most other people don't enjoy.) As we finished our lunch, he surprised me by asking if I wanted to go canoeing in Canada. He didn't have to ask twice. When I was younger we made several family camping trips to Canada, and one year we stayed at a family run lodge just north of Wawa, Ontario. One day the proprietor led us on a day trip canoeing up the University River. The fishing and the adventure were wonderful, but the birth of my younger brother steered us toward less adventurous family trips for several years thereafter. Now my dad was proposing that just he and I return to the University River and take enough supplies to spend the better part of a week fishing on the lakes that dotted that area.

We packed as lightly as we could because we would have to carry everything we took over several portages, but we still wound up packing an incredible amount of food, camping gear, and fishing tackle into the Falcon station wagon. Early one summer morning we climbed into the Falcon and headed north. (My dad always started

46

trips early in the morning. His goal was to drive 100 miles before breakfast.) The drive through Michigan was uneventful, and we crossed into Canada at Sault Ste. Marie early in the afternoon. Once we got out of the city, Dad let me drive while he dozed in the passenger seat. I was doing about 70 mph, and with the canoe on top that was just about as fast as the Falcon would go. Suddenly, amid a great cloud of oil smoke, the transmission shifted into low gear. This caused the engine to revolve at an unwholesome rate of revolutions. Despite its best efforts, the Falcon was not capable of maintaining 70 mph in low gear so we began a rapid deceleration. My father was thrown into the dashboard while the engine sounded like it was trying to climb into the seat between us. I managed to steer the car onto the shoulder while loudly protesting that it wasn't my fault.

We had the car towed back into Sault Ste. Marie and engaged a room at the Beaver Hotel, a quiet little family establishment nestled between a copper refinery and a sawmill, tucked underneath the bridge to the US. The hotel was clean – the cracks in the wall were well scrubbed and the patches on the sheets were freshly laundered – and we had free use of a bathroom down the hall. For entertainment the hotel featured a black-and-white TV in the lobby. The best thing about the hotel was that it was within walking distance of the transmission shop where the Falcon was being repaired. My dad and I read, played cards in our room, ate dinner in the hotel, and took an after dinner walk to the famous Soo Locks. Unfortunately there were no ships going through the locks at the time, and looking at empty locks doesn't provide much long-term entertainment. The next morning we had a leisurely breakfast at the hotel and spent the rest of the morning looking at the empty locks again. Fortunately the car was finished after lunch, and we were able to proceed on our way.

The canoeing and fishing were fantastic, and the memory of that trip with my father remains fresh to this day. After several glorious days in the bush we reluctantly paddled back to the spot where we had left our car. Dirty, unshaven, and totally relaxed we packed up the gear and headed south. As we neared Sault Ste. Marie it was my turn to doze while Dad drove. Once again, the transmission belched forth a cloud of blue smoke and shifted into low gear. The one saving grace about this mishap was that it removed all traces of doubt that I was somehow responsible for the previous incident. Once again we had the car towed to the transmission shop, and fortunately we arrived just before they closed for the long Labor Day weekend. The owner of the shop was extremely helpful, and he came in to work himself over the holiday to get us back on the road. It turned out one of the seals they'd replaced during the first rebuild was defective, causing the second breakdown. We booked a room in the Beaver Hotel (we were becoming their best customers) and played cards while we listened to the rumbling of cars driving on the bridge as thousands of other drivers cruised to the US without incident.

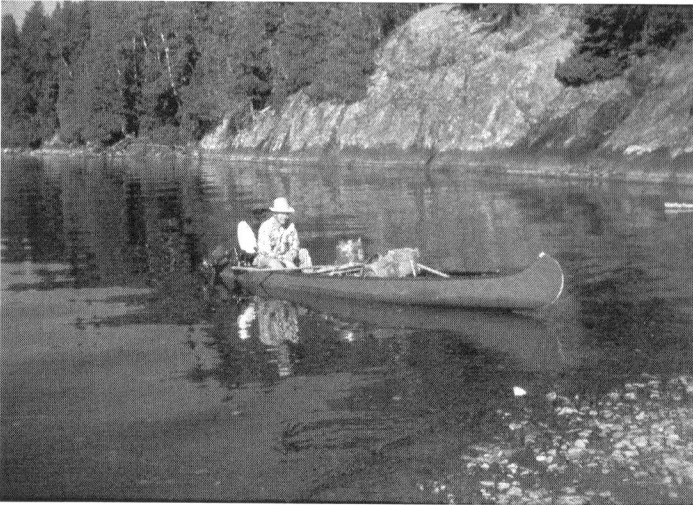

Canoe Camping with Dad

Despite the inconvenience of two blown transmissions, my dad and I repeated that trip several times in the years to come. The trips were always fantastic and we never again had car trouble, although we did have a bit of a shock when we returned from a trip in August of '74. We had been back for a few days, long enough to shave, clean up, and run out of camping stories to tell to my mom. We were watching the news on television and the announcer made a reference to President Ford. "President Ford?" we asked in amazement. "Oh that's right," my mother replied. "I forgot to tell you. Nixon resigned." I can't say that this development actually made any difference in our lives, but it did drive home the point that when you're in the bush, you really are out of touch with the rest of the world.

As the last few weeks of summer slipped imperceptibly into the first weeks of fall there was a definite chill in the air – and not just because the weather was changing. The time was fast approaching when Andy, Don, and I would head off to different colleges. This began to cast a pall over everything. Even the drive-in theater wasn't quite as thrilling as it was at the start of the summer. People think of show biz as being a glamorous profession. They think you spend all your time hobnobbing with stars and cavorting at the wild parties they read about in the tabloids, but it's not always like that. At least, it's not always like that if your connection to show biz is working at a drive-in theater. The only perk we got from that job was free admission on nights when we weren't working. Even that wasn't quite the windfall it sounds like. For one thing, we worked every weekend unless the movie was so stinko that nobody wanted to see it. More to the point, we heard the dialog of every movie they showed and we occasionally watched bits of the movie if the concession business was slack, so we had very little interest in spending our time off watching the same movie we'd already listened to over and over again. You had to be really bored to do that. One night in early September Don and I were really bored. So bored in fact that we not only decided to go to the theater, we decided to go in costume. I wore a white shirt, pinstriped vest, arm garters, spats, and my straw hat. Don sat in the back seat of the Model A wearing a trench coat with a tan fedora pulled low over his eyes, the wooden Thompson resting on his lap. By sheer chance, there was a new girl in the ticket booth who didn't recognize us. She stared at the car, stared at us, stared at the car again, and finally said "Uh, three dollars please."

Don lifted the Thompson slightly and said "We don't need tickets. Drive on." I tipped my hat slightly to the open-mouthed girl in the ticket booth and drove on. Sadly, my days of driving on were about to end, at least for a while.

Chapter 6 – Grounded

They say there are three things that are true at any university. The alumni want a winning football team, the students want sex, and the faculty wants parking. At Purdue the students joined the faculty in wanting parking, in addition to their other desires of course. Like most universities, Purdue had a shortage of parking. When I arrived as a freshman, Purdue chose to solve the parking problem by only allowing upperclassmen to have cars. And by "have cars" they meant "have a car anywhere near Purdue." If an underclassman so much as got a parking ticket in Tippecanoe County, where Purdue was located, their continued enrollment in the University was in jeopardy. So, with great reluctance, I parked my Model A in the garage at the lake and began my college career as a pedestrian.

My parents drove me to Purdue on a sunny September day and helped me carry my few boxes of belongings up to my dorm room. The dormitory was built in 1928, but it had been extensively repainted since then. I was in what was known as a small double. The "small" designation came from the fact that forty years of repainting had made the walls so much thicker that the room now offered significantly less floor space than it had in '28. Other than that, not much had changed. Plaster walls, metal frame bunk beds, a battered oak desk, a hard wooden chair, and a clanking steam radiator beneath a solitary window. (The radiator gave off more noise than heat, owing to the insulating qualities of all those layers of paint.) A phone booth in the hall provided the only hint of modern technology. Since I was to share that phone with 30 or 40 other students it was easy to see I wouldn't be spending much time on the phone. All in all, I'd seen prison movies with more appealing quarters. At least they had a toilet in their room. I had to make do with a gang latrine down the hall.

Mom, Dad, and I had lunch at the Student Union and then walked back to the visitor parking area. We said our good-byes, my mom hugged me, and then they got in the car. They drove off, giving me a cheery wave as they left. Then I was alone. Don and Andy were going to a different school. Cory was going to a different school. Everyone I knew was going to a different school. Somehow, on a campus of 35,000 students, I felt utterly alone. I stared down the vacant street where my parents had disappeared from sight. If tumbleweeds had grown in Indiana, one would have been rolling down that street. I turned toward my dorm and slowly walked down the sidewalk. I was thinking about the past, as it seemed like a golden age had just ended: aimless driving in the Model A, the drive-in theater, skiing at the lake. Graduation had been fun. My parents had given me a Samsonite suitcase and a radio alarm clock as graduation presents. My grandparents gave me a box fan, and Father Dupree honored me with a set of nail clippers. That last present seemed like an unusual graduation gift at the time, but as the years went by I realized it was one of the most fundamentally useful presents I had ever received, and it's the only graduation present I still use today. Fr. Dupree also gave me a word of advice. "Never be average" he said. "If you're average, you're just the best of the worst or the worst of the best." That turned out to be very good advice, but it wasn't of much comfort as I walked to my dorm room. Suddenly, I heard a familiar "chuffa-chuffa-chuffa" behind me. I turned, and watched a 1931 Model A Ford pull into the dormitory parking lot.

I tried to act casual as I sauntered over to take a closer look, but I was so excited to find something familiar in my new surroundings that I set a new record for the fifty yard saunter. By the time I got to the car the driver was, not surprisingly, fussing with something under the hood. He wasn't blowing out a gas line, though. The cross he had to bear seemed to be an alternator which someone had installed in place of the original generator. This needed to be fiddled with whenever he started or stopped the car. Or at least, that was the general impression I gleaned from the stream of profanity he was spewing at no one in particular. He was a big bear of a man with a full beard and a gruff voice that sounded a little like W.C. Fields. I think he was aware of me because some of his comments seemed to be a response to my questions, but it was obvious I didn't have his undivided attention. I didn't even seem to have his divided attention. He sort of grunted an acknowledgement when I told him I had a Model A myself, but all in all he made me feel about as significant as a fly buzzing around the aft end of a mule. After a brief visit I made some excuse about having work to do and left him muttering under the hood.

I walked back to my dorm room and tried to think of something to do for the rest of the afternoon. It took me about 15 minutes to unpack. I got out my campus map and my class schedule, and tried to figure out how I was going to make it from one building to another in the 10 minute break between classes. A few minutes later there was a pounding on my door, with someone shouting "Hey! You got a phone book?" I opened the door and there was the Model A owner. This time he was surprisingly friendly. It turned out he lived just across the hall from me. His name was Al, he was a senior, and he was from southern Indiana. We chatted about cars and Purdue for a few minutes, and then he said "Come on. You've got to meet Viktor."

Viktor was a tall, thin Bohemian from Chicago. He also was a senior and had a full beard. Later I learned it was a tradition at Purdue for men to show up for their senior year with a full beard and shave it off after Purdue won its first home football game. (Sadly, that tradition was fading fast, and by the time I was a senior I seemed to be the only student who grew a beard for the occasion. In my case I had to shave it off before my first ROTC class, as the military's love of tradition apparently didn't include senior beards.) Viktor owned a 1930 Model A pickup truck, although he hadn't brought it to Purdue. Viktor also had a rich, expressive vocabulary that would make a drunken sailor blanch. Al tended to simply hurl a few crude expletives at anything and everything that offended him, but Viktor chose his profanity with great care, using precisely the correct word, always the correct tense, and often improvising complex adjectival phrases to suit the occasion. Al and Viktor introduced me to Raymond, another senior and an agriculture student from a tiny farming community in southeastern Indiana. Surprisingly, for someone who grew up with a cow for a pet, Raymond was the most refined of the three, and far and away the smoothest talker. Sadly, Raymond did not own a Model A, but in all other respects he seemed quite normal.

Returning to my room, I noticed a pile of boxes and suitcases on the top bunk. I assumed I had a roommate, but it wasn't until after dinner that I actually got to meet him. He popped into the room with a couple of his high school buddies who lived in a different dorm, dug through the boxes on the top bunk until he found the record he wanted, and headed for the door. Then almost as an afterthought, he introduced himself and his friends. As soon as the "hellos" were finished they disappeared. I read for a while, turned out the lights, and went to bed.

Somewhere on the north side of 2:00 AM I woke to the agonizing squeals of a pig being pulled through a knothole. There was a deep thumping noise, too. Maybe I was back at the Beaver Hotel, and the steam whistle was announcing the start of the morning shift at the copper refinery. Or maybe the sawmill had run out of grease and the machinery was howling in protest as the bearings melted. I'm a sound sleeper and I'm sometimes a little confused when I'm awakened suddenly. It takes a lot to wake me up, but in this case not only was there this God-awful din in the room, the place was filled with the glare of a thousand arc lights. Squinting against the brightness, I gradually discerned that my roommate and his friends had returned. They were standing in the room drinking sodas and shouting to be heard over a stereo that was playing at full volume.

"Hope we didn't wake you" my roommate shouted in my direction. Then he jerked his thumb toward the stereo. "Steppenwolf" he announced.

In addition to 20's jazz, I liked to listen to Henry Mancini, movie sound tracks, show tunes, and folk music - or at least, folk music where the singers didn't descend into politics. Every once in a while I'd be in the mood for some classical guitar music, but I regarded electric guitars as an abomination. OK. Some of the early Les Paul stuff was amusing, but I hated the modern players who deliberately distorted the music. I especially detested players who made the guitar squeal, like a microphone held too close to a speaker. Whoever or whatever Steppenwolf was, they seemed to enjoy tormenting their instruments. To this day whenever I hear obnoxious music on the radio I assume it must be Steppenwolf.

"That's OK" I replied to my roommate, with what I thought was extraordinary courtesy under the circumstances. "I sleep better when there are bright lights and loud music in the room." I lay back down and pulled the pillow over my head. The party continued unabated. Evidently this group didn't grasp the concept of sarcasm. Fortunately I have always been able to fall asleep under almost any circumstance, and I gradually drifted off again.

The next day was quieter, with just my roommate and me in the room. We may have gotten off to a rough start the night before, but once we got a chance to get to know each other it took almost no time at all to discover we had absolutely nothing in common. Books, movies, music, cars, hobbies, sports – you name it and we didn't share it! He seemed like a nice enough guy, but after a few minutes conversation neither one of us could think of anything more to say. Fortunately he spent most weekdays with his friends in the other dormitory and he went home every weekend, so I had the closest thing possible to a private room.

I soon discovered the only reason my roommate and his friends got away with playing loud music at 2:00 AM was because the dorm counselor hadn't arrived yet. In 1969 Purdue still took the concept of "In Loco Parentis" seriously. While you were a student, the university acted as your local parent. They stopped short of nagging you to eat your vegetables in the cafeteria, but in all other regards they were even stricter than my mom and dad. Quiet hours were from 10:00 PM to 7:00 AM. No running or shouting in the halls. No alcoholic beverages anywhere on campus, and you could only have one empty beverage container in your room "for decorative purposes." On most nights you had to wear a shirt with a collar and slacks (no jeans) to get served in the cafeteria. The exceptions were Wednesday night and Sunday dinner, when a coat and tie were required. You could have a girl visit your room once per semester, for not more than 15 minutes, between the hours of 1:00 PM and 4:00 PM on a Sunday afternoon, if accompanied by your parents, her parents, or a dorm counselor. Many of these rules had been enforced since the mid 1800's, when John Purdue beat William Digby in a poker game and won the right to name the school. The rules were fading fast when I began at Purdue, and by the time my younger brother enrolled they had vanished altogether. (Isn't it always true that your younger siblings get all the breaks?)

Strict rules do not necessarily create saints. The three seniors I had met on my first day at Purdue took me under their wing and spent the rest of the year making certain I got a well-rounded education. Purdue taught me chemistry, physics, and calculus. They taught me how to drink, swear, smoke a pipe, and indulge in other vices, all of which took me years to unlearn. (We didn't do drugs, though. Even at the height of the "psychedelic era" we knew that drugs were for losers.) They also taught me a variety of practical jokes, which for some reason were known locally as "pimp jobs." Most of them were relatively mild, such as covering someone's doorknob with Vaseline. Not only did that leave a disgusting mess in your hand when you grabbed the doorknob, most of the latches were so stiff you couldn't possibly open the door until after you'd thoroughly degreased the doorknob. Filling a manila envelope with shaving cream was another favorite. You could then slit open one end of the envelope, slip it under someone's door, and stomp on the envelope. If you did it right, there would be an explosion of shaving cream inside the room. More elaborate schemes, such as placing a cherry bomb inside a bag of flour and setting it off inside someone's room, were talked about but never executed.

One afternoon Viktor, Al, and I were sitting in Al's room, discussing what to do about the junior who lived in the room next to mine. He was one of those guys whom Viktor claimed could "tick off Santa Claus" (or words to that effect.) The fact that he inexplicably lined his walls with tin foil which rustled and crackled whenever he made the slightest movement was a minor irritant. More annoying was the fact that he would blast out "Give My Regards to Broadway" on his stereo every morning at 7:00 AM, the moment quiet hours ended. He also rode a 2-cycle motorbike with straight pipes which made a highly obnoxious "Rrrrringgg – dinga – dinga – Rrrrringgg – dinga – dinga" noise when he warmed it up before going for a drive. The fact that the bike rack was just below my window and he warmed it up for at least 5 minutes before driving away made this particularly annoying.

"Why don't we wait until some night when he's got a hot date, penny him in his room, and make a big mud hole underneath his window" suggested Viktor. "He'll be all dressed up, and when he can't open the door he's sure to try climbing out the window."

"What the hell do you mean by 'penny him in his room?'" asked Al.

"You've got to be sh---ing me!" exclaimed Viktor. "You're a senior and you've never pennied anyone in their room?"

"Never even heard of it" snorted Al. He sounded a little defensive. His reputation as a world-weary senior who'd seen it all and done it all was being challenged.

"It's not that difficult" explained Viktor. "You just wedge a penny or a stack of pennies between the door and the doorframe and it jams the lock."

"That wouldn't work, would it?" asked Al. "I don't see how that would jam the lock."

"I'm not kidding" said Viktor. "It really works. Here, I'll show you. Have you got some pennies? You can do it with a pencil, too."

Al found a pencil on his desk and gave it to Viktor. I followed Viktor into the hall and he instructed Al to lock the door behind us. When we heard the deadbolt click into place Viktor pushed in hard at the top of the door and created enough of a gap to wedge the pencil between the door and the doorframe. He then pounded it down as close to the lock as it would go, calling through the door to Al to explain what he was doing. When he couldn't get it to go down any farther he told Al to try opening the door.

"Hey! That's pretty cool" said Al. "I can't budge the lock."

"This has got to be the pimp job of the century!" Viktor called through the door. "I told you what I was going to do every step of the way and you still let me do it." He then turned and walked down the hall to his room, whistling happily as he listened to the increasingly frantic pounding and shouts of "Let me out!" from Al's room.

Since I was condemned to the life of a pedestrian that year I didn't have many adventures of interest to this story. After all, this is supposed to be a book about cars, remember? I did experience one automotive incident, however, which even today leaves me a bit bewildered.

When Dad and I rebuilt my Model A engine, I bought a junk engine for parts. One day I happened to notice an unfamiliar pipe in the box of miscellaneous effluvia which came with the junk engine. After much head scratching, I discovered it was an oil return line which went from the tappet cover to the block. My engine had no such line, and in fact the junk engine had castings on the block and the tappet cover which my engine lacked. At first I thought the junk engine was an oddball, but after mentioning this to several Model A collectors I discovered that my engine seemed to be the only one anyone had ever heard of that didn't have this oil return line. It seemed hard to believe that Ford would have cast one Model A block that was different than the other 4,320,445 Model A blocks, but that appeared to be the case. Viktor was active in a large Model A club in Chicago and he knew the president of the nation-wide Model A Restorer's Club, so I gave him some photographs of my engine which he shared with the club. They searched the Ford Archives but could find no record of any car ever having been built without this oil line. Ford was experimenting with repositioning the line when my car was built, and apparently one experiment involved removing the line completely. Henry was never one to let anything go to waste, and it seems that when they had finished their experiment they sold the car. I was now the lucky owner of that car. The Model A Restorer's Club published photographs of my engine in their monthly magazine, and that was the end of it. Or so I thought. Then one night I got a phone call.

Although we had no phones in our rooms, each room had a bell and every resident had a unique phone number. When someone called your number, the bell would ring in your room and you could pick up the call in the phone booth down the hall. On a cold January night my bell rang, so I walked to the phone booth and picked up the receiver. There was an operator on the line.

"Long distance person-to-person phone call for a Mr. Steven Tom" she said. I had never gotten a person-to-person call before in my life. I've never gotten one since, for that matter. This was long before the phone system was deregulated. The phone company was a monopoly and even ordinary long distance calls were outrageously expensive. I called my parents maybe once or twice a month while I was at school, and then only for a few minutes because the calls were so expensive. I had no idea how much a long distance person-to-person call would cost.

"This is Steve Tom," I said.

"One moment while I connect your party." There was a short pause, and a clicking of connections. Then a man's voice was on the line.

"This is Mister Model A of America. Are you the feller that's got the Model A with no oil return line?"

"Yes, that's me."

"You're dead, son!" I didn't know quite what to make of this phrase. His voice didn't sound like it was a threat, but it certainly was unsettling. I thought he meant I was dead right, but I wasn't absolutely certain. Then he continued.

"I got one just like it, but it's got a Lincoln starter/generator and an automatic transmission."

"I, I didn't know they ever made a Model A with an automatic transmission." I was trying to be polite. I knew damn well Ford had never made a Model A with an automatic transmission, and I was pretty sure the automatic transmission wasn't even invented until about 20 years after the last Model A had been built. Still, when you're talking to someone who seems to be crazy, it's best to be polite. Especially if he's just told you you're dead.

"Naw, this ain't in a car. But it's just like yours, except for the Lincoln starter/generator and the automatic transmission. You ain't gonna sell yours, are you?"

"No, I don't think I'll ever sell mine."

"You're dead, son!" There was that phrase again. A long silence followed, during which I was trying to figure out just what it was that this guy wanted.

"You hang onto that car now, you hear?"

"I will."

"You're dead son! I'll let you go now. I just wanted to let you know I got one just like yours."

The phone went dead. I walked back to my room trying to make some sense of the call. It must have cost him at least $10 or $20 to make a long distance person-to-person call, and all he did was tell me he had an engine just like mine. Except it wasn't just like mine. It had a Lincoln starter/generator and an automatic transmission. Oh, and he also wanted to tell me I was dead. I was tempted to just write him off as a crackpot, but then again, how could he be a crackpot? After all, he was Mister Model A of America!

(Postscript: I recently found a web site created by a Model A collector who takes his hobby seriously. He has spent years researching Ford archives, trying to identify every engine variation that ever left the factory. He found a document that indicated approximately 1,350 experimental engines were built without this oil line. On his web site he asked if anyone had ever seen such an engine, so I sent him photos of mine. I checked his blog just before going to press, and to date I have the only known surviving car with one of these experimental engines.)

Chapter 7 - New Horizons and a Minor Setback

I was a little more cheerful about beginning my second year at Purdue. Al, Viktor, and Raymond had all graduated and moved on, but Don had transferred to Purdue. He had visited me a couple of times the previous year, and was impressed by the fact that the people he met actually seemed to be interested in their classes. True we were using our newfound engineering skills for challenges like wiring an ignition coil to a doorknob so it would shock the wee-willikers out of anyone who tried to open the door, but apparently that was a step above the pranks that were being pulled at his school. At his school the sole focus of students seemed to be on how drunk everyone got at last weekend's parties and who was throwing the best party next weekend. Although Don was not an overly conscientious student, he did feel he ought to be getting something more than a party experience out of his tuition. Don and I shared what was known as a "large double," a corner room which had two primary advantages over the small double I'd lived in the year before. First, it was in fact a larger room, providing a gross floor area of roughly 100 square feet, or 50 square feet per student, a number which brought it into compliance with Federal Prison standards. Second, being a corner room, it had a vastly improved climate control system, namely two windows and two clanking radiators.

Since I was still an underclassman I couldn't bring the Model A to Purdue. Early in the semester I met an extremely rare student – an underclassman (a freshman no less) who actually had a car on campus. His name was Nick and he was a tall, solidly built Italian with dark hair and an ever present smile. His dad owned a sports car dealership in a nearby railroad town and Nick had somehow convinced the Purdue authorities that he was indispensable to the family business. This meant he needed a car to drive home every weekend. Nick was a hard worker, but I'm not certain he spent every weekend working the family business. Then again, his car was probably not something most students would want to be seen in, let alone put in the spotlight by arguing for a special privilege. In addition to selling MGs, Triumphs, Jaguars, and other exotic foreign sports cars, his dad also sold Ramblers. If you had a lot filled with MGs, Jaguars, and Ramblers, which car would you trust your son to drive to college? Right. Nick drove a 1965 Rambler Classic convertible. Affectionately known as the Kenosha Koach since

Ramblers were built in Kenosha Wisconsin, this car had been wrecked by a salesman who "borrowed" it off the showroom floor one weekend, got drunk, and ran it through a barbed wire fence. Nick's dad fixed it up after the accident, but no one wanted to buy a brand-new car that had been run through a fence so they used it as the shop "mule" for several years. It was loaned out to customers who had cars in the shop, driven to Chicago for emergency parts runs, used as a tow car by various amateur racers, and generally abused for years before Nick got it. By the time Nick showed up at Purdue it had the patina of neglect about it. Dents, scratches, rust, and silver duct tape repairs to the white convertible top (or at least the "used to be white" convertible top) were the first things one noticed about this car.

Appearances notwithstanding, the Kenosha Koach had the distinction of being the only brand-new 1965 Rambler on campus. Possibly it was the only brand-new 1965 Rambler in the world. Since the car had never been sold, it had never been titled. Never mind the fact that it had over 100,000 miles on the odometer. It was still carried on the dealership's books as a new car, with a certificate of origin which could be exchanged for a title should anyone ever decide to buy it. No one ever decided to do that, so Nick was "forced" to use dealer plates when he drove the car. This eventually led to an impasse with the campus police, who issued the coveted parking stickers that were absolutely essential to having a car on campus. The speed with which the campus police could ticket an illegally parked car was legendary. Just as the university hosted visiting professors who came from around the world to study under Purdue's esteemed engineering faculty, campus police departments from around the country sent their meter maids to study the miracles Purdue was achieving with three-wheeled golf carts. This ticketing system was backed up by a thoroughly entrenched bureaucracy that issued parking stickers. The form required to get a sticker had a space for the vehicle registration number. There was no place for a certificate of origin. The lady who issued stickers was adamant that Nick would have to register the car before he could get a sticker. In vain Nick argued that such a move would be pointless, and that it would cost his father thousands of dollars. Currently the Kenosha Koach was a new car, a very rare condition for a 1965 Rambler. If he registered it, it would just be another used car, and not a particularly valuable one at that. He also suggested that it would be untruthful, perhaps dishonest for him to write up a bill of sale and register it, as the car would still belong to the dealership no matter what the paperwork said. In response, the sticker lady said it was no concern of hers what the car was or was not worth. If he didn't have a registration number he wouldn't get a sticker. She went on to say that in her opinion it was untruthful and perhaps dishonest to drive a car on dealer plates when it wasn't actually being used for dealer business. She went on to suggest that she might be able to use her influence to get Nick transferred to an institution where he could learn to make his own license plates. (In Indiana, stamping out license plates is one of the useful occupations they teach at the men's penitentiary.)

I learned a valuable lesson that day. I learned that when a knight battles a dragon, sometimes the dragon wins. Sometimes, no matter how well the knight prepares for battle or how proudly his banners are flying, the dragon takes one "huff" and then flicks the smoldering remains onto the pile of rusting armor left by all the other knights who had challenged it. Bureaucracies are a lot like dragons. Nick registered the car, and the Kenosha Koach became just another well-worn Rambler.

Late that fall Viktor came to visit driving his latest acquisition – a 1949 MG TC. He had told me about this car over the phone but I was a bit skeptical about it, primarily because he sold his Model A pickup to buy it. I didn't see how any car except a Stanley could be better than a Model A. Then I drove his MG. I wouldn't sell my Model A for one because I had too much sentimental attachment to my A, but the MG was certainly a revelation. I had heard a lot about sports cars from my friend Chris, but I had never actually driven one. Chris's mother had sold the Jag about the time Chris turned 16, a move which I didn't fully understand until I had kids of my own. In its place, she bought an Austin-Healey Sprite for Chris to drive. Chris had told me about its precise steering, tight cornering, and phenomenal gas mileage, but the words had failed to impress me. I'd driven friends' "hot" Novas, Mustangs, Camaros, and similar performance cars which were loved by their owners, but they didn't hold much appeal to me. There was something about this MG, though, which captivated me in a way that Chris's words and my friends' muscle cars never did. To begin with, the handling was astounding, at least compared to my Model A. True, with roughly 50 hp under the hood, it couldn't keep up with the muscle cars. Actually, it had only a little more horsepower than the Model A. It used an engine about a third the size of the Model A's to generate those horses, though, and the engine was much quicker to rev. Since the car itself weighed about half what the Model A weighed, the acceleration seemed quite peppy in comparison. The cornering was what really amazed me. A mere twitch of the steering wheel was all that was needed to send the car off in another direction. Indeed, until I got used to it I was hard pressed to keep the car going in a straight line, as I was constantly overcorrecting with the steering wheel. Again, as far as absolute performance figures are concerned, the MG probably couldn't have out-cornered any of my friend's muscle cars or even my Dad's Maverick. (He had finally traded in his Falcon.) Those skinny 19" bicycle tires made certain this car was not going to set any new records on a skid pad. There is, however, a certain "feel" to a sports car, an agility, an eagerness to snap from one direction to another, that isn't captured by performance numbers but which can make them an absolute delight to drive. This car had a true sports car feel to it.

Viktor's 1949 MG TC

I must confess that at least some of the appeal of this MG came from the fact that it was old. I've always been fascinated by the past, and by antique machinery in particular. I like to see how the designers made use of the materials and technology available to them at the time. I also like the straightforward driving controls that were used when the only intelligent subsystem in the car was the driver. This car bore a lot more similarity to my Model A than to anything in a dealer's showroom. Clam shell fenders, giant chrome headlights, an upright radiator, a fold-down windshield – this was one of the most beautiful cars I had ever seen. It also had more than enough "quirks" to make it lovable. A giant wire-spoked steering wheel, a tachometer the size of a dinner plate, right-hand drive, and a hand crank in case the electric starter ever died. I may not have been willing to trade my Model A for one, but I knew someday I would have to own an MG TC.

First semester came to an end amid the icy blasts of an Indiana winter, and my tenure as an underclassman ended with it. By testing out of a couple of introductory classes and taking 18+ hours per semester, I completed my freshman and sophomore years in three semesters. Maybe there was some benefit to not allowing underclassmen to have cars, as it certainly left me with lots of time for studying. In any event, after my last final exam was graded I was officially an upperclassman, and that meant I could have a car on campus.

After spending an enjoyable semester break with my parents, I proudly packed my suitcase and a tool box into the Model A and set off for Purdue. It was a rather balmy day for January. The temperature was below freezing, but the sky was clear and the sunlight was sparkling off a fresh layer of snow. I had the manifold heater bolted into place, but being no fool I was wearing heavy boots, a winter coat, thick gloves, and a woolen cap. The Model A had never run better and it was just eating up the miles. Or at least, it ate up the first 30 miles. As I was sailing through the town of Palestine Indiana there was a sudden bang from under the hood. This was followed by a horrible crunching noise, as though an evil gremlin had just thrown a handful of gravel into my engine. I killed the ignition and coasted off to the side of the road. It's amazing how silent the world is at a time like this. After an hour of the rumbling, creaks, rattles, and roars that constitute normal Model A sounds followed by a few seconds of that agonizing death rattle, there was no noise. No traffic sounds, no birds singing, no crickets chirping, just the labored breathing of a very disappointed kid with a broken car.

Mentone Indiana is known as the Egg Basket of the Midwest. There's a giant concrete egg in the middle of town to advertise this distinction, but that's not what brought me to Mentone that afternoon. What brought me to Mentone was a tow truck. Palestine didn't even have a gas station, much less a garage. Fortunately it did have a pay phone. So I had the A towed to Mentone, where it sat outside a Marathon station with a two stall garage. Both stalls were occupied, so I lay down in the snow and began unbolting the oil pan. Suddenly, the weather didn't seem nearly a balmy as it had that morning. After much shivering and some frantic digging through the snow with numb fingers looking for dropped bolts, I got the pan off. There was a pile of ground up metal pebbles in the bottom. Peering up into the engine, with an occasional drop of oil in my face thank you very much, I could see the problem. The bottom half of the number two piston had decided to detach itself from the upper half and drop down into the oil pan, where the spinning crankshaft smashed it to pebbles in the few seconds it took me to turn off the engine. Being aluminum it was much softer than the crankshaft, and as near as I could see the only thing that was damaged was the piston. Not an ideal situation to be sure, but it was repairable if I could find another piston.

Luck was with me that day, as there was a machine shop in Mentone that had a decent used Model A piston I could use as a replacement. Actually, luck was with me on several fronts. The old piston hadn't seriously damaged the engine, the machine shop had a replacement, my parents had talked me into leaving for school a couple of days early just in case I had trouble on the road, and the people in the Marathon station took pity on me after a few hours and found a spot where I could work inside. By noon the next day I had the Model A running again. The weather wasn't nearly as balmy as it had been the day before, and it was threatening to get worse, so I reluctantly decided to drive home. It was only 30 miles to get back home, and about 100 miles to get to Purdue, so I decided discretion was the better part of valor.

That turned out to be one of the wiser decisions I've made in my life, as the following day the number 3 piston decided to shed its skirt. Dad and I had tried to keep the costs as low as possible when we rebuilt the engine, and that included re-using the 40 year old pistons. They looked fine, but apparently they weren't up to prolonged high speed cruising. ("High speed" in the Model A meant

65

55 mph. Top speed was around 65 mph, but at that speed the steering was very dicey and the brakes were a bit scary as well.) So, I ordered a new set of pistons from J.C. Whitney and reluctantly let my parents drive me back to school. A few weeks later I got a chance to come home for a weekend. Dad and I put in the new pistons, and I eased the car to Purdue at 45 mph. Finally I had wheels again!

It's amazing what a difference a set of wheels can make to a boy at college, even if they are 40 year old wheels. Suddenly, Don and I weren't confined to the dormitory any more. Movies, bookstores, restaurants, even road trips to visit friends at other colleges were suddenly possible. Naturally we made a few trips to visit Don's old college. He may have decided he wanted something more than a party school for an education, but that didn't mean it wasn't a good destination for a weekend. The Model A even proved to be pretty reliable on these trips. We only had to blow out the gas line once or twice per trip, and the generator even held up to night driving. Then one week we got invited to the mother of all road trips – a weekend at Indiana University!

To understand why this trip was so exciting, you need to understand the relative positions held by Purdue and IU. The Indiana state legislature didn't want to waste money on competing programs, so they divvied up programs between the major universities. IU got the medical school, the law school, the pure sciences, and the liberal arts. Purdue got the veterinary school, the school of pharmacy, the engineering schools, and the agricultural department. That meant IU was filled with actresses, musicians, French majors, and various other artists of the female persuasion. Is it any wonder IU sounded like a magical city? The mysterious Land of Oz where all your wishes would be granted? By comparison Purdue was filled with, well, geeks and nerds. (Except for Don and me, of course.) This was especially true in Engineering. As an engineering student I spent most of my life in classes, labs, and the engineering library. These locations were packed with engineering students, and almost all of them were male. It wasn't that the engineering schools weren't open to women. The students would have gotten down on their hands and knees and begged for more women students. It's just that back then most women weren't interested in engineering - especially mechanical engineering.

Mechanical engineering students studied thermodynamics and worked on greasy machinery, and for some reason this didn't appeal to the fairer sex. Thankfully this has changed dramatically in the years since I was a student, but during my undergraduate program I can only recall two women in any of my mechanical engineering classes. One appeared to have chosen Purdue because her physique was a dead ringer for Purdue Pete, the Boilermaker mascot. The other was quite attractive, or at least on the few occasions when I was able to catch a glimpse of her she looked nice. Just as it would be difficult to see a solitary candle in a room full of moths, so it was difficult to see this student through the throng of admirers who swarmed around her. Needless to say, the prospect of a road trip to a school where rumor had it the women actually outnumbered the men was exciting.

The specific justification for this road trip was an invitation from Jill, who was Corey's girlfriend. Corey had hitchhiked to Alaska the previous summer and then discovered it wasn't as easy to hitchhike back. He decided to drop out of school temporarily and spend the winter working a series of incredibly high paying odd jobs. (Alaska was in the midst of an oil boom at the time.) Don and I knew Jill from high school and had shared a few Model A adventures with her, so she invited us to come visit her at IU. Jill was off limits as far as dating was concerned - she was still Corey's girlfriend even if he was stranded in Alaska - but we were looking forward to seeing her again and we figured there was a good chance she'd know a couple of other girls who might be free that weekend. After all, this was IU! So one Friday afternoon Don and I packed the Model A with a bag of Cheetos, a six-pack of Vernor's ginger ale, Don's portable Victrola, and an album of 78's. We were ready for a road trip to the Emerald City.

The trip there went great. As the warm, spring afternoon melted into a glorious evening we stuffed ourselves with Cheetos and Vernor's as the miles slid effortlessly by. The Model A seemed to be enjoying the trip, as the gas line stayed clear, the radiator stayed cool, and the generator continued to generate. No doubt it enjoyed the crooning voice of Rudy Vallee, as Don would periodically wind up the Victrola and play a tune for the road. We found IU with no problems, and even managed to follow Jill's directions to her dorm. That's when our troubles began. We called Jill's room from the phone in the lobby, but her roommate said Jill wasn't there. It turned out Corey had earned so much money in Alaska he was able to buy a plane ticket home. He had surprised Jill that morning by calling her from Yodersburg, whereupon she frantically searched the ride boards until she found a ride home herself. In all the excitement of Corey's return, she totally forgot she had invited Don and me to come for a visit.

We weren't totally out of options. Marianne Kressler, my high school dream girl, was a student at IU. Well, perhaps "dream girl" was too strong a phrase, since I had never actually found the courage to tell her that I liked her. On the other hand, we had gone out together on more than one date and I had never seriously injured her with my hat. In my book, that made her special. It only took a moment to find her address in the phone book, and we set off to surprise her at her dorm. We managed to surprise her all right, just as she was leaving to fulfill a babysitting commitment she'd made with one of her professors. Somehow, when her roommate told her the parking lot contained "two guys in an old car playing 'Yes! We Have No Bananas' on a wind-up phonograph" she guessed it was us. She barely had enough time to lean out the window and shout "hello" before she had to leave.

Our one last hope was another girl we knew from high school. We hadn't actually spoken to her since graduation, but the last we'd heard she was planning to go to IU. We found her name in the phone book, but her roommate said she'd gone out on a date and no one knew when she'd be back. Three strikes and we were out. Our spirits crushed, Don and I climbed back into the Model A and headed north, leaving the land of milk and honey behind us. The drive back to Purdue was a lot quieter than the drive to IU. Fortunately the Model A didn't let us down that night, and we got back to the dorm around 2:00 AM. In the months and years to come we would have more road trips in the Model A, but we never again set out for IU.

I did learn one more important lesson that spring. Whenever you feel like you're the top dog, there's always somebody just around the corner who can take you down a notch or two. Picture a warm, sunny day in April. You're driving across campus in a 1928 Model A Ford, one of the finest cars ever built. No matter what it looks like to others, to you it's a gleaming gem of a car, the envy of all the lesser peons who scatter before you like chickens. That was me, driving the Model A. The fairy tale ended when a car pulled out of a side street a block ahead and passed me going the other direction. It was a Duesenberg SJ Town Car, around 1930 vintage. Perfectly restored, supercharged, with gleaming chrome pipes and an exposed chauffeur. Never before or since have I seen a Duesenberg on the road. I think maybe the good Lord sent one that day just to remind me not to get too cocky.

1929 Duesenberg Town Car

Chapter 8 – New Love

That spring Don and I discovered a new source of entertainment – searching for derelict sports cars. Nick's Dad was always looking for old sports cars that could either be fixed up and sold or used for parts. The field behind the shop was filled with cadavers that had already donated vital organs to keep customers' cars on the road. In the years to come, I'd learn a lot about foreign cars just by walking through the back lot. There was the usual crop MGs, Triumphs, Fiats, and Healeys, along with a few less common cars. I'd never heard of Jowett before, but they had both a Jowett Javelin and a Jowett Jupiter. The back lot was where I saw my first Sunbeam Alpine, my first Volvo P1800 Sportswagon, and my first Renault Dauphine. (Some cars clearly belonged in the back lot!) I remember the Dauphine in particular, as some previous owner had painted the name "Barney" across the back in large black letters. The back lot was a veritable cornucopia of automotive delicacies, but there was still a need for fresh meat and we were the hunters.

College schedules are wonderfully flexible, and it was surprising how many sunny afternoons there were when neither Nick, nor Don, nor I had any classes. Or at least we didn't have any critical classes. On these afternoons we'd pile into the Kenosha Koach and go sports car hunting. We weren't looking for the kind of sports cars that you see parked in garages, driveways, or used car lots. We weren't even looking for cars you'd see advertised in the Classifieds section of the local newspaper. We were looking for cars lying abandoned behind a garage or hidden amidst the weeds in a back yard. Cars that had been forgotten by their owners, or better still, forgotten by a previous tenant. Cars that could be bought for a song and towed to a life of more productive abandonment.

I was surprised at how many of these cars we found. There was a Triumph Spitfire with no wheels rusting behind a garage. (The owner refused to part with this one, which was probably just as well as the lack of wheels would have made towing difficult.) An MG Midget was quietly rusting away in the weeds behind a rental house, the back porch of which was filled with parts which had inexplicably been removed from the Midget. This car impressed itself upon my memory for two reasons. First, because it taught me that some cars have engines so small that it is indeed possible for two people to pick them up and carry them to the trunk of a waiting Rambler. I was staring at the engine, wondering how we'd ever get an engine hoist around to the back of the house, when Nick simply said "Give me a hand, will you?" and grabbed the front of the engine. Nick was a pretty strong guy and I suspect he could easily have handled the engine by himself, but I dutifully grabbed my end and lifted. The second reason I remember this car is because it taught me to always look to make certain the carburetors aren't filled with chocolate milk before I lift an engine. I have no idea why there was chocolate milk in the carburetors, as that is not a location where chocolate milk occurs naturally. Probably some kid had poured it in there for one of those reasons that only make sense to kids. Or maybe a previous owner thought it would be a magic elixir that would breathe new life into a tired engine. Wouldn't be any stranger than some of the "ring job in a can" products you see in low budget car parts stores. Wherever it came from, it dumped all over my left leg when we hoisted the engine.

We also found a Morris Minor convertible slowly decomposing behind a chicken coop. While not exactly a sports car, it was still an interesting find and Nick thought it would make a good project car for his younger brother AJ to work on. (AJ was maybe 9 or 10 at the time, but apparently the kids in his family started working on cars at an early age.) The lady who owned it insisted it had run fine the previous fall, but the moon pin had gotten stuck in the transmission so it wasn't drivable at the moment. "You just ask anyone who knows anything about transmissions and they can fix it real easy" she assured us. Nick nodded his head in agreement.

When the lady went inside to look for the title I asked Nick what a moon pin was. "I have no idea," he replied. "But I'm sure Dad will know. He knows everything about these cars. I just don't want to let on to this lady that I don't know much about transmissions."

Whatever the problem with the moon pin was, it had the effect of leaving the car stuck in gear. Nick didn't seem to think this would prevent us from towing it back to the shop. We bought the car and he tied it to the back of his Rambler with a long rope. "You just sit inside and steer" he told me. "Watch my brake lights, and hit the brake whenever I start to slow down. Oh, and hold the clutch to the floor while we're moving."

We set off down the road and at first everything went fine. I kept my eyes glued to his brake lights and managed to keep from ramming into him as we stopped for various intersections and traffic lights. Then we got out onto the open road and there were no more stops. Ten minutes went by, and my left leg started to get a little tired holding the clutch pedal. Twenty minutes went by, and holding down the clutch pedal was definitely becoming painful. After half an hour my left leg started shaking uncontrollably and I was pushing down on my knee with my left hand to hold it in place while spasms of pain racked my thigh. Fortunately, at that moment the transmission started making a horrible "grunching" noise and Nick stopped to check it out, so I didn't have to wimp out and tell him I couldn't take it any more. I hobbled around rubbing my leg while Nick crawled under the Morris and disconnected the drive shaft. He had it out in less than five minutes, which made me wonder why I'd spent the last half hour torturing my left leg holding that damn clutch pedal to the floor. We made the rest of the trip without incident.

When we got to the shop, AJ was thrilled to see the Morris. It turned out he collected Morris Minors (or Morris Manures, as he called them) the way other kids collected baseball cards. He already had a variety of sedans, a delivery van, and a pickup truck. With this convertible, he only needed a "woodie" to complete his collection. His dad was less thrilled about our latest acquisition.

"What the hell did you buy a Morris for?" he asked Nick. This was the first time I'd met Luis Riccotto, the proprietor of Riccotto and Sons Imported Motors. He was short and powerfully built, with black hair and a close cropped black moustache. He wore black pants and a white Riccotto and Sons uniform shirt, which distinguished him from everyone else in the shop who wore blue uniform shirts. The stub of a cigar seemed to have taken up permanent residence in the corner of his mouth. In the years to come I would occasionally see him light it, but most of the day it was dead and lifeless. His eyes, by contrast, shone with energy and sparkled when he laughed. He was friendly and talkative, but there was something about him that was just a bit intimidating. At least, he was intimidating to a college kid who felt way out of his league discussing cars with Luis. Somehow, I knew I never wanted to get on his bad side. At one point while we were talking AJ ran screaming through the shop, being chased his younger brother Mario. Luis briefly interrupted our conversation to call over his shoulder "Aww shaddup or I'll break

72

both your necks." The words were spoken without emotion and he barely raised his voice, but both kids stopped dead in their tracks and tiptoed out of the garage. I wondered how many other kids he'd once had who hadn't stopped quickly enough.

Nick started explaining how we'd gotten a great deal on the Morris. "It's in good running condition," he said. "The only thing wrong with it is the transmission. The moon pin is stuck."

"The moon pin?" Luis snorted. "What the hell is a moon pin?"

Several weeks later Nick, Don, and I were again exploring the back alleys and side streets of Lafayette, looking for derelict cars. Nick spotted a tarp covering something with a promising profile sitting in the grass behind a ramshackle house on the edge of town. We knocked on the door, and a blond man in his twenties came to the door. He was shirtless, with disheveled hair, a stubble beard, torn jeans, beat-up sneakers, and no socks. Somehow he didn't fit my image of a sports car driver.

"We're looking to buy old sports cars." Nick announced. "What's that you've got in the back yard?"

"It's an MG." the man replied without enthusiasm. "It ain't run in several years." He walked around to the back yard and we followed. A dog on a chain started barking furiously until the man took it off the chain and shoved it in the back door. Then he pulled off the tarp. Underneath were the remains of a 1957 MGA. The car was mostly blue, with multiple bondo and primer spots interrupting its dull chalky paint. The trunk lid was white, but the rust holes in the rocker panels showed whoever had attempted to do the bodywork hadn't gotten very far. The fact that the entire front end of the car was caved in at least six inches gave further proof to the futility of the spot repairs. The top was mostly intact, with an opaque rear window and heavily scratched Plexiglas side curtains on the doors. Opening the doors, we could see tears in the leather upholstery and smell mildew in the carpet. I immediately fell in love with this car.

I'd never seen an MGA before, and I thought it was one of the most beautiful cars ever built. The long sloping hood was accented by smoothly rounded fenders which blended seamlessly into the door. The door dipped rakishly low toward the rear, giving the driver plenty of elbow room. Behind the door the body kicked up over the rear wheels before sweeping back down to a streamlined tail. Viktor's MG had looked like an antique, but although this car was less than 10 years newer it looked like it came from another century. I could easily visualize this car tearing down the back straights at Le Mans. (Later I would learn that the body design was in fact based upon a Le Mans car, and the MGA prototypes had run at Le Mans.) Somehow it looked more Italian than British, and there was something about it that just screamed "Red. I need to be painted red."

Nick, of course, had seen lots of MGAs in his life, and he was not particularly impressed by this shabby example. After much haggling he talked the owner down to $50. We tied it to the rear bumper of the Kenosha Koach, I hopped in, and we set off for the shop. This was a completely different experience than being towed in the Morris. For one thing, I didn't have to keep my foot on the damn clutch pedal. More than that, though, this car just felt like a fast, responsive race car, even when it was being towed. You sat low in this car, almost on the pavement, with your legs extended straight out in front of you, and your right hand rested naturally on the shift knob. The hood seemed to stretch half-way to the horizon. There was a bewildering array of gauges and knobs scattered from one side of the dash to the other. The windshield was low, and with the top up it felt like the car had been molded around my body. I could tell that the car would respond instantly to the slightest twitch of the steering wheel, although since it was tied to the back of Nick's car I resisted the urge to test that theory. Despite the mildew, an enticing aroma filled the interior. There was a hint of gasoline, of course, or perhaps I should say "petrol" since this was a British car. The smell of old grease and wool carpeting reminded me of the Model A, but there was also a background scent of old leather from the upholstery. This was definitely a car I could get used to.

We dropped the MG off at the shop and I didn't think much more about it. Several weeks later, after final exams were finally over, I stopped by the shop on my way back home for the summer. I noticed they had a red MGA sitting up front. This one was definitely in much nicer condition than the hulk we'd towed in. Nick explained that this was a customer's car, or at least it had been. The customer had towed it in and told them to do whatever was necessary to get it running. "Whatever was necessary" ran up a bill which Nick thought was around $500, and when they gave the customer the bill he refused to pay. He then skipped town. After many unsuccessful attempts to contact him, Riccottos had issued a mechanics lien against the car and were going to sell it for the repair bill. This piqued my interest, as $500 didn't sound like an unreasonable price to pay for a car like that. Still, I already had a car.

A few weeks later as my parents and I were sipping coffee after dinner, they said they wanted to talk to me about my car. For some reason they were worried about me using a 40 year old car as a daily driver. I think maybe they were overreacting to the two broken pistons, but in any event they seemed to think I needed something newer to drive back and forth to school. They were even willing to help pay for it since they suspected (with good reason) that I might be unwilling to sell the Model A to buy another car. Then they asked if this Riccotto fellow might be able to make me a good deal on a used car. All the forces in the universe were suddenly in alignment. I told them about the $500 MGA, and although that wasn't exactly what they had in mind when they suggested I get a more reliable car, they were at least open to the idea. The next morning I called Nick on the phone and he said they still had the car and I could come by any time to look at it. I left immediately.

After I called, Nick told his dad I was driving down to look at the MGA. "We can't sell him that car," his dad replied. It turned out there had been some new developments while Nick and I were taking our final exams, developments Nick hadn't been aware of when he told me about the car. For one thing, the total repair bill was $750, not $500. More importantly, it turned out the reason they hadn't been able to contact the owner was because he was in prison. Under state law, they couldn't use a mechanic's lien to claim title to the car until six months after he was released from prison. Until then, they were stuck storing the car at their own expense. If I really wanted an MGA, his dad suggested they could rebuild the one we had towed into the shop. I'd have to live with them for a week or two and help work on it, but Nick could rebuild the engine while his dad helped me with the bodywork. With my help, they could make it look like a brand new car for $500.

Nick explained this to me when I arrived. Actually, the idea of spending a couple weeks rebuilding the car didn't sound too bad to me. The Air Force had already told me I had to go to a training camp for four weeks in the middle of the summer (I think it had something to do with the papers I signed for an ROTC scholarship) so I couldn't get a real job anyway. Rebuilding the car would be a good way to get to know it inside and out. Somehow I suspected that might be useful in the years to come.

As Nick and I were discussing the details of rebuilding the MGA, his dad came up with a new idea. Luis told me they had just taken a Triumph Herald in on trade, and it would be a much better car for me. I already had the Model A for my fun car, he explained, so I didn't need another toy like the MGA. The MGA only carried two people, and you couldn't carry anything at all in the trunk. The Triumph had plenty of room for four people – you could squeeze in more in a pinch – and it had a full size trunk. Plus it was a convertible, just like the MG.

Luis led me around to the side lot and showed me the Triumph. It was, as he'd said, in beautiful condition. Light blue with a black convertible top, it looked like it had just left the showroom. The interior was immaculate, there wasn't a spot of grease in the engine compartment, and the carpet in the commodious trunk wasn't even dirty. It was also about the dorkiest looking car I'd seen since the last time I looked at a Nash Metropolitan. Everything that was sleek and sexy on the MG was perky and cute on the Triumph. The front of the car was absolutely flat, with a grill that looked like a big toothless grin. The chrome trim around the headlights reminded me of the harlequin eyeglasses middle-aged ladies wore in the 50s. The hood was short, the windshield was tall, and the boxy trunk was framed by cute little forked tail fins. I'm sure that in some quarters the Triumph Herald is considered a classic today and there are people who lovingly restore them. It probably is a fine car, but in the summer of '71 it wasn't a car that college students dreamed of. At least, not this college student. Still, Luis had a point. This was a much more practical car than the MGA. I had always been a kid who tended toward the practical, a kid who faced every decision with the question "what would Dad do?" I was pretty sure Mom and Dad would like this car better than the MGA. And of course, Luis was recommending it, and Luis knew a lot more about cars than I did. For $500, I'd probably never find a car in better condition. And it was a convertible. . . I left the shop without having made a commitment, but with my mind pretty much made up to "do the right thing" and buy the Triumph rather than the MG. This was a Friday, and I promised to get back to them on Monday with a decision.

Triumph Herald

When I told my parents about the Herald that night they didn't seem very excited about it. I thought they'd be happy that I was choosing a practical car instead of the flashy MG, but it didn't seem like it made much difference to them. All that my mom said was "Oh. I thought you wanted an MG." It almost sounded like there was a touch of disappointment in her voice. The next day I had a chance to talk about it with Jill. I'd known Jill all through High School and she had been Corey's girlfriend ever since I could remember. This made her one of the few girls I could talk to just like she was a regular person. I didn't have to get nervous, be entertaining, be overly polite, or worry about accidentally belching. I'd described the MGA to her previously, so now I explained why it made more sense to get the Triumph.

"I suppose it is a more practical car" she said. Then she cut right to the heart of the matter. "Do you want the Triumph?" she asked. I'd never actually thought about it that way. I'd been weighing the pros and cons of the two cars from a transportation standpoint, and everything pointed to the Triumph being a better car for me. When I stopped trying to play accountant, however, I realized I didn't want the Triumph. I wanted the MG. I would probably have years and years of practical cars in my future, but for the moment I could get by with something wildly impractical. There was only one obstacle. I'd have to call Luis and tell him I was rejecting his advice and buying the MG.

I spent the rest of the weekend dreading that phone call, and when Monday morning came I screwed up my courage, called Luis, and told him I'd decided to buy the MG. To my surprise, he didn't seem at all offended that I wasn't taking his advice. "OK" was all he said. "We'll get started on it as soon as you get here." It began to dawn on me that I'd almost bought a car I didn't want because I thought it was what everyone else wanted me to do, and all the people I was worrying about didn't really care which car I bought.

By the time I'd packed a few things and had driven to the shop, Nick already had the engine out of the MG. Luis handed me a power sander and showed me how to cut through the many coats of paint the car had accumulated over the years. Meanwhile, he set to work on the front end, pounding it out until it roughly followed the original body lines and then smoothing it out with Bondo. I'd always heard people speak disparagingly of Bondo, but I'll have to admit it did the trick on my car. When Luis was finished it looked great, and it continued to look great for years and years. After we finished the bodywork Luis sprayed the entire car with the reddest paint we could find.

Once the bodywork was complete, I set to work on the electrical system, finding all the shorts, broken wires, and bad bulbs. I also helped Nick with the engine, although my help mostly consisted of handing him tools and watching him work. Finally it was time to put the engine back in. The trickiest part was getting the engine to slide over the shaft sticking out of the transmission. The engine and transmission have to be perfectly aligned for that miracle to occur, and there's not much room in an MGA to squeeze the engine past the steering gear and frame members to the point where it will line up. Nick got called away at this critical point and left me to try and slip it in by myself. We had the engine hanging from an engine crane and a floor jack was underneath the transmission. I tried to "tickle" things into place – raising the transmission a half inch, lowering the engine a half inch, twisting the engine to a slightly different angle, lowering the transmission again, etc. After a half-hour of this I had made no progress whatsoever. The engine still refused to slide over the transmission shaft. At this point Nick came back.

"Haven't you got that in yet?" he asked. Then he wrapped his arms around the engine and began to shake it the way a terrier shakes a rat. The whole car shook, and I would swear there were times when he lifted all four wheels off the ground. After about 15 seconds of this punishment the engine slid neatly into place. "There you go" he said while wiping his hands. "Now bolt her into place."

By the next afternoon, everything was finished. The engine ran, the brakes stopped, the lights worked, and the new paint gleamed. What more could you ask for? We stood back and admired our work. Luis summed it up. "If you can't get $1000 for that car you're a mighty poor salesman." I drove the car home and showed it off to my parents and my younger brother.

After dinner, I drove the car over to Andy's to let him admire it. It was a warm summer evening, just after dusk. The air smelled sweet, and a gentle breeze rustled the leaves on the trees. The first stars were just beginning to show in the night sky. I knew all this, of course, because I had the top down. Life was good. Suddenly, a black cat darted out in front of me and then froze, its eyes glowing green in my headlights. There was a car in the oncoming lane so I had nowhere to go. I swerved slightly to make certain I straddled the cat, praying that it would stay put and not dart under my wheels. After I passed over it I looked in my rearview mirror and saw it scamper off to safety. I breathed a sigh of relief. Then I inhaled, and nearly gagged. That wasn't a cat – it was a skunk! He rewarded my concern for his safety by spraying the wooden floorboards as I drove over him. It would be a long time before I could stand to put the top up on this new car.

New Love - A 1957 MGA

MGA From Above

Chapter 9 – The Healey

When I first got my MG home, I couldn't immediately show it to Don because Don's family had moved to North Carolina. The company his dad worked for had opened a new plant there and they needed him to run the lab, so they transplanted this Hoosier family to the sand hills of North Carolina. In Don's case, the transplant was rejected. I got an occasional phone call or letter from him, and he wasn't enjoying North Carolina at all. To begin with, he didn't like the heat. He said the lyrics to the song "Nothing could be finer than to be in Carolina in the morning" was correct as far as it went because the mornings were beautiful, but you could forget about the rest of the day. He also didn't get along too well with the locals. He had a summer job working as a waiter in a pizza parlor, and the people there razzed him unmercifully about his "brogue." I couldn't understand how anyone could razz a Midwesterner about his accent because we lived in the only part of the country that didn't have an accent. (It was years before I realized that everyone in the country, from Maine to Texas to Hawaii, thought they were the only ones who spoke English correctly and that everyone else had an accent.) In any event, Don was not happy in North Carolina and he decided to move back to Indiana. His plan was to take a year off from school and work full time, both to earn money to go back to school and to establish Indiana residency so that when he did go back he could pay in-state tuition.

Don moved back to Indiana in late August, shortly before school started, and he moved into an apartment with Andy. He liked my MGA and decided he wanted a sports car too, so I drove him down to Riccotto's. Don's budget was even more limited than mine, and he couldn't spend a couple weeks rebuilding a car, so he followed a different path. He found a 1959 Austin Healey 100-6 decomposing in their side lot. It was gradually making its way to the infamous back lot, but it hadn't quite sunk to that level because it still could be driven under its own power. It would need a lot of work before it could pass the Indiana safety inspection, so Luis at first refused to sell it to him. Don finally talked him into accepting $350 for "parts only," with the understanding that Don would fix all the safety problems before he ever tried to register it. Somehow Don forgot about that part of the plan, and the local license branch didn't seem to be bothered by the fact that Luis had written "parts only" on the bill of sale. They asked no questions and gave Don a license plate.

If the value of a car were based on appearance alone, Don got robbed. This car had originally been painted red, but over the years it had mutated into a two-tone: red over rust. A previous owner had attempted to repair the bodywork with racing stickers. Round holes were covered with STP stickers, square rust-outs were patched with Castrol stickers, and a giant American flag covered what was left of the trunk lid. The top was a dirt-streaked white, with a slightly translucent amber rear window. The famous "Kilroy was here" caricature and fence were scrawled on the top in red paint. Like an old family horse, it was swaybacked. The doors still opened, but the frame had sagged to the point where the latches no longer met the sill and it took a pair of screen door hooks to keep the doors closed. The wheels gave mute testimony to the ingenuity, though not the craftsmanship, of America's backyard mechanics. The center "knock off" hubs of the original wire wheels had been welded into the center of a much wider set of steel wheels. Three wide strips of steel plate, roughly cut with a torch, served to brace the wheels to the hubs. Through luck or divine intervention (even the most charitable observer would not attribute it to skill), the wheels turned true without a trace of wobble. A set of Goodyear Wide Oval bias ply tires graced these mangled mags. It was easy to measure how far the tires protruded beyond the bodywork, as the fenders had cut grooves in the tires where they bottomed out on bumps. The crowning glory, the pièce de résistance of this automotive objet d'art, was a pair of two foot long chromed boat horns mounted prominently on the right front fender. Resplendent in all their gleaming brightness, they were even more conspicuous because they were the only piece of metal on the entire vehicle that still had a shine to it. All in all, the appearance of this car was enough to elicit comment from even the most apathetic non-enthusiast, and it made true sports car aficionados retch.

Beauty, as they say, is only skin deep, and in the case of the Hurtin' Healey that applied to Ugly as well. Despite its appearance, despite the cracks in the main frame members, and despite the bewildering array of hardware store switches someone had installed on the dashboard, this Healey could move! It took a great deal of faith and patience to coax the big six cylinder engine into life, particularly on a cold, damp morning, but once it caught it roared with a ferocity that shook the entire car. First gear was engaged with a "crunch" which tortured the mechanically cognizant. The gear lever had to be held forward with brute force lest it pop back into neutral when the clutch was engaged, but if you could hold it in gear the car would leap forward like a jackrabbit. Second through fourth gears were well behaved by comparison, and with each shift the car would surge forward as though it was riding the crest of a wave. I'm sure the "muscle cars" which several of my friends owned were technically faster than the Healey, but they didn't convey the same sensation of speed and power. Possibly this was because they didn't also convey the sensation that they were going to disintegrate at any moment, or maybe it was because they gave the driver some reassurance that if he relaxed his concentration for a moment the car would continue to travel in a straight line. Whatever the reason, that Healey seemed like the fastest car in the world. It could reach 100 mph in almost no time at all, and with Don at the wheel, it frequently did. A slight ripple in the pavement would cause it to leap into the air like a champion steeplechaser. It would slam back to earth with a sickening crash, then hurtle down the road searching for the next pothole. It seemed accustomed to these leaps, probably because the shock absorbers had given up the ghost years earlier. In fact, the first major jump we attempted somehow "healed" the long dormant electric overdrive. Luis had assured us the overdrive was beyond repair, but when Don accidentally turned onto an abandoned dirt road on our test drive the overdrive kicked in as soon as we crashed over the first pothole. It continued to function properly for the rest of the time Don owned the Healey.

If a day trip in the Hurtin' Healey could be described as "exhilarating," a night trip was downright terrifying. I can still vividly recall the way that car would hurtle through the blackness of an Indiana country road, with one feeble headlight intensifying the darkness by illuminating a small patch of pavement and a shadow of cornfields on either side. (The other headlight, owing to a small rust problem with the adjusting screws, would be helpfully illuminating any tree branches that hung over the roadway.) Don would be hunched over the steering wheel, his grinning face intermittently visible as the dash lights flickered on and off. Like a hapless passenger in a roller coaster from Hell, I would be hunched forward too, trying to spot the next pothole in time to brace for the impact . . . There's one now! . . . Crash!!! The Healey would leap into the air, then fall to earth with a bone-jarring crunch. Sparks shot from the fenders each time the car landed, as the long eroded fenders bit deeper into the Wide Oval tires. A sudden crash, a brief shower of sparks, and the Healey would plunge deeper into the darkness, the moonlight sparkling off those gleaming boat horns.

Like most of us, Don had changed a bit since he graduated from high school and was still experimenting with different personality traits as he blazed his path to adulthood. At this point in his life he was at least as remarkable as the Healey he drove. Six foot four of gangling leanness, he had an unruly mop of dark hair, a slightly continental manner, and a smile that could charm the socks off a centipede. He could infuse a simple phrase like "I'm sorry officer, was I doing something wrong?" with a mixture of courtesy and innocence that would soften the heart of even the most jaded County Sheriff. The fact that he generally drove with the top down, even in the rain, while wearing a deerstalker hat, a pair of gold pince-nez glasses, and smoking a curved pipe served to further disorient the gendarmes. The appearance of the Healey led one to expect it might be driven by Charles Manson, or maybe Ché Guevara, but certainly not this polite mixture of Sherlock Holmes and FDR. On at least one occasion an officer who began with the intention of handcuffing the idiot who was blasting through the countryside with no taillights wound up holding a flashlight and offering suggestions while Don experimentally connected various loose wires in the trunk, hoping to find the combination that would coax his taillights back to life.

On the rare occasions when he had the top up, his appearance was no less remarkable. The top had gradually shrunk over the years to the point where he could put up the top bows or he could fasten the top, but he couldn't do both. As long as he was moving, the bows were superfluous because the wind would puff up the top like a bloated white mushroom. When he stopped, say for a red light, the top would slowly deflate, draping itself over his head and shoulders. He then flailed his arms against the collapsed billows in a vain attempt to see through the windshield, making the whole affair reminiscent of a scene from "The Blob." When the light changed to green he would be off. The top would begin flapping in the breeze like the sail of a schooner that was coming about, and then it would catch the wind and puff back into its dome shape, straining at the snaps that secured it to the car. Occasionally the strain would prove too much, and it would leap into the sky like a dove unleashed, then gracefully flutter back to earth. The unscheduled pit stops that followed these ascensions were actually beneficial from a safety standpoint, as it was usually time to tighten the knock-offs anyway.

Don couldn't see spending the money it cost to buy a copper wheel hammer, so he used a rubber mallet to pound the knock-offs. This mallet did more bouncing than tightening, so every twenty or thirty miles the wheels would start wobbling and Don would once again flail away at the knock-offs with his rubber mallet.

Although the Healey engine proved to be indestructible, the same could alas not be said for the rest of the vehicle. Healeys were a fragile thing of beauty when they left the factory, and this one had seen a lot of hard miles since then. The sides of the oil pan were corrugated, like an accordion, owing to the fact it slammed into the ground quite frequently. The bottom of the pan had originally protruded an inch or so below the frame, but no longer. It was now pounded up to the level of the frame, and both were deeply gouged from moving encounters with rough pavement. The only parts of the car that hung beneath the frame were a few sections of bright copper wire, long since stripped of their insulation. These were flexible enough to push up out of the way when the car bottomed out, and they still occasionally conducted electricity to the nether reaches of the car. The frame itself was cracked in several places, and the first time we put the car up on a hoist we marveled at the fact that the floorboards were made from old antifreeze cans. We never understood why they lasted as long as they did, but long after the factory bodywork crumbled into rust you could still scrape the mud off the floorboards and read the correct amount of antifreeze needed to protect the car to -40°F.

The Healey also suffered from a fair amount of battle damage during our acquaintance. Once, while driving through Chicago, Don made the mistake of stepping on the brake. Ordinarily this was not a hazardous maneuver. It was usually pointless, but once in a while the Healey would surprise everyone by stopping. On this particular occasion, however, a rusted cotter pin allowed the hood support rod to slide forward when Don applied the brakes. Its forward motion was checked when it encountered the spinning fan blades, which bent forward when they struck the rod. Unfortunately, this brought them into contact with the radiator, and they bored the center out of the radiator as neatly as if it had been sliced with a chain saw. Needless to say, Don was not amused when the front end of his car erupted in a fountain of steam and antifreeze. An overnight stay at Viktor's house, a few pounds of solder, and a can of Bars-Leak soon put matters right, or at least as right as anything else on that car.

On another occasion, Don and Jill made a spectacular leap over a railroad crossing, easily the most impressive jump the Healey had ever made. I was following them in my MG (we were on our way to a pizza parlor), but I slowed for the crossing and they left me far behind. When I arrived at the pizza parlor, I found the Healey parked in the middle of a gorgeous rainbow of color. Red, orange, blue, and other iridescent colors shimmered on the oil slick that surrounded the Healey. We could see this was a job for experts, so we took the car to a nearby blacksmith. It turned out a coin would easily cover the hole in the oil pan, and they brazed a shiny new penny into the pan in practically no time.

Probably the most memorable escapade occurred the following spring, when Don was driving the Healey to Purdue for a weekend visit. It was raining cats and dogs when he left, so he was forced to put up the top and reduce his speed to a mere 60 or 70 mph. When he got within about 50 miles of the school, the rain stopped and the moon came out. He then proceeded to make up for lost time. He was traveling on the high side of the century mark when the top decided to make one of its celebrated ascensions. He stopped to retrieve it and, since it was no longer raining, he decided to fold it up and stow it in the trunk. There was a security light shining beside a nearby barn, and Don decided to drive under the light so he could see what he was doing. Having driven his rolling junkyard through a blinding rainstorm at an unholy rate of speed without incident, Don proceeded to drive into a ditch at about 3 miles per hour. It was a little after one o'clock in the morning, and passing motorists were few and far between. Eventually a pickup truck filled with friendly drunks pulled him out of the ditch - a ditch that was now filled with motor oil. The blacksmith who brazed the penny into the oil pan had underestimated the amount of abuse his repair was expected to withstand. It was shortly after this that I got a call: "Buy all the oil you can find and meet me in Clymers." At that time of night all the oil I could find or afford consisted of four gallons of Everest (The Height of Protection) motor oil. A one gallon can of this oil sold for 79¢ and was very popular with the student set. Eventually I found Don and the Healey and followed them back to campus, stopping periodically to slosh a little more oil into the engine. A quick trip to a welding shop the next day and the penny was reattached to the pan, as good as the day it left the factory.

As it turned out, it was neither rust nor mechanical failure nor maniacal driving which doomed the Healey - it was the long arm of the law. Don's winning smile and polite manners might influence the police on the borderline cases, but there was nothing borderline about the sticker on the windshield that said the Healey had last passed Safety Inspection back when LBJ was president. For a while Don tried driving only at night, when it was harder to see the sticker, but even he had to admit this was not a satisfactory compromise. With a heavy heart and a pocket full of court summons, he traded the Healey in on a 1965 MGB. The MG was a vastly more refined car. It still had all its factory bodywork, and it was 100% street legal. It would prove to be one of the best cars Don ever owned, but it wasn't the Healey.

Just as parents have a special place in their hearts for a wayward child, mechanics take a special interest in their "problem children." Whenever I stopped by Riccotto's I would ask the mechanics what was happening with the Hurtin' Healey. After Don traded it in, it was sold to a man who had high hopes of restoring it. He spent over $1000 on bodywork (a princely sum to invest in that car), but there was not enough solid metal left to hold the Bondo together. Great chunks of it flew off when he towed the Healey back from the body shop. Disgusted, he sold it to a man who frittered away several hundred dollars in a vain attempt to make it pass safety inspection. When this proved to be an impossible quest, he sold it to a high school student who used it for stoplight racing. The kid fiddled with the ignition timing, and the carburetors burst into flame one night as he was leaving a gas station. He sold it on the spot to the pump jockey, who soon traded it to Riccotto's for a set of driving lights. It sat forlornly in the side lot for two years, until a passing Healey owner tried to buy parts off it. Luis didn't want to sell parts and be left with a stripped hulk, so he sold the entire car (with title) for the price of the parts. The buyer came back in the dark of night, stripped all the parts he could use off the car, and left the carcass on the lot. (For some inexplicable reason, he didn't take the boat horns.) That was the final blow for the Healey. With no title and several major parts gone, Luis moved it to the infamous back lot. A couple of years later a traveling junk man came by with a portable car crusher and bought what little remained for scrap. Ashes to ashes, rust to rust. The Healey passed into immortality.

Chapter 10 – Learning to Live with an MG

You don't really know a car until you've depended on it as your daily driver, and you don't know it well until you've depended on it for at least a year. As the weeks and months went by, I began to learn more and more about my MG. The looks, the handling, the brakes, the steering – these things I learned pretty quickly. I also discovered other things very quickly, such as the fact that this car literally cooked my feet as I drove. The first time my mother drove the car she actually stopped and got out to look under the hood, as she was convinced the car was on fire. The carpeting that had once served as insulation between the engine and the cockpit was long gone, the exhaust system ran directly under the driver's seat, and there were lots of holes that let hot air from the engine compartment blow into the cockpit. At the time I naively thought this meant the car would be nice and toasty in the winter. When winter came, I learned that all the gaps and holes that let hot air flood the cockpit during the summer were non-discriminatory. They let cold air blast through the car to freeze my derriere during the winter.

One of my first memorable lessons was taught on a balmy June day, shortly after I brought the car home from Riccotto's. I was proudly driving through the neighborhood when I spotted Marianne Kressler standing beside her mailbox, sifting through the day's mail. I stopped to say hello, something I wouldn't have had the courage to do had I been driving a lesser vehicle. I then surprised myself by inviting her to go sailing after lunch. More surprising still, she said yes. I rushed back to my folk's house, as I had a lot to do to get ready. The car had to be washed, interior vacuumed, and the windshield cleaned if I was going to take Marianne for a ride. I also needed to replace my left rear wheel with the spare, as the tread on the spare was much better. Finally, I wanted Mom to help me figure out how fast the car was going, as the MG speedometer didn't work. It would be awfully embarrassing to get a speeding ticket with Marianne in the car. My tachometer worked fine, so I wanted to find out how fast the car was going at different engine RPMs. I figured the easiest way to do this was to follow Mom as she drove at various speeds, signaling her speed by holding up an appropriate number of fingers.

The first several jobs took longer than I expected. By the time I changed the rear wheel I was definitely rushed for time. I figured if I skipped lunch I would still have time to calibrate my speed against the tachometer. Just as I lowered the car down off the jack I got a phone call. My insurance company was having some sort of a problem with the paperwork for the MG. When I finished straightening that out Mom was sitting in her car, ready to go for the test drive. I threw the jack & lug wrench into the MG trunk and we took off.

We drove out to a nearby country road and Mom held three fingers out the window. Thirty miles per hour. Got it. Kind of boring driving 30 miles per hour on this nice straight road. We sped up a little and she held four fingers out the window. Still kind of boring, but something didn't feel quite right. The car didn't want to go in a straight line by itself. I had to keep correcting the steering. When my mom held five fingers out the window the car definitely seemed twitchy. I couldn't understand it. Here I was in a snazzy British sports car, a car that was known for its excellent handling, and I'm feeling nervous just trying to keep up with a big bloated American sedan on a straight country road. A sedan that's being driven by my mom, no less! When she signaled 60 mph I definitely knew something was wrong. It was almost as though the back end of the car had a mind of its own. It was darting right and left at random intervals while I was struggling to keep the car going straight. A sudden, cold chill passed over me. Did I remember to tighten the lug nuts after I took the car off the jack? Maybe I ought to pull over to check them. . .

Thud! The left rear corner of the car dropped down to the pavement as the wheel shot crazily off to the side. With the sickening sound of metal dragging on asphalt I went skidding down the road. I could steer well enough to pull off onto the gravel shoulder. I stopped the car and got out to survey the damage. Fortunately the most serious damage was to my pride. I could see, though, that it was not going to be easy to get the wheel back on the axle. The MG jack was designed to slide under the axle. That's easy to do when the wheel is holding the axle above the ground, but not so easy when the wheel is off in the weeds and the axle is down in the dirt. I was going to have to dig a trench under the car to give me room to slide the jack under the axle. It wasn't going to be easy digging in that hard packed gravel, especially since the only tool I had to dig with was the lug wrench. This was going to take a while. I took a lug nut off one of the remaining wheels and gave it to my mom, asking her to drive to a local parts store and pick up four new lug nuts while I dug the trench. She asked if there was anything else she could do to help. I hesitated for a long time. Dreams die hard. "Yes" I finally replied. "You'd better stop by Marianne's and tell her I won't be able to take her sailing this afternoon."

It wasn't easy to scrape a ditch under the MG but I persevered, muttering curses at my own stupidity all the while. Eventually I got the jack under the car and raised the rear axle enough to slip the wheel back on. I was hot, disheveled, and discouraged, and Mom still wasn't back with the lug nuts. When she finally arrived, the first thing she told me was how cute Marianne had looked in her swim suit. I really didn't need to hear that. Then she told me she went to every parts store in town, but nobody had any metric lug nuts.

"What?" I asked in astonishment. "This car isn't metric! Did they even look at the lug nut I gave you?"

"They just asked me what car it was for. When I said MG they said MG's were metric and they didn't have it." (Foreign cars were still something of a novelty in 1971, and a lot of parts stores didn't carry metric hardware.)

Mom gave me back the lug nut. I was about to put it back on the wheel I'd taken it from when it occurred to me that I probably didn't need all four lug nuts on every wheel, at least, not for a short trip. By taking one lug nut off each of the remaining wheels I had three lug nuts to bolt the left rear wheel back on. Then I drove to a parts store myself and gave them a nut without telling them what it came from. They had a whole bin of nuts that size for 25¢ apiece. I learned a valuable lesson that day. (Well, two if you count the importance of tightening your lug nuts.) Car parts stores have more parts that will fit an MG than they think they have. You just can't let them know it's for an MG. The metric question is particularly vexing, as I've met a great many parts store clerks and more than a few MG owners who swore up and down that MGs were metric. They didn't seem to be aware of the fact that the British invented the inch. Not only did they invent the inch, in the early 1800's England joined several other nations in a war with France to keep Napoleon from spreading his metric pestilence across Europe. The US joined this effort in 1812 by declaring war on England. Admittedly this might not have been the most helpful thing we could have done to oppose metrification, but at least we weren't sitting on the sidelines. Napoleon ran into a spot of bad luck at Waterloo, the good guys won, and the metric system should have faded into obscurity. Unfortunately, in this case the victors did not get the spoils. Legend tells us that when Perseus slew Medusa every drop of spilled blood produced a brood of serpents. So too did metric broods sweep across Europe in the aftermath of Napoleon's downfall. Eventually even England succumbed, but not before she produced the MG. (Please don't misinterpret this unbiased presentation of historical fact as meaning I don't like the metric system. I recognize the inherent logic of the system and I know it makes sense for the US to go metric. It's just going to be a big pain for those of us who have no idea of whether a "McDonald's Quarter Kilo with Cheese" is a big burger or a slider. Sooner or later we're going to have to bite the bullet and make the change. I suggest we begin the week after I die.)

Other lessons I learned while working on my MG weren't quite so painful. The turn signals, for example, were an unusual design to say the least. Most cars put the turn signal lever on the steering column, so when you finish making a turn and straighten the steering wheel it turns off the signal. MG put the switch on the dash with a lever you pushed one way or the other to indicate which direction you intended to turn. When you pushed this lever it activated the turn signal, or "trafficator" as the Brits called it. It also started a timer that turned the signal off after about 30 seconds. Of course, if you were stopped waiting for a traffic light, the turn signal would time out before the light turned green so you might have to turn it back on several times before you could make your turn. On the other hand, if you turned quickly you might drive half a mile or so before the signal turned off, but at least it would turn off eventually. Mine wasn't working quite right so I took it out of the car and disassembled it. It turned out to be a wonderfully complex electro-pneumatic switch that used a cam, a spring loaded piston, and a bleed valve to control the time delay before the switch turned off. I cleaned everything, replaced a burned out contact with a piece of copper I cut from some scrap piping, and put everything back together. It worked perfectly, or at least it did after I spent an hour or so fiddling with the adjustment of that damn bleed valve. In many ways, this turn signal was typical of the way MG built cars. It was an unusual design, it could be taken apart and rebuilt using ordinary hand tools, it was well built, it lasted practically forever, and it wasn't particularly reliable unless you fiddled with it every now and then. It also wasn't made by MG but was instead made by Joseph Lucas and Sons, who supplied electrical parts to virtually every British car manufacturer.

As the years went by I learned that although MG was probably the best known sports car manufacturer in the world, they were never much more than a shoestring operation. A lot of the parts that went into an MG were standard, "off the shelf" items made by other companies. Lucas made the electrical components, the heater was made by a company called Smiths, Lockheed made the brakes, and a company with obviously mixed heritage named British Jaëger made the instruments. The horn was made by a company with the wonderfully descriptive name of "Clear Hooters Ltd." (Hoot! Hoot! I heard that quite clearly!) Other parts were marked with the mysterious word "MOWOG." Was this a company? A good luck talisman? A curse? Viktor claimed the letters stood for "Might Occasionally Work Out Good." Whatever the letters stood for, it was obvious that either MG's design philosophy or their budget didn't include designing every part that went into the car.

The batteries also gave me some insight into the MG design philosophy. Yes, I did use the plural term "batteries." The car had a twelve volt electrical system, but it relied upon two six volt batteries wired in series to produce 12 volts. These batteries were located behind the seats, under the cockpit floor, just in front of the rear axle. This location has caused full grown mechanics to burst into tears when asked to change the batteries. Why did MG use two batteries, and why did they put them in such an inaccessible location? Earlier MGs had a single twelve volt battery under the hood, like any other car, so it's not like MG never thought about putting a battery there. There's not much extra space under the hood of an MGA, but that doesn't mean MG couldn't have rearranged things to make room for a battery. Alternatively, they could have put a single twelve volt battery in the trunk, like Healey did. I think the real reason MG designed the batteries the way they did is because it gave at least a theoretical performance advantage. Car batteries in the 1950s were much bulkier and heavier than their modern equivalents, and putting the battery "amidships" helped MG achieve a near perfect 50/50 weight distribution between the front and rear wheels. There wasn't enough room for a large 12-volt battery, but they could put one 6-volt battery on either side of the drive shaft, and these two batteries gave more cranking power than a small 12-volt battery would have. Also, by spreading the weight between two batteries on either side of the car they kept the center of gravity low and achieved a high roll moment of inertia which made the car less likely to roll over. The midship location gave the car a low turning moment of inertia which meant you could steer the car right or left very quickly.

Using two 6-volt batteries was definitely more expensive than one 12-volt battery, and the difference in handling would probably only be noticeable if you were driving the car to the absolute limit during a race, and maybe not even then. What kind of a car company would make thousands of owners swear and bark their knuckles over a design feature that few if any would appreciate? The more I learned about my MG the more curious I became about the company that built it. (Author's note: There are many excellent books on the history of MG which I did not bother to consult before writing this chapter. The following is a brief history of the company based upon a hazy memory of things I've read. Serious researchers would be well advised to look elsewhere.)

MG has been in business almost as long as its anagrammatically confusing rival GM, but it never achieved quite the same production volumes as its American competitor. MG was really an offshoot of Morris Motors, a company that built sedate family sedans in England. William Morris produced bicycles in the late 1800s, briefly turned his attention to motorcycles, and began building cars around 1910. Cars were still a bit of a novelty then and there weren't many places to get them repaired, so Morris also opened a garage to service his cars. By 1913 business had grown to the point where he opened several garages, and the name of the service company officially became "Morris Garages." In 1921 a man named Cecil Kimber became the manager of Morris Garages, and he soon expanded the business to include modifying cars for improved performance. By 1924 he was modifying brand new cars and selling these Morris Garages specials under the MG name. In 1924 he also designed and built a one-off race car (using a lot of Morris parts, of course) which today is affectionately known as "Old Number One," the first true MG. It was about this time that William Morris incorporated MG as a separate company, managed by Cecil Kimber but owned by Morris. The cars were manufactured in a town with the delightfully British name of "Abingdon-on-the-Thames."

Over the next 10 years MG made an astonishing variety of cars, ranging from race cars to sedans. I suspect it was a lot of fun to work for MG back then, at least if you worked in the design shop, as the company was always experimenting with new ideas, new models, and racing, without much concern for the mundane business of churning out large numbers of identical (and profitable) cars for sale. One of the most popular cars they built was an extremely tiny two-seat sports car called the Type M Midget. Profits from the sale of these Midgets helped finance limited production single-seat race cars with superchargers, high performance double overhead cam engines, and four-wheel independent suspension. Not surprisingly, in 1935 William Morris decided to reign in the company a bit. He reorganized his empire and put MG directly under the management of Morris Motors. (Morris also owned the Wolseley car company, and shared parts were often marked MOWOG. Sadly, this stood for Morris Wolseley MG. I liked Viktor's explanation better.) Race car development came to a standstill, and MG's efforts were redirected toward designing a two-seat sports car for mass production. This car utilized a slightly modified Morris engine and a more traditional suspension. Hard-core enthusiasts were horrified, but the car, introduced in 1936 as the MG Midget Type TA, performed far better than its mundane design would suggest. More importantly, it sold well. In 1939 it was given a number of minor improvements and introduced as the Type TB, but then World War II erupted and put an end to all car production in Britain.

During the war, Cecil Kimber managed to keep MG together and contributed to the war effort by producing everything from light tanks to airplane cockpits. The executives at Morris tried to micromanage everything he did, and eventually he left the company in disgust. Shortly afterward, he was killed in a freak railroad accident. When the war finally ended, the remaining managers at MG tried to pick up the pieces and resume car production. There were shortages of almost everything in post-war Britain and MG had no budget for development, so they dusted off the design of the Type TB, made a few minor improvements, and released it as the MG Midget Type TC. Steel was tightly rationed at the time, and since England had run up enormous foreign debts during the war car companies could only get steel if a large percentage of their production was sold overseas. MG began to look for new markets and found an unexpected demand for their cars in the US. At least part of this demand came from US servicemen who had been stationed in England during the war and who found the light, responsive MGs a refreshing change from the bloated sedans and ponderous handling that were typical of

American cars. MG sales picked up, and between 1945 and 1949 they sold 10,000 TCs! Never mind the fact that Ford, Chevy, and others made that many cars in a week. For MG, this was big time production. Even more important for the survival of the company, nearly three quarters of these cars were exported, with over 2,000 going to the US – despite the fact that they never made a TC with left hand drive. MG was clearly on a roll, and in 1950 they replaced the TC with the TD, a car which looked very similar but which had such modern innovations as independent front suspension, rack and pinion steering, and (for the colonists) left-hand drive. Between 1950 and 1953 they sold almost 30,000 TDs, over 23,000 of which were exported to the US. (Note: These numbers are approximate, as MG didn't always keep good production records, particularly in the early years. On the other hand, you have to admire a company that assigned chassis number "0251" to the first production car of each model, even if it did lead to confusion about the number of cars built. Why did they pick that number? It was the telephone number of the MG factory in Abingdon!)

With MG production (and profits) showing such remarkable gains, the company began to ease its way back into racing. They built several land speed record cars based on the T-series which set a number of class records at the Bonneville salt flats, eventually culminating in a car with a 1500cc engine which reached 254 mph. They also assisted private owners in a number of racing projects, most notably a series of cars which ran at Le Mans in 1951 and 1952. These were in fact concept cars for a new sports car which MG wanted to build. They presented their plans to the head of BMC (British Motor Corporation, a new conglomerate which had absorbed Morris and MG) in the fall of 1952. Unfortunately, they had an afternoon appointment, and that morning Donald Healey had presented his plans for a similar looking sports car that would become the Austin-Healey 100-4. BMC executives thought Healey's radical new sports car was enough risk for one year, so they told MG to shelve plans for their new car and just "tart up" the TD. The result was the MG TF. MG did as much as they possibly could to update the T-series design, and the result was that the TF no longer looked like a car that had been designed in 1936. Instead, it looked like a car that had been designed in, say, 1940. It was a nice car, but it was obviously a dated design and it never sold as well as the TD. Finally, MG was given approval to build their new sports car. They'd pretty much run through the alphabet with car models, and since this new car was a radical departure from the square-rigged T-series they decided to start over and call it the MGA. Prototypes ran at Le Mans in 1955 and production started that September.

The MGA was a very successful car for MG, and they sold over 100,000 MGAs between 1956 and 1962. Most were roadsters, but the car was also produced in a coupe version. For the ultra-enthusiasts, a highly tuned double overhead cam model with four wheel disk brakes was also available. MG also manufactured Austin-Healey sports cars at their Abingdon-on-the-Thames factory, and MG helped Donald Healey design a tiny sports car known as the Austin-Healey Sprite. In 1961 they began selling a specially trimmed version of this car as the "new" MG Midget. MG also designed a larger sports car to replace the MGA, and in 1962 the MGB went on sale. It was originally designed to use a six cylinder engine, but when BMC shelved plans for that engine an updated version of the MGA four cylinder engine was substituted. Later, an aluminum V8 engine was available in England. The body was a completely new monocoque design, which was much more solid and handled better than the traditional ladder frames on all previous MG sports cars. The MGB even included revolutionary features for the driver's comfort such as roll-up windows and day/night mirrors. The car was a phenomenal success by MG standards, with over 500,000 MGBs being produced between 1962 and 1980.

Sadly, the introduction of the MGB marked the apex of MG's fortunes. BMC was absorbed into an even bigger conglomerate called British Leyland, and the entire British car industry went into a decline during the 1960s and 1970s. MG tried to design a replacement for the MGB within a few years of the car's introduction, but BL had bigger problems to worry about. MG was only given enough development money to make minimal cosmetic improvements and to implement engineering changes needed to keep up with emerging safety and emissions standards. Concept designs for new mid-engine sports cars were left to gather dust in MG offices while profits from MGB production were plowed into other hemorrhaging BL companies. The first time a top BL executive even bothered to visit the MG factory was in the 1970s. He was appalled to discover their "mass production" consisted of small teams of skilled craftsmen who worked on a car and then pushed it by hand to the next team of workers, much as they'd done in the 1920s. Each completed car was driven by a factory test driver as a final quality check. This test drive was done over public highways, as MG never had enough money to build a test track. The quality of components supplied to MG plummeted during the 1960s and 1970s (especially electrical components) and MG's reputation suffered accordingly. In 1975 British Leyland decided to celebrate MG's "Golden Anniversary." Somehow it seems a fitting tribute to BL's management that the Golden Anniversary would be celebrated 51 years after the car known as "Old Number 1" was built. Even if the celebration was a year late, MG got into the spirit of things and introduced a Golden Anniversary trim package for the MGB. The town of Abingdon also caught the spirit and sponsored a week-long festival to honor MG, culminating in a massive picnic on Sunday. In a remarkable display of community spirit, on the following Monday BL announced they were closing the factory at Abingdon. Enthusiasts on both sides of the Atlantic tried to change this edict, but BL had decided to focus all sports car development on its Triumph brand and phase out MG. Production dragged on for five more years, but in 1980 the last MGB rolled off the assembly line at Abingdon.

1980 marked the end of the Abingdon factory and the end of MG exports to America, but BL hung on to the MG name and produced several modified sport sedans with MG nameplates in the 1980s. Then, as BL itself was collapsing, it merged MG with Rover (best known in the US for its Land Rover vehicles) and spun the two off as a separate company. MG actually built an updated MGB called the MGRV8 for a few years and then designed a completely new mid-engine convertible sports car to be known as the MGF. About this time the German company BMW bought Rover-MG, and although there were some concerns that the MGF would compete with BMW's new Z3 sports car it allowed production of MGFs to begin. The MGF was fairly successful in England, but the Rover/BMW merger was not and in 2000 BMW sold Rover-MG to venture capitalists. Production of MGFs continued, and in 2001 MG returned to Le Mans. Rover wasn't doing too well financially however, and even changing its name to MG-Rover didn't help. (Rover was a huge company compared to MG, but MG had much better name recognition.) In 2005 the company went into bankruptcy and production of MGs stopped as a result. The bankrupt company was purchased by the Chinese Nanjing Automotive Group, who announced plans to resume MG production in England and build a new MG factory in Oklahoma. The announced dates for these blessed events slipped several times and Nanjing stopped talking about an Oklahoma plant, but they did eventually begin building a small number of MGs in England. It was a slightly modified version of a passenger sedan, but maybe they're just paying homage to the early MGs. Unfortunately, the press releases for this car claim the letters "MG" no longer stand for "Morris Garages" but instead mean "Modern Gentleman."   Of course, MG's rival GM hasn't been faring too well either. Only time will tell which of the "two-letter marques" will survive the longest.

Returning to my story, in 1971 I didn't know the full history of MG but I did know there was something special about the hand-crafted parts which periodically fell off my car. After years of driving a Model A Ford, the MGA seemed like a wonderfully fast, comfortable, and reliable conveyance. It was also an absolute blast to drive. It never replaced the Model A in my affection, of course. Instead, it taught me how it's possible for parents to love all their children equally. Each has its own personality, its own talents, and its own quirks. Each one is your favorite. When I headed back to school that fall, I had the Model A for formal affairs, double dates, and elegant touring; and I had the MGA for blasting around town, long-distance travel, and top-down driving on twisting country roads. I was on top of the world.

Chapter 11 – Back to School

Having two cars wasn't the only thing that changed when I went back to school. For one thing, Don wasn't there. He was taking a year off to work and earn enough money to continue his schooling. This meant I had a new roommate – actually a series of them as it turned out – who was just as nice, just as normal, and just as forgettable as my freshman roommate. Marianne Kressler transferred to Purdue that year, but she immediately acquired a steady boyfriend so there were no new developments in my love life. Of more impact was the fact that Luis offered me a Saturday job, cleaning up and doing odd jobs around the shop. And, of course, my engineering courses were getting more and more demanding as I progressed toward my degree. Some people look back on their college life as an endless series of parties and social events, with an occasional class to break the monotony. That was not my experience. I look back on college as an endless series of classes, labs, homework, and tests. If I wasn't doing homework, I was worrying about the homework I was supposed to be doing. I told myself at the time that I was giving up four years of my life in exchange for a good job and a higher standard of living after college. That's not to say I never had fun while I was in school. I had fun, and I have fond memories of the friends I made in college. It's just that the fun was tightly rationed, and was an explosive release from the pressures of studying. At times I felt like a World War I pilot having a rollicking night in Paris, knowing full well that the next day he'd go back to the front and face death in the air. Perhaps that's why so many of my college memories involve cars. These were unplanned, forced breaks from the pressures of academic life. They weren't always fun, but they were better than studying.

A Saturday morning in the fall of 1971. Cool, crisp, clear air. I'm driving to work at Riccotto's and there's a light dusting of snow on the ground. This is the first time it's actually been cold enough to put up the top and turn on the heater. The cockpit's a little drafty and the side curtains are rattling, but my feet are warm and I'm enjoying the drive. The sun is shining and there's a pleasant smell of burning firewood in the air. Someone's enjoying a cozy morning in front of the fireplace! A few miles further, and I notice the smell of burning firewood seems to be getting stronger. Or maybe it's burning leaves. Odd, because I haven't seen anyone burning leaves this morning. I stop the car and check under the hood. Everything looks fine, and nothing seems to be burning. I get back into the car and drive on. The smell of burning leaves is definitely getting stronger. I stop again, but everything still looks fine under the hood.

As I get to the town of Clymers Indiana, smoke fills the cockpit. I immediately pull over and throw open the hood. Everything's fine there, but when I look back I see smoke streaming out of the side curtains and the half-open driver's door. I throw open the door and see a column of smoke rising out of the driver's seat. I lift the seat cushion and flames leap up into the cockpit. Holy Cow! It's like some demented cartoon! I've been driving around sniffing at the smoke while my butt was on fire! I hadn't drunk any coffee that morning so I didn't have an organic fire extinguisher, but I see a little snow in the ditch. I scoop up a handful of snow and douse the flames.

The flames are out, but there's a big, smoldering hole in my floorboards. The MGA, like the Model A Ford, has floorboards that literally are made of boards. Wood actually has a lot to offer as floorboard material. It doesn't rust, it deadens noise, and it's easy to work with. Its one minor disadvantage is that it catches fire when it gets hot. In this case I apparently ran over something a while back that bent my exhaust system until it was touching the floorboards. Could it have been that unmarked speed bump at the Barf & Gag, the infamous all night student eatery? Whatever it was, it's now burned a big oval hole in the floorboards, and the edges of the hole are glowing red with burning embers. I need some water.

I look around. There's not much in Clymers. No gas stations, no stoplights, no stop signs, not even many houses. Just a bend in the road, a reduced speed limit, and a farm supply store just a little ways up the road. It only takes me a minute or so to walk to the store, but nobody's there. The door is unlocked and they've apparently just opened for the day, but there's nobody behind the counter. I see an open door behind the counter leading to what appears to be a shop area for repairing farm machinery. On the wall of the shop there's a hose spigot, and a bucket sits on the floor beneath it.

I call out, but no one answers so I walk into the shop and start filling the bucket. Just as I'm finishing, someone walks into the shop from the parking lot out back. He seems surprised to see me there. "Can I help you?" he asks.

"Yes, please" I reply. "My car's on fire and I need something to put it out. Is it OK if I borrow a bucket of water?"

That got his attention. "Of course!" he answers. "Are you sure that will do it?"

"Oh, I think this will take care of it" I reply, as nonchalantly as possible. Then I casually stroll out of the shop, walk to my car, and dump the water on my floorboards. That takes care of the immediate problem, but I still have another 15 or 20 minutes of driving until I get to the shop. I gather up as much snow as I can find and build a pillar of snow underneath my seat. I'm guessing there's enough snow there to last until I get to Riccotto's. I return the bucket. "Thanks for letting me use your bucket" I say with a wave. When I get to Riccotto's a few minutes work with a pry bar moves the exhaust system back where it belongs. Then I nail a plywood patch over the hole. The patch has held for over 40 years now. One of these days I really ought to replace that floorboard.

One positive result of this incident is that I have always since carried fire extinguishers in every old car I've owned. Fortunately I've never had to use one. I like to think the mere presence of the fire extinguisher has been enough to intimidate incipient conflagrations. That didn't prove to be the case with my younger brother, though. When he was in college he drove a 1958 MGA which I had rebuilt and loaned to him, and one day he drove for several miles wondering who was burning firewood before he discovered that his floorboards were on fire. He pulled off the road, grabbed the fire extinguisher I'd mounted in the car, and then hesitated as he thought "I wonder how much it will cost to buy Steve a new fire extinguisher?" Fortunately he didn't ponder this question long before he broke the seal and doused the fire.

Thanksgiving break. Much to my surprise, Marianne Kressler asked if I could give her a ride back to Yodersburg. I'm looking forward to the trip, as it will give us three hours to chat. We'll have to chat, as there's no radio or other source of entertainment in the MG.

The day of the trip is cold and blustery. No surprise, as it is late November in Indiana, but still it means we'll have to make the trip with the top up and the side curtains rattling. I notice when I get in the car that there's a thin dusting of snow on the passenger floor. Must have blown in through the cracks around the door and the side curtains. I wonder if maybe this car had weather-stripping when it was new.

I drive to Marianne's dorm and pick her up. There's not much trunk space in the MG, but by tying my suitcase to the luggage rack there's room for her stuff in the trunk. I help her into the car and seal the side curtain as well as I can. Then I get in and we take off. For some reason she starts putting on nail polish. Who puts on nail polish in a car? She seems to have a little trouble as we bounce over railroad tracks and potholes, and once or twice I think I hear a muffled curse. Maybe she's not used to the taught suspension and quick handling of the MG. After it dries she puts on her mittens to warm her hands.   Later, when she takes off her mittens her fingernails are covered with mitten fuzz. I guess maybe the nail polish froze before it dried.

Three hours later I drop her off at her house. Her mother is glad to learn that the wheels stayed on for the entire trip. (I guess I'll never live that down.) The conversation lagged now and then, and we had to shout to hear each other over the rattling side curtains, but all in all I thought the trip went well. I help her carry her things inside and say good-bye. As I'm getting back into the car I notice the passenger's floorboards still have that dusting of snow. Damn. And I had the heater on full blast the whole way. I spend several hours over Thanksgiving sealing up the cracks and putting weather-stripping around the doors, top, and side curtains. This improves the effectiveness of the heater significantly. I call Marianne the day before we're scheduled to head back to find out what time she wants me to pick her up. She says her parents were going to drive to Purdue anyway, so she'll just ride with them. I guess what they say about never getting a second chance to make a first impression is true for cars, too.

I wonder if her parents really were planning on driving to Purdue or if somehow she just didn't enjoy riding in the MG?

It's a cool night in early spring, and I'm driving across campus to the library. A light mist is falling and I have the wipers on. Suddenly, the wipers stop dead. Naturally they stop in the middle of the windshield, where they obstruct as much vision as possible. I pull off into a parking lot, get out my flashlight (I learned a few things about preparedness from the Model A) and pop open the hood. I know there's a fuse box in there somewhere. Turns out it's in the middle of the firewall, and there are only two fuses in the entire car. I pull each one out and examine it, but the fuses seem to be fine. I put the fuses back and crawl under the dash. It's pretty easy to see the problem. There are two connectors on the back of the wiper switch, but only one is connected to a wire. There's a loose wire hanging next to the other one.

The connectors are wonderfully British. A block of solid brass that has been carefully machined with a hole for a wire which intersects a threaded hole with a small brass set screw in it. In theory, you tighten the set screw against the wire to hold it in place. Expensive to manufacture, they will last for hundreds of years. Of course, they won't hold the wires that long, because as you drive the vibration jiggles the set screws loose and the wires fall out. No problem, as long as your periodic maintenance schedule includes crawling under the dash and tightening all the set screws every now and then. Viktor calls them "Lucas Casual Connectors." (I will soon learn that there is an entire genre of jokes about Lucas electrics. Why do the British drink warm beer? Because they have Lucas refrigerators. What's the Lucas company motto? "Home before dark.") It's a bit of a pain to reach past all the other wires to get to the wiper switch and I have to hold the flashlight in my mouth while I'm doing it, but in a few minutes I have the wire back in place and my wipers are working again. Success. I drive to the library without further incident.

When I'm finished with my research at the library and get back into my car I notice the ignition light is on. This is unusual, as the key is still in my pocket. I pull on the starter knob (you don't turn the key to start an MGA, you pull a knob) and the car starts immediately. Not very good theft protection. Just to be safe, I take the key out of my pocket, put it in the ignition switch, and turn it on. When I get back to the dorm the car doesn't turn off the first time I turn the key off, but I jiggle the key on & off several times and eventually the engine stops. "Oh great" I think. "My switch is going bad."

For the next several days my ignition switch is intermittent. Sometimes it works fine, sometimes the car turns itself on without the key, and sometimes I have to fiddle with the key to turn the car off. Finally the inevitable happens. I drive back to the dorm and the car won't turn off. No matter how much I jiggle that key, the car keeps running. Very carefully, so as not to short anything out, I crawl under the dash and start disconnecting wires from the switch. One by one, making a sketch of where they go so I can put them back again. Finally, I remove the last wire from the switch. The car is still running. I take the switch out of the dash, just to make certain I haven't overlooked any wires. The car is still running. I'm holding the ignition switch in my hand, the nexus of all things electrical, and still the car keeps running. It's like a bad horror movie – The Car That Would Not Die! I used to get frustrated at my Model A when it wouldn't start, but that was nothing compared to a car that won't stop. In desperation I flip the seats forward, remove the access panel above the batteries, and disconnect the batteries. The car is still running. I have a moment's panic while I consider that maybe the car has been possessed by some evil spirit before I realize the generator is still supplying electricity to the ignition system. I push in on the clutch, put the car in gear, stand on the brake, and let up on the clutch. The car stalls and dies. Silence. Blessed silence.

For the next several days I don't bother with the ignition key. Why should I? The ignition switch is sitting on a desk in my room. When I want to drive the car I connect the battery, pull the starter knob, and drive off. When I'm finished I disconnect the battery, then stand on the brake and stall the motor. In my spare time I pour over the workshop manual, trying to figure out what's gone wrong.

I was lucky to find an original MGA factory workshop manual at an antique car swap meet. It makes wonderful reading. In addition to the British terminology and spelling (bonnet, boot, tyre, colour, moulding, etc.) the Brits have a wonderful sense of style. "Always use a good grade of anti-freeze solution when frosty weather is anticipated." "Carefully prise the two halves apart, examine the sealing ring, and renew if perished." I also learn that my car is equipped with an "anti-dazzle device." This wondrous invention "dips the headlamps to prevent dazzle of oncoming drivers." Fascinating, but it doesn't help solve my problem. Finally I resort to studying the wiring diagram. The wiring on the MGA is simple enough that the wiring diagram is laid out the way the wires are run in the car, so you can actually see which wires run close together. I'm guessing that somewhere in the car I have a wire that's always hot shorted to a wire that's only supposed to be hot when the ignition switch is on. The result is that the electricity is bypassing the switch and turning on the ignition regardless of whether the switch is on or off.

After several fun-filled hours of tracing wires, my suspicion centers on the fuse box. Of the two fuses in this box, one is always hot and the other is only hot when the key is on. The fuse that's always hot goes to the horn. I don't know what's so damned important about the horn that it deserves its own special fuse, or why this fuse is always hot. Do the British like to sit in their driveways and honk their Clear Hooters with the ignition turned off? The other fuse supplies electricity to everything else in the car that's fused. Not everything is fused, of course. The headlights have no fuse, for example, so they're just sitting there waiting to fry the wiring harness at the first sign of trouble. But the ignition, the wipers, the turn signals, and almost everything else in the car runs through that second fuse – but only when the key is turned on. Then I remember that rainy night when I pulled out my fuses and replaced them in the dark. I walk out to the car and look at the fuse box in the light of day. The horn fuse is sitting in its fuse holder, just the way it's supposed to. The other fuse is wedged in between the two fuse holders, shorting the horn circuit to the ignition circuit. It's not a very good short, however. There is enough dirt and corrosion in that fuse box so the two circuits were only intermittently shorted together. Sometimes the ignition switch worked, and sometimes it didn't. I pull out the fuse and put it back where it's supposed to go. The car is fixed. That certainly was a hell of a lot of trouble for such a simple problem.

A few weeks later, while I'm at work, Luis calls me over to my car. For no apparent reason whatsoever, he has chosen this moment to share some tidbit of knowledge with me. "Pop the hood open, Steve" he says. "I want to show you something." I open the hood. "Don't ever worry about losing your key" he says. He points to the fuse box. "If you lose your key, just pull one of those fuses out and stick it in between the two fuse holders. That will bypass the ignition switch and you'll be able to drive your car."

Thanks, Luis.

A Friday night in April. I'm sitting in my dorm room, trying to get a head start on the weekend's homework so I won't have to worry about it while I'm working at the shop tomorrow. It's a warm night, and I have the window open. Suddenly I hear a familiar sound: Ahhoooooga! Ahhoooooga!. The chances of there being two cars outside my window that sound like that seem pretty slim. I look outside, and there appears to be a pretty lively party going on inside my Model A. I rush outside, and there must be at least seven or eight drunks crammed into the car. They're leaning out the windows, shouting clever phrases like "Twenty-three Skidoo!" to passersby as they rock the car back and forth. The driver is honking the horn and wearing my straw hat. I let them know that this is my car, as politely as possible under the circumstances. Gradually it dawns on them that maybe I don't want them in my car. They pile out, each one shaking my hand in turn while telling me that it's a great car and they didn't do anything to hurt it. The driver starts to walk off with the others, and then realizes he is still wearing my straw hat. "Here" he says, returning it with the exaggerated courtesy of a drunk. "This is for you." He rushes off to join the others while I roll up the windows and close the doors. I wonder how they'd react if they found a pile of drunks sitting in their car.

Final exams. I'm up late studying Advanced Thermodynamics. I've already emptied my jar of instant coffee trying to force my groggy brain to grasp the importance of the Gibbs Free Energy equation. I'm not having much success, but I know it's going to be on the exam tomorrow. There's a warm breeze blowing in the window. It rained earlier in the evening, but now the clouds are clearing off and the air smells fresh and clean. Finally I say "screw this," grab my car keys and go outside. The MG is parked at the curb. The top is down, of course. It's spring. I unfasten the driver's half of the tonneau cover, tuck it behind the seat, and hop in. In no time at all I'm heading out of town on South River Road.

There's no one else on the road at this time of night. A full moon is shining brightly, occasionally shaded by the few wisps of clouds that are rushing off to the east. The road runs along the banks of the Wabash River and the river glitters in the moonlight. It's a nice twisty road and I'm enjoying the drive immensely. I'm not really pushing it, but the pace is brisk enough to keep things interesting. Spring is in full bloom and the night air is glorious. After about 15 or 20 minutes my conscience begins nagging me. Reluctantly I turn around in the parking lot of a closed tavern and head back toward campus. The return trip is almost as enjoyable as the outbound trip, spoiled only by the knowledge of what awaits me at the journey's end. Finally I get back to the dorm. I button up the MG and go back inside. Thermodynamics isn't any more interesting than it was when I left, but at least now I'm refreshed and ready to hit it anew.

Classes are finally over, and it's time to head back home for the summer. Don has driven his MGB to campus to help me pack up. Today we're going to drive our MGs to Yodersburg, and tomorrow Don will drive me back to campus to pick up the Model A. Don's a good friend.

We're about half an hour south of Berrytown, stuck behind a slow pickup truck. There aren't many places to pass on this stretch of State Road 25, and every time we come to a passing zone there's oncoming traffic. Finally we get a break. I pull out and scoot around the pickup truck. I look in my rear view mirror expecting to see Don passing the truck, but all I see is the truck. Then I see a cloud of dust off to the side of the road with a spinning blue MGB at the center. I pull off, let the truck pass, and go back to Don. His car is hunkered down in the dirt, with the right front wheel jutting out at right angles to the fender. We examine the wheel and see that the lower wishbone, the piece that holds the bottom half of the suspension to the car, is broken in two. I remember that a couple of weeks earlier Don had come down for a weekend visit and had hopped a curb with that wheel. At the time I had peered under the car and noticed that the lower wishbone was bent, but I couldn't see how bad the damage was. I had advised Don to take it to someone who could put it up on a lift and take a good look at it, but Don has a degree from the "No Tomorrow" school of automotive maintenance and is sometimes prone to defer maintenance longer than a more nervous person would think prudent.

"Did you ever have anyone look at that suspension arm?" I asked.

107

"Not yet." Don replied laconically. Then he changed to a more introspective tone. "You know, you really can't steer very well with only one wheel. The car just sort of goes wherever it wants to."

There's not much we can do in terms of a roadside repair so we call a tow truck. Fortunately it's only a short tow to Riccotto's in Berrytown. When we get there all the stalls are filled with customer's cars, but Luis says we can work on in the driveway. We manage to get the car up on jack stands, but run into a new problem. Normally you loosen the lug nuts before you jack up a car, so the weight of the car will keep the wheel from turning. There's no way we could put any weight on this wheel, so now we're faced with trying to hold the wheel from turning while we break the lug nuts free. Don and I trade off, one of us wrapping our arms around the wheel and trying to keep it from turning while the other one tugs at the lug wrench. It's no use. The nuts are on too tight, and we can't keep the wheel from turning. Both of us are filthy from hugging the wheel. Nick is working on a car in the shop, and finally we give up and ask Nick for help. Nick looks at us like we're dumber than a box of rocks. "Did you try stepping on the brake?" he asks. The dummy look illuminates both our faces. It never occurred to us that even though the suspension was broken, the brake would still work. I step on the brake and Don removes the lug nuts with no problem.

It's getting dark, and Luis is ready to close the shop. Don and I have gotten the broken suspension arm off the car and obtained a replacement from one of the junkers out back, but there's no way we can finish the job that night. Nick warns us to take everything out of the car and lock it up in the shop. For some reason, thieves scour the area around the shop every night. It seems that people who would never dream of stealing from their neighbors have no such scruples against stealing from a business, even if it is a small family-run shop. We lock up the tools, jacks, nuts, bolts – everything anyone could walk off with. Then we drive back to campus in my MGA. We are absolutely filthy.

The next morning we drive back to the shop and discover thieves have picked the car up and stolen the jack stands out from underneath it. Luis is furious that we lost a good set of jack stands. We're furious that they dropped the car down on the ground after they stole the stands. Once again I have to dig a tunnel under an MG so I can get a jack under it and lift it off the ground. The rest of the job proceeds smoothly. We thank Luis for letting us use his tools, apologize for losing his jack stands, and drive back to Yodersburg, having learned a few things about suspension repairs and thieves.

The MG Mechanics

There's a postscript to this story. Replacing the lower wishbone on Don's MG pretty much trashed his alignment. At the time, I didn't know how to set the alignment so I advised Don to take it to an alignment shop. The going rate for an alignment back then was $17. This struck Don as an outrageous waste of money when the car drove fine, with the minor exception that he wore through a set of front tires in less than 1,000 miles. This wasn't a big problem for Don because there was always a pile of old tires in back of Riccotto's and Luis let Don pick through the pile any time he needed another tire. Not all of Luis's customers were starving college students, and some of them replaced all four tires at the same time even though only two or three were actually worn out. Whenever Don's front tires wore out he could always find a couple of tires in the pile that had enough tread to last another six or seven hundred miles. It wasn't long before Don got enough practice using the tire machine that he could rip his old tires off the rims and mount a new set of tires in less than 10 minutes, although he did have a tendency to pinch the tubes now and then. (His rims had long since deteriorated past the point where they would seat tubeless tires.)

One summer weekend we drove Don's B to Riccotto's for some long forgotten errand and while we were there Don picked out a nice pair of tires for his front wheels (one Dunlop, one Pirelli) and a Sears Allstate "*Ted Williams Approved*" tire for his spare. (Between the bad alignment and the pinched tubes his spare saw a lot of service.) He finished mounting them just as Luis was closing shop, and after a brief stop for dinner at Mr. Happy Burger we headed north on US 25 for a nice summer night's drive back to Yodersburg. Unfortunately, we didn't make it out of Berrytown before the right front tire went flat. We tossed that into the trunk along with a few mild curses, put the spare on, and set off once again. It didn't take us long to discover that the spare had a slow leak. Fortunately there are a lot of gas stations along US 25. This was long before the advent of those #%$& air machines that demand a handful of quarters before they'll put air in your tires. Gas stations were actually service stations, with a mechanic on duty and a couple of stalls to work on cars, and they kept an air compressor in the shop, with a courtesy hose outside for customers to use if they needed air in their tires. These stations had long since closed for the night when Don and I were making our trip, but most of them left the courtesy hose outside when they locked up and they had more than enough air left in the compressor to fill an MG tire. For the rest of the trip, we kept our eyes peeled for service stations and stopped at every one we saw to top up the tire. Even if it had only been a couple of miles since the last fill up, we didn't know how far it would be to the next air hose so we topped off the tire just in case. As the night wore on we realized the leak was getting worse, but we persevered. We almost made it. We got as far as New Paris, which was only a couple of miles from the farm house where Don was spending the summer and where my MG was parked. There was a gas station in New Paris, but by this time the air was leaking out of his tire as fast as we could pump it in. Reluctantly, we left the car at the station and began walking to the farm house.

By this time it was well past midnight on a dark, moonless night. Even the stars were hidden behind a low, horizon to horizon cloud cover. If you've never walked down an Indiana country road on a moonless night you wouldn't believe how dark it can get. Don and I couldn't see each other and we couldn't see the road. Only the sound and feel of the pavement beneath our feet told us we were

110

still on the road. When we heard crunching gravel we knew we had strayed onto the shoulder and we'd have to scout around a bit to find the road. Things can get a little spooky when it's that dark, especially when the guy walking beside you suddenly lets out a blood-curdling scream. A large, shaggy dog had come out of nowhere, padded noiselessly up behind us, and suddenly nuzzled Don's hand. Later it was my turn to jump when an unseen horse leaned over an unseen fence and went "PBPBPBPBPBPBPB" in my ear. (How do you spell the sound a horse makes when it exhales through closed lips?) Fortunately there was a light on in the bathroom of Don's farm house or we would have walked right past it and continued walking until dawn.

On Monday Don got a lift back to the gas station and paid them to patch his tube. The mechanic started to feel inside the tire for a nail or other leak-causing protrusion but Don told him not to bother because he was certain he had pinched the tube in a tire machine. The patched tube lasted just long enough for Don to make it to the next gas station before he once again had a flat tire. This time he kept quiet while the mechanic checked the inside of the tire. A look of shock flashed across the mechanic's face. "What the . . .?" he exclaimed as he hauled a handful of broken glass out of the tire. Don explained that he had gotten the tire off a junk pile and it was just possible that he hadn't looked inside before mounting it. Actually, I was pretty impressed with that used Sears tire. We drove over 75 miles with a handful of broken glass between the tire and the tube. I don't think you can expect much more than that from any tire, regardless of price.

Senior year! Don has managed to work his way back to school, so we're sharing a dorm room again. I've got the MGA and the Model A waiting for me in the parking lot, so it looks like it's going to be another good year. I seem to be the only senior who showed up with a beard, however. When I was a freshman, all male seniors showed up with a full beard which they shaved off after Purdue won its first home football game. It's amazing how fast some traditions die out. Unfortunately, I can't keep mine until we win a football game because the Air Force is helping to pay my way through school and the ROTC instructors don't seem to fully grasp the importance of this tradition. So, I head out to my first ROTC class a little early and stop by the village barber shop on my way. For the first and only time in my life I ask for a "shave and a haircut." Only this barber shop no longer shaves customers. They say no one's asked for one in years and they don't even have a razor in the shop. I have a minor panic attack until they offer to mow my beard off with electric clippers. Not the best shave I've ever had, but it will do.

Senior Beard

Later that fall I get a surprise phone call from Cory. Cory's decided to take a few years off to go through a hippie phase. He's living in an informal commune on a farm outside of Yodersburg with Jill and an assortment of other ragged looking individuals. They don't actually farm, they take turns working at factory jobs to buy groceries and pay the rent. Cory is obviously excited about something. "Hey, man" he says. "I scored a duck."

For some reason I briefly thought he was talking about a DUKW, the World War II amphibious landing craft you see in old war movies, but I immediately dismissed that idea as being preposterous. However, I couldn't seem to come up with any other plausible ideas that would explain why he was calling me to talk about a duck. "You scored a duck?" is all I could think of to say.

"Yeah, man. I scored it today."

"Did you hit a duck with your car?" I asked. The last time I visited the farm Cory was working on an old Triumph Spitfire out in the barn. It wasn't running at the time, but if he'd gotten it running and hit a duck with it, I thought it was just possible the duck had done some damage that he wanted to ask about. A Spitfire isn't all that big, and his was pretty rusty, so it might have come out second best in an altercation with a duck.

"No man. I scored it. You know, bought it. A 1943 duck. D-U-K-W. One of those World War II things."

Hard to believe, but Cory really had bought a DUKW. Somehow he'd met a hippie who was living way out on the lunatic fringe, and this guy had bought it at a truck and farm equipment salvage yard. At the time he had some vague notion of using it to squash cop cars, but then he sobered up enough to realize that not only was this not a very peaceful thing to do, it might actually get him into some serious trouble. He was going to restore it, but so far his restoration had only gotten as far as painting a small peace symbol on the prow of this noble vessel. When Cory offered to buy it from him he didn't mind letting it go.

A DUKW is a rather large vehicle, being over 30 feet long and weighing in at about 7-1/2 tons. This particular one wasn't in the best of condition. It had a few rust holes in the hull and the propeller shaft bearings were shot so it wasn't seaworthy, but its six-wheel drive system was intact so it could still be driven on land. You could fit up to 40 people on the deck, and Cory figured that if we could get it seaworthy it would be the perfect vehicle for parties at the lake.

A World War II DUKW

113

A few weeks later Don and I were poking about in an Army/Navy surplus store near campus when we found the perfect accessory for the DUKW. It was a very large cube-shaped cooler with extra thick insulation on the sides. An ice storage bin formed the core of this chest, and a couple of heavy duty wire racks held bottles in place around this bin. The racks would hold 24 bottles, so it would be the perfect thing to keep a case of beer cold. The best part was the stenciled lettering on the top and all four sides. In bold, red military stenciling against the olive drab surface were the words "Human Blood. Handle with care."

There was no way we could ever fit this into the MG, so after we bought it we came back with the Model A. We carefully lashed it to the top of the car and proudly drove back to campus with our new treasure. That weekend we drove to Yodersburg and delivered it to Cory, filled with bottles of dark red beer of course. (You can do wonders with food coloring.)

Sadly, we never used the DUKW for parties at the lake. I helped Cory work on the engine a few times (it was a conventional 6-cylinder Chevy truck engine) and we drove it around the farm, but we never did get it seaworthy. A year or two later Cory moved to California, and believe it or not the DUKW made the trip with no problems. It also saved Cory from having to rent a moving van. Finding a 30 foot parking spot in California proved to be difficult, though, and eventually Cory sold it to a collector who had the time and the money to restore it.

Delivering a Blood Chest

114

Mid January. One of the coldest nights of the year. Five below zero, which is pretty cold for this part of Indiana. Don and I and a couple of girls are driving back to campus from a movie theater. We're driving the Model A, of course, as we couldn't fit four people in either Don's MGB or my MGA. It's pretty cold in the car, and neither the manifold heater nor the lap robe can keep the chills at bay. There aren't many other cars on the road tonight. I'm stopped at a traffic light and we're all talking about how cold we are. Suddenly all conversation stops, as we stare at a car that drives past us on the cross street. It's another Model A Ford. I recognize the car, as I saw it once in Yodersburg. I don't know what it's doing in Lafayette, but I'm sure it's the same car. For one thing, there aren't many white Model A's with red running boards and red pin-striping. For another thing, there aren't many Model A sedans that have had the top hacked off with a metal saw. The driver looks awfully cold in this homemade convertible. No top, no side curtains, just a windshield to huddle behind as he scoots down the road. Suddenly my Model A doesn't seem quite so cold anymore.

Spring break. I'm headed back to Yodersburg, but I promised Nick I'd stop by the shop on the way and help him get his car ready for a race. Over the past few years I had occasionally helped Nick and Viktor work on their race cars. Both raced at an amateur sports car track in Wisconsin. Viktor drove a 1959 Austin-Healey 100-6 that was just a little too heavy to keep up with the MGB's, despite its six-cylinder engine. Nick drove a 1960 Fiat Abarth 600D Allemano Spyder, a marvelous little gem of a car which had the misfortune to leave the factory with an engine that was only about ¾ the size of the next smallest sports car. This meant that even though Nick raced in the smallest displacement class possible he was still blown away by the "big" Bugeye Sprites with their 850cc engines. This plus the fact that he was trying to race on a college student's budget inspired him to name his racing team "Scuderia Banca Rotta" - Bankrupt Racing Team. He claimed this was the final achievement of all the great Italian racing teams and that if we started there maybe we could build upon their success. I designed a logo for the team and we had some T-shirts made. The T-shirts turn out to be much more successful than the team, and they last longer, too.

Scuderia Banca Rotta

When I get to the shop I expect to see Nick doing the final "fine tuning" on the Abarth, since the race is the following day. Instead I discover he has the engine on a bench and he's just now putting the pistons in. He's running a little behind schedule. He doesn't want me to help him with the engine, though, he wants me to drive to Chicago to borrow Viktor's new racing helmet. The track where Nick races has new safety rules this year and his old helmet won't pass tech inspection. Viktor's expecting me. It's a nice, sunny day so a six hour drive to Chicago and back sounds a lot better than sweating over a greasy car engine.

The drive to Chicago is uneventful, although the sun quickly disappears behind a heavy cloud cover that's moving in from the North. I pick up the helmet and have dinner with Viktor. By the time I'm ready to head back it's dark and the temperature has dropped significantly, so I put up the top. The first flakes of snow appear as I reach the outskirts of Chicago. By the time I reach the Indiana state line it's a full-fledged blizzard. Thick, wet snow is blanketing my windshield despite the feeble efforts of my wipers. (MGA's have an incredibly lethargic, single-speed windshield wiper motor. When the MGB was announced enthusiasts rejoiced over the news that it would have a two-speed wiper motor. Unfortunately, it turned out

MG had added a new "glacial" speed that was apparently designed for people who thought the MGA wipers were too fast.) The wipers pack snow against the top of the windshield, where it freezes into a miniature glacier that slowly creeps downward. Eventually it stops my wipers dead in their tracks and I have to pull over and clear the snow to free them. Then I can drive until the next time they get stuck. Once they stick just as a tractor-trailer roars past in the other lane, splashing bucketfuls of thick brown slush on my windshield. I'm in a total brownout and can't see a thing. I throw open the side curtain and reach out to free the wipers just as another truck roars past. This time the bucketfuls of brown slush fly in through the open side curtain, drenching me in an icy slime.

The blizzard slows traffic to a crawl, and I don't make it back to Berrytown until after 2:00 AM. I drive to Riccotto's house, but I'm too intimidated by Luis to ring the doorbell and wake everyone up at this hour. I decide to sleep in the MG and give Nick the helmet in the morning. It's amazing how fast an MG cools off on a cold spring night. I try wrapping the tonneau cover around my body and wearing the racing helmet, but it's no use. My teeth are chattering madly and sleep is out of the question. Then I notice Nick's car is not in the driveway. I drive to the shop and he's just starting to put the engine back into the car. This is a 45 minute job if everything goes right, but of course tonight everything doesn't go right. Dawn breaks as we tighten the last bolt. Nick jumps into the driver's seat to start the engine, but it won't turn over. We put jumper batteries and battery chargers on it but it still won't budge. Luis shows up and helps us try to push start it, but every time Nick lets out the clutch the rear wheels lock up. Nick finally has to admit that maybe he built the engine just a little too tight. Normally he checks the tolerances on everything as he assembles an engine, but last night he was in a hurry and he just slapped it together. There won't be any racing for us today. We poke dejectedly at the breakfast Nick's mother makes for us, and I tank up on extra coffee. I haven't slept in over 24 hours and I still have to drive to Yodersburg. After breakfast I climb into my MG and – my starter dies. All in all it's not a good day for Scuderia Banca Rotta.

Later that spring. It's a Friday night, and Don and I are going to take a couple of girls to a movie. We've still got an hour before we have to leave, so Don decides to walk to a local drug store to get a pack of cigarettes. It's just one block away. I stay in the room, as I've got some homework I want to get out of the way before we go to the movie. Time passes. 15 minutes. 30 minutes. 45 minutes. I call the girls to let them know we'll be a little late. Finally, after about an hour, Don staggers into the room. His pants are torn and he's covered with mud from the knees down.

When Don walked out of the dorm on his way to the drug store, he saw his MG parked at the curb. He hadn't driven it much recently, as he had parked it at Riccotto's with a "for sale" sign in the window trying to raise a little extra cash for school. No one was interested, so we had just brought it back to Purdue the previous weekend. It was a beautiful spring night, and Don decided to drive the MG to the drug store.

Driving a block wasn't very satisfying, so Don decided to take the long way back to the dorm. Basically he was just driving around the perimeter of the campus, but on the north east corner his route took him a little way out into the country. I knew the road well. Evidently Don didn't. As he crested a small hill he was surprised to see a speed limit sign dropping the speed from 45 to 30. He was doing about 60 at the time, so he was even more surprised to discover the reason for the speed limit change was that the road changed from asphalt to gravel. Worse still, the gravel road curved to the left. Don didn't.

Don had gotten into trouble a few times previously by slamming on the brakes and locking up his wheels when things got dicey. That was how he had hopped the curb the previous spring. I had tried to talk him out of that, explaining that when you lock up the wheels you can no longer steer. The car just becomes a projectile following a fixed trajectory. Brakes are very useful when you need to slow down, but don't lock the wheels if you have to steer. That night he followed my advice and almost made it through the curve. Almost wasn't quite good enough, however. Once he left the gravel he was on wet grass and spring mud, and there wasn't much he could do. He flew through a fence and came to rest in a farmer's corn field. When he opened the door there was the sickening sound of bending metal. Apparently his left front fender had been jammed back against the driver's door. As he waded through the mud to get back to the road he barked his shin against a piece of twisted metal lying in the field. It was his rear bumper.

By the time Don finished walking back to the dorm he was thoroughly disgusted with himself, his car, and life in general. I suggested we drive back to the car to survey the damage but he didn't want to spoil what was left of the evening. The car was in the middle of nowhere, and it would still be there tomorrow. So we climbed in the Model A, picked up the girls, and drove to the movie. The movie was sold out by the time we got there, so we decided to go back and look at Don's car. It's a good thing we did. There were at least a half-dozen police cars there and a group of men with flashlights were searching the cornfield, looking for the body of the driver. They called off the search when the driver asked them what they were doing.

The police had already called a tow truck, and the farmer who owned the field was there too. Don settled up with the farmer for the damage done to his fence while the tow truck dragged his car back out to the road. As the farmer counted his money he told Don "You're lucky you went out into the field. Most people slam on their brakes and slide right into that telephone pole."

Fortunately, a few minutes bodywork with a big hammer made Don's car drivable again, although it didn't look quite as nice as it did before the accident. The bumper was beyond salvaging as an automobile part, but it made a lovely conversation piece when it was suspended it from the ceiling in our room. We hung it in a corner, as its twisted shape matched the angle of the two walls perfectly.

Don's Bumper

Chapter 12 – More of the Same

Under normal circumstances, I would have gone on active duty with the Air Force immediately after graduation. I signed up for ROTC when I first entered Purdue, while the Viet Nam war was raging. My great-great grandfather had fought to end slavery in the Civil War. My grandfather had fought to make the world safe for democracy in World War I. My father had fought to save the world from Hitler during World War II. It seemed like the least I could do was to save Southeast Asia from the Godless commies. As it turned out, the war ended before I graduated and the Air Force suddenly discovered they had signed up a lot more lieutenants than they needed for the post-war military. One of the programs they offered to help alleviate this situation was called an Educational Delay. If any new officer wanted to go back to school to get an advanced degree, the Air Force would delay their entry into active duty until they finished the degree program. I had memorized a jumble of equations over the last four years, but somehow it didn't seem like they added up to any kind of engineering expertise. I didn't feel like I was really qualified to design anything, and I thought maybe a Master's degree would make it all come together. I applied for a one year educational delay so I could get my MS – "More of the Same" in academic parlance. The Air Force's only concern was "are you sure one year will be enough?"

Continuing my education meant I had one last summer vacation. One last chance to work in a factory and kick back at the lake. It also meant I could make one last trip to North Carolina with Don. The last couple of summers Don and I had taken a week off from work to drive down to North Carolina to visit his family. This year we were going to make the trip in my MGA, as his MGB was getting a little the worse for wear. First, however, I took my MGA to Riccotto's to have them fix an oil leak. It's normal for old cars to leak a little oil, as oil seal technology didn't used to be very sophisticated. The Model A, for example, just used a piece of rope to try and block some of the oil that was desperately fighting to escape from the engine and relax on the driveway. British cars had improved on this technology a little, but they still were not known for the quality of their oil seals. I always suspected this was a deliberate design decision to help owners maintain their cars. When you back a British car out of the driveway, you should see three spots of oil – one from the engine, one from the transmission, and one from the rear axle. If any one of those spots is missing, you're probably low on oil.

My MGA was doing more than just spotting the driveway, however. When I backed up I could see the outline of the entire car in the oil that had dripped off the frame. I was slinging oil out the back of my engine at the rate of about one quart every 50 or 60 miles, and had been ever since Nick and I rebuilt the engine. I had to stop for oil more frequently than I stopped for gas. I figured that would be a real drag on a cross-country trip to North Carolina. Nick promised to see what he could do, but things were pretty backed up at the shop and he didn't actually get a chance to look at it until the week before Don and I were leaving for North Carolina. (Over the years I have learned that one of the universal laws of sports car shops is that they are always pretty backed up.) Nick finally had to pull the engine and dissect it to find the problem, and then he called me with the bad news. The guy who had owned the car before we bought it had driven it with bearings that were so bad it let the crankshaft rub against the block. Specifically, it had worn out the oil slinger on the crank and the grooves for this slinger in the block. In practical terms, the engine was toast. Neither Nick nor I had noticed this when we rebuilt the engine, and we had basically invested a lot of time and money in an engine that was beyond repair. It ran great, but there was no way to stop the oil leak.

One of the features that gave Riccotto's its charm was that they almost never threw anything away. The dusty corners of the shop were piled high with spare engines, gearboxes, wheels, radiators, and other cast-off automotive artifacts. There was a small room with an enticing sign over the door that said "Competition Department." Rumor had it this room contained a lathe, a cylinder boring machine, a vertical mill, and other machine tools that could be used to make or modify almost any part you could envision. I had to take Nick's word for it, though, as the room was packed so full of dead car parts that none of the machine tools were visible. There was also the infamous "back lot," filled with automotive cadavers just waiting to be plundered for whatever parts you needed. Surprisingly, however, there were no spare MGA engines lying about. Nick and I searched all the nooks and crannies looking for another engine for my car, but there were none to be found. We even peered as deeply into the Competition Department as we could (there was no way to actually enter that room without a tunneling machine) but with no luck. Then, as if on cue, a mysterious stranger known only as "STP" stopped by the shop to see if anyone wanted to buy an MGB engine.

An MGB engine is virtually identical to an MGA engine except that it's bored out a little bigger and has about 25% more horsepower. It would bolt right into my MGA and Nick said if I came to the shop to help we could have it running in time to make the trip to North Carolina. The down side was that nobody knew much about this STP character or his engine. He had told Nick "It runs good" and he wanted $100 for it. Not having any other options, I pulled $100 out of the bank, got a ride to Berrytown, and arranged to meet STP at the shop.

STP showed up on schedule with the engine sitting in the back of a rather disreputable looking pickup truck. STP looked a little disreputable himself. When he introduced himself he said he had a Polish name that nobody could pronounce, but it sounded sort of like STP. The engine was covered in grease and obviously was well used. STP was a little vague as to how it had come into his possession, but it seemed that either he or a friend of his had once had an MGB that had met with an untimely demise and the engine was all that survived. There were no cracks in the block or other obvious defects, so I handed him $100 and helped him unload the engine. He then drove off to oblivion, never to be heard from again. Nick and I proceeded with the transplant operation. It did in fact bolt right in, and the extra power made driving the MGA even more enjoyable. We changed the oil and filter, but other than that I put my faith in the fact that STP said this was a good engine. Don drove down from Yodersburg, we threw our suitcases into the MGA, and we took off for North Carolina.

The trip to North Carolina was uneventful from an automotive viewpoint. The only minor problem I had was that the return spring on the MGB carburetors wasn't strong enough to slow down the car when I took my foot off the gas pedal. That made driving through the mountains a bit dicey, especially trying to navigate the switchbacks on the downhill sections, but I soon learned to hook my toe under the gas pedal and pull it up whenever I wanted the car to slow down. Don and I had a great time in North Carolina, we put a stronger return spring on my gas pedal, and we made the drive home without incident. About three days after we got back, however, a bearing in my gearbox let go as I was backing out of my driveway. One minute I was backing up, and the next minute the rear wheels locked up while there was a horrible crunching noise underneath the gear shift. I guess the extra power from the MGB engine was just too much for a worn out gearbox. Having the gearbox go bad in Indiana was a royal pain, as you can't remove the gearbox from an MGA without pulling the engine, but at least in Indiana I had my tools, my Dad's garage, and the support of Riccotto's. I still have nightmares about what would have happened if that gearbox had let go during the trip. To begin with, it wouldn't have been much fun to have my rear wheels lock up while I was barreling down a twisty mountain road. Then, if I survived the initial breakdown, I'd be faced with trying to rebuild my gearbox in some tiny little mountain town like Bat Cave North Carolina. Bat Cave had beautiful scenery and wonderful people, but it didn't have an MG dealer. This was long before the Internet, overnight delivery, and specialty shops that shipped nationwide. These were the days when you carried your greasy parts into an equally greasy car parts store and said "Have you got a cluster gear bearing for a 1957 MG? I think they used the same bearing through 1959, but they changed it in 1960."

Time was short and I had never tackled a gearbox before, so I decided to pull the gearbox in my Dad's garage and take it to Riccotto's for a rebuild. For once Riccotto's finished a project on schedule, and I had the MG running again by the time I headed back to school. Grad students couldn't stay in the dorm, so at the end of the spring semester Don and I had gotten together with an Italian engineering student named Tony and signed a lease on a broken down apartment just off the south end of campus. The only problem was, Don wasn't sure he was going to be able to go back to school after all. He hadn't earned as much money as he'd hoped over the summer, the bank was having an unexpected delay in processing his student loan, and the prospect of paying for 1/3 of a $150/month apartment plus groceries was becoming more than a little frightening. It was about this time that I got a surprise phone call from Viktor. Viktor had decided to come back to Purdue to get a Master's degree in business, but he was having trouble finding a place to stay. After several rounds of phone calls to Don, Viktor, and Andy, Don decided the odds of his actually making it back to school were slim to none and Viktor picked up Don's portion of the lease. (As it turned out, Don's student loan came through about three weeks into the school year. It was a scramble to find professors who would let him join their courses at that late date, but Don persevered and became a student again. He spent several weeks sleeping on couches in friends' apartments until he found a permanent place to stay, but everything worked out in the end.)

The apartment which Viktor, Tony, and I shared was basically half the downstairs of an old two story house which someone had subdivided into apartments. There was a small bedroom with a lumpy bed, a slightly larger bedroom with moldy bunk beds, a worn-out kitchen, a living room with a broken down couch, and a mildew-encrusted bathroom. The water was brown, fuses blew regularly, and you could hear people whispering in the other apartments. In short, it was a typical student apartment. One section of the yard had been converted into a gravel parking lot, so there was plenty of room for our cars. Actually, I was the only one who had more than one car at the apartment. Viktor had stored his TC in Chicago and was driving a Mazda RX-2. This had Mazda's first generation Wankel engine in it, and it really was the ultimate sleeper car. It looked like a typical Japanese econo-box, but it would outdrag a lot of American V8's and it would top 130 mph. Mazda's slogan was that most cars went "boing-boing" but their cars went "Hmmmmm." Viktor liked to quote that saying a lot. I predicted my MG would still be going boing-boing long after his Mazda was humming a different tune. As it turned out I was right, but Viktor had so much trouble with that Mazda in the years that followed that I didn't have the heart to remind him of my prediction. Mazda would go on to build some great cars, but the RX-2 wasn't one of them.

Tony, on the other hand, drove a clapped-out Fiat station wagon. This wasn't too surprising, as he had grown up in Turin, the city where Fiats were made. (Fiat actually stands for "Fabrica Italiana Automobili Torino," or "the Italian automobile factory at Turin." Why is it that I can remember useless trivia like that, but I can't remember to set the trash out on Thursday night?) When I first met Tony I would not have guessed that he'd only been in this country a few years, as he spoke very good English. I thought maybe he'd learned it growing up, as magazines and editorials were filled with stories about how kids in other countries learned five languages in elementary school, while at the same time mastering calculus and astrophysics. That wasn't Tony's experience, though, and he once confessed to me that when he got off the plane in New York he had to stand outside the rest rooms to see which one the men walked into. He had obviously learned English very quickly, although he still had a noticeable accent. I'm not certain I would have identified it as an Italian accent, though, and I certainly wouldn't have guessed he was Italian just by looking at him. Short, skinny, with blond hair and steel-rimmed glasses, he looked more German or Austrian than Italian.

If you ever rode with Tony in his Fiat, though, you would have immediately identified him as an Italian. Even a quick trip to the corner store for a loaf of bread was an occasion for squealing tires, honking horns, and Italian curses. Tony seemed to believe that every lane was placed there for his personal convenience, and that every other driver on the road was a *bastardo* who was deliberately trying to block his progress. Tony would swerve from one lane to another, cutting other drivers off with reckless abandon, while simultaneously shaking his fist and cursing at any driver whom he felt was driving too slow, too fast, or committing the ultimate sin of trying to merge into his lane. One afternoon I was washing dishes and looking out the kitchen window into the parking lot when Tony drove in. I watched his Fiat come sliding around the corner and skid to a stop in front of our apartment. I could see Tony waving his hands while his mouth was moving a mile a minute, but that wasn't unusual. Tony often shouted like that while he drove, even when he was alone. What was unusual, though, was that he continued to shout and gesticulate at the car even after he got out and was standing in the parking lot. Then, ever so slowly, I saw three heads peek up from behind the seats. They looked surprised to find they were still alive, and they peered carefully in all directions to make certain they were safely parked. When they were absolutely sure the car wasn't going to move again, Viktor and two of his study partners bolted from the car and began kissing the ground. Tony had driven them to a burger joint to get a snack, and on the way back he had driven with even more enthusiasm than usual. The final blow came when Tony was driving uphill on the busiest street in town, a street that was jammed with traffic that filled two lanes going uphill and two going downhill. Tony was in the far right-hand lane when he decided traffic was not going to make way for him no matter how much he honked his horn, and he could make better time if he turned onto a side street. He jerked the wheel to the left, bringing the three other lanes to a screeching halt while he bolted onto a side street. It was at this point that Viktor and his friends threw themselves to the floor and assumed the time honored "duck and cover" position. Tony thought they were overreacting. "They did not hit me" he shouted. "I had plenty of room!"

In addition to the fact that Tony let go of the steering wheel to gesture as he drove, he had an unsettling habit of looking people straight in the eye while he talked. This was bad enough when he was talking to someone beside him in the passenger seat, but it was positively frightening when he talked to someone in the back seat. This wasn't just a quick glance to see if they'd grasped his point. Tony would let go of the wheel with both hands, turn completely around in his seat, and wave his hands about as he stared into the terrified face of his passenger. Everyone else in the car would be shouting "Turn around! Watch where you're going!" but it had no effect on Tony. He would finish his story, and then reluctantly turn back to the business of driving. One day I discovered a fact that helped explain this habit, while at the same time making it even more frightening. I have always preferred 3-D pictures to flat photographs, and I have a couple of old stereo cameras which I use to take stereo slides. (OK. I guess maybe my hobbies are a little out of the mainstream. Someday I'll tell you about my collection of razor blade stropping machines.) You view stereo slides through a special slide viewer, sort of like a Viewmaster but with bigger pictures. I was showing some of my slides to Tony and trying to explain how the system worked.

"The camera has two lenses" I said. "They're the same distance apart as your two eyes, and it takes two pictures at once. The two lenses see things from slightly different angles, just like your eyes do, and the viewer lets you look at the left picture with your left eye while your right eye is looking at the right picture so you see things in 3-D."

Tony seemed to be having a hard time grasping this concept. He said my stereo slides didn't look any different than any other slides, so I tried a different approach.

"You know how if you close one eye and then the other it looks like things sort of jump back and forth? That's because you're eyes see things from slightly different angles. This is the same. Try looking into the viewer while closing one eye and then the other. You'll see how the two pictures are slightly different."

Instead of closing one eye or the other, Tony began to move the slide viewer back and forth so his left eye looked first at the left picture and then at the right picture. "I don't see any difference" he said.

"No, don't move the viewer." I said. "Just close one eye and then the other."

"Do you need both eyes to see 3-D?" Tony asked. "Because I can't see anything out of my right eye."

Suddenly I knew why Tony turned all the way around to look at passengers in the back seat.

Not surprisingly, Tony and Luis hit it off from the moment they first met. Not that Luis had any great admiration for Tony's driving skills or for his mechanical ability. "That kid could screw up a steel ball with a rubber mallet" he once muttered after watching Tony try to fix his Fiat. What Luis admired was Tony's fluency in Italian. Luis had been born in Italy, but his family moved to the US when he was three years old. He learned to speak a little Italian from his parents, but not much. He liked to have Tony come by whenever he was having problems with one of the exotic Italian cars that occasionally showed up in the shop. There was one Italia in particular that was a frequent visitor. Its owner smashed it up every six months, just like clockwork, and sometimes Luis had to scramble to find the parts he needed to get it back on the road in time for its next accident. Not only could Tony talk to the people at the factory to order the parts, he could explain things to them in terms they understood. There may have been a lot of shouting and Italian profanity whenever Tony was on the phone, but the parts arrived much quicker than if Luis ordered them.

One Saturday night, after a particularly successful phone call to the Italia factory, Luis invited Tony, Tony's girlfriend, and me to come to the house for dinner. An invitation to Luis's house for dinner was not something you wanted to turn down! His parents had run a popular Italian restaurant in Berrytown and Luis had learned some great culinary secrets from them. Not that Luis ever did any cooking, mind you. His wife Leto always did the cooking, but Luis had obviously taught her well. Leto was Greek, and she occasionally added a Greek appetizer or a touch of Greek seasoning to the meal. The food was simple, abundant, and unbelievably delicious.

On this particular Saturday night Luis was in an exceptionally good mood. After dinner he opened a bottle of Lambrusco and we sat around the table drinking wine and telling stories. I took it easy on the wine because I was driving, but Tony had no such restriction. Normally an animated speaker anyway, he became more and more outspoken as we solved the problems of sports car design, American politics, and Italian politics. We also managed to kill more than one bottle of Lambrusco in the process. Tony's most dramatic gesture came late that night when he stood up and tore open his shirt, sending buttons flying in all directions. "See!" he shouted. "There is no red S on my chest! I am not Superman!" Luis and Leto roared with laughter, but I sensed it was time to head back to the apartment.

Tony's girl friend and I helped guide Tony out to the Model A. Luis actually came out on the porch to wave good-by, a sign that he too had partaken freely of the Lambrusco. Normally you were lucky to get a good-bye grunt from Luis, let alone a personal farewell. It was also nearly midnight, extraordinarily late for Luis to be up. If everything had gone smoothly we would have been back at the apartment by 1:30, but of course this was a night drive in the Model A so everything did not go smoothly. Somewhere between Rockfield and Delphi the generator died. It was a bright, moonlit night so I didn't really need my headlamps to see where I was going, but I suspected other drivers would regard it as a polite courtesy if I fixed the generator so I could turn on my lights. A Model A doesn't exactly hurtle through the darkness, but it goes fast enough that drivers about to pull onto the highway would be unsettled if an unlit black Ford sedan suddenly emerged from the night. I parked on the shoulder beside a corn field and began fiddling with the wires under the hood. It was then that I heard the inevitable from the back seat.

"Ohhh" Tony started moaning. "I think I am going to be sick."

"Not in the car!" I shouted.

Tony did open the door and tried to lean out before erupting, but he didn't quite get his head all the way out of the car. I could hear the Lambrusco splattering against the coachwork and the running board, as his girlfriend stroked his hair and said "Oh, poor baby." I'm afraid at that moment I wasn't feeling quite as sympathetic as she was. A little while later she stepped out of the car and tapped me on the shoulder.

"Tony has to go to the bathroom, but he can't walk. Can you help him?"

There was a clump of bushes not too far away, and I thought maybe I could help Tony stagger to the bushes. I knew the bushes wouldn't matter to Tony, but to me it seemed like the right thing to do. Tony had never been as shy about natural functions as most other people I knew. Viktor and I discovered that one day when we drove to a girl's dormitory to pick up our dates. We were about half-way to the front door when we heard Tony call out "Hey, guys. Wait up a minute." We turned around and were horrified to see him relieving himself in the parking lot. He insisted everybody did that in Italy, although I sincerely hope he just meant all the men did it. In any event, I wasn't surprised tonight when he stopped about half way to the bushes and announced "This is good." His girlfriend had stayed in the car for modesty's sake, and it was all that I could do to hold him upright. I was totally unprepared for what happened next. Instead of unzipping his fly, he suddenly unfastened his belt and squatted down.

"Tony!" I shouted. "Pull down your pants!"

"I did that already."

"No you didn't! You just unfastened your belt!" My words had no impact on him. After what seemed like an eternity, he stood back up with as much dignity as he could muster and fastened his belt. "False alarm" was all he said. His eyes had that strange, seriously puzzled look of one who is trying very hard to make sense of a world that refuses to stand still.

The rest of the night was relatively uneventful. I fixed the generator, dropped Tony's girlfriend off at her dorm, dumped Tony onto his bed, and covered him with a blanket. Tony didn't look too good the next morning, but he didn't utter a word of complaint when I handed him a bucket of soapy water and a sponge and pointed at the Model A.

The generator problem had been relatively easy to fix. A few weeks later, however, I had a problem that wasn't quite so simple. I was driving the MGA on I-465 around Indianapolis. It was a nice day, I had the top down, and everything was going great. I wasn't in a hurry, just keeping up with traffic in a 75 mph zone. That's about 4500 rpm in the MGA. (It's geared low.) The water temperature was fine, oil pressure was good, and the engine was purring. Then I heard a tremendous "bang" from under the hood and everything behind me disappeared in a cloud of blue smoke. I killed the ignition and coasted onto the shoulder. Not having a clue as to what had gone wrong I popped open the hood and peered into the dim recesses of the engine compartment. Everything appeared to be in the right place. The smoke I had seen in my mirrors was obviously oil smoke so I pulled out the dipstick to check the oil level. The oil level was fine, but I got my first hint of how serious the problem was when I noticed the little metal tube that the dipstick fits into pulled out with the dipstick. Worse yet, the tube was still screwed into a small piece of the block. This was not going to be a roadside repair.

To this day I don't know what caused that engine to blow. I guess maybe $100 just didn't buy much of an engine, even back then. MG engines are normally pretty tough. It takes some serious abuse and/or neglect to trash one. This engine ran smoothly, had good oil pressure, and was never over-revved during the few months that I owned it. For some reason, though, the number 3 rod decided to separate just below the piston. This meant it was no longer constrained to go up and down with the piston but could instead explore other regions. In engineering terms, it had one more degree of freedom than it needed. In layman's terms, it was flailing away like a chain on a buzz saw. At 4500 fpm (flails per minute) it didn't take long to wear the rod down to a nub, but that was more than enough time to trash the engine. The block was shattered into a dozen pieces, loosely held together by the oil pan. The cam was broken in half, and the broken ends were sticking out of the block like a compound fracture. The only good news was that (A) it didn't break in Bat Cave North Carolina, and (B) now I had an excuse to build a dream engine. My experience with Scuderia Banca Rotta, helping Nick and Viktor campaign hopeless race cars, had an influence on me. I was never seriously tempted to invest the time and money required to go racing myself, but I was intrigued by the idea of building a street engine that was at least a little hotter than stock. Since my stock engine had just donated a few vital pieces to the Indianapolis pavement, I had a blank slate to work with.

This time there was no shortage of junk engines lying around Riccotto's, and Luis let me pick out an MGB engine with five main bearings, which would make it a little stronger than my previous engine. I wasn't trying for a full race engine, but I did get some forged 10:1 racing pistons, had the rods hardened, installed a competition clutch, balanced everything, and generally spared no expense to make a hot street engine. Viktor helped me port & polish the head, an operation that involved a minor amount of panic when we broke through to a pushrod hole, but we managed to repair that. The only part of this whole operation that caused me any consternation was the cam. I was pretty sure I'd need something hotter than stock to let the engine breathe freely but Luis immediately dismissed that idea. "You don't need a hot cam in that thing" he said. "That'll just screw up the idle and drink gas." I respected Luis a lot and he was no stranger to racing himself, having raced MGAs when they were brand new. Nevertheless, I was convinced he was wrong on this account. The problem was, how could I slip this by him? Then I had an idea.

I was still working at the shop on Saturdays, and I did most of the work on my engine late at night, after the shop had closed. Luis left me with the keys and I had free run of the parts department, as long as I wrote down everything I took so we could settle up later. If I needed something they didn't have in stock, I just wrote down the part number and the parts lady ordered it on Monday morning. Pouring through the MG parts book I found what was billed as a "half-race cam." The part number was virtually identical to the stock cam, so one Saturday night I just slipped that part number into a long list of parts I was ordering. Luis never said a word about it. I was relieved when it arrived in a standard MG package, looking no different than any other MG part.

Finally the day arrived when I had the engine back in the car. It was a slow Saturday, so Luis gave me the afternoon off to get everything hooked up. I'm always a little nervous when it's time to start an engine I've rebuilt, and my mind is plagued with doubts. Did I get the valve timing correct? Did I remember to put the gasket on the oil pickup? I did torque those rods, didn't I? In this case the engine started immediately. It had good oil pressure, and everything seemed great. It wasn't idling very smoothly, but that just meant I needed to adjust the carburetors. So I fiddled with the carburetors. And I fiddled some more. And some more. And still the engine was idling "ta-da-dump" "ta-da-dump" "ta-da-dump." Luis walked by the stall while I was trying yet again to get the idle to smooth out. He didn't look my way, didn't even slow down. He just called out over his shoulder "You ain't never going to tune that out. It's that damn cam you ordered when you thought I wasn't looking." To this day I have no idea how he found out about the cam.

My Master's research was related to automobiles, but only just barely. My major professor had gotten a research grant to develop a way to measure pavement roughness. He and a couple of PhD students had developed a trailer that they towed behind a car to measure how a wheel "bounced" over irregularities in the road. They then performed what was known as a "power spectrum analysis" of the way the wheel vibrated. They also developed an equation to describe these vibrations, using variables they called the "P" and "Q" parameters. The vibrations depended on how fast the car was moving, but when they looked at the equation they realized that if they picked certain values for "P" and "Q" the vibrations would be independent of the vehicle's speed. They called this an "isoroughness road." They had no idea of whether or not a real road would actually behave this way, or if it was just a mathematical quirk of the equation. If such a road did exist, they had no idea of whether or not anyone could intentionally build such a road, and if it could be built, they didn't know if it would be any better than a normal road. But my professor thought it was an interesting question, and he assigned me to work backwards through the equations and discover what such a road would look like. After endless computer simulations, I discovered that an isoroughness road would have to be smoother than a sheet of glass. My entire research project was of absolutely no practical use whatsoever, but that put it squarely in line with many other research projects. My professor was delighted with the results. The only problem was that he had to come up with a title for this project to list on my course records.

My professor stared for a long time at the form the university had provided him to describe my research project. "What you're really doing is describing the effects of the P and Q parameters on the pavement roughness spectrum" he said, "but they don't give me enough space to write that." After thinking a while longer he finally said "I'll just abbreviate it, and if anyone is interested they'll ask you to explain it." And that's what he did. So today, somewhere in the dusty archives of Purdue University student transcripts, is an official record that I completed an independent research course in "Eff of P Q Par on Pave Rough Spec." I devoted countless hours of my life to that project, and no one has ever asked me to explain the title.

By the time I finished this research project I had the MG back on the road, and we were well into spring. Final exams were just around the corner, and almost before I knew it they were over. I was the proud owner of a Master's of Science degree in Mechanical Engineering. I still didn't feel like I had a clue as to how to go about designing anything, but my research project had convinced me another degree wouldn't fix that problem. Now it was time to go back home, pack my things, and begin my Air Force career. Or so I thought.

Chapter 13 – A "Professional" Mechanic?

After saying good-bye to Viktor and Tony, I headed back to Yodersburg. I still didn't have active duty orders from the Air Force, but I expected them any day and I had no shortage of car projects to keep me busy while I was waiting for the Air Force to call. Indiana dumps tons of salt on the roads during the winter, which leads to a lot of corrosion, and both my cars needed work to take care of that old demon rust. I wasn't considering body work, although Lord knows they were both in need of that, but they also needed mechanical work to take care of some serious rust problems. The MGA kingpins were rusting up, which made it hard to steer. It took a lot of effort to muscle it into a turn, and then it would keep turning until I forced the steering wheel back the other way because the wheels couldn't overpower the rust to straighten out by themselves. The Model A needed brake work, as the mechanical brakes were rusting up. It would still stop, but you really had to stomp on the pedal to make it shudder to a stop and it let out loud groans of protest in the process.

I stopped by the shop to say hello to Luis on the way, and he asked what my plans were for the summer. When I told him, he said he could really use some help getting a Jaguar back on the road for a customer. He asked if I could spend a couple weeks working for him at the shop. That sounded like a good idea to me, as I really couldn't do anything else until I heard from the Air Force. I offered to start work in a week or two, just as soon as I got the MG and the Model A fixed. Luis said he really needed the help now, as he'd promised to finish the car by the end of the month. He wanted me to start the next day, spend a couple weeks working on the Jaguar, and then fix my cars. I could stay at his house while I was working on the Jag. The idea of spending a couple of weeks eating Leto's cooking sounded great to me, so I said OK. I had no idea that "a couple of weeks" would turn out to be nearly a year and a half.

The Jag he wanted me to work on was an XK-150 drophead coupe that needed bodywork and a complete paint job. I spent the better part of a day sanding fenders and removing trim, until a Fiat came in with an unusual electrical problem. The regular mechanics were great at recognizing and fixing electrical problems they had seen before, but new problems tended to baffle them. They would try changing any part they thought might be related to the problem.

If it fixed it, they'd know how to fix this problem the next time a customer brought in a car with these symptoms. If it didn't fix the problem, they'd put the old part back and change something else. Eventually they'd find the problem, but the process wasn't pretty and they sometimes burned up a few new parts along the way. I'd taken a few electrical engineering courses at Purdue, and while electrical theory was never one of my strengths I could study a wiring diagram and work through the circuit, checking voltages and testing theories, until I isolated the problem. My way was slower than theirs on problems they'd seen before, but faster and safer than their trial and error approach on new problems. In this particular case it took me a couple of hours to find a bad fuel pump safety relay which Fiat had recently added to the car without bothering to notify its dealer network.

The next day I started back to work on the Jag, but Luis pulled me off that because one of his mechanics had called in sick and a lot of customers had scheduled maintenance that day. And so it went, day by day, for the first couple of weeks. I probably spent two or three days total working on the Jag, but mostly I worked as a mechanic. That suited me fine, as I preferred mechanical work, and it suited Luis fine as I proved to be something of a Jonah in the body shop. It wasn't that I couldn't do decent body work, I was just bad luck. If I sanded a fender, the primer would run when Luis sprayed it. If I replaced a body panel with one that was primed at the factory, the color coat wouldn't match the rest of the car. As it happened, the mechanic who had called in sick wound up retiring. It wasn't exactly a formal retirement, he just kept calling in sick and he never came back to work again. We saw him around town so we knew he was all right. He was just tired of working. Luis gave me his stall and hired an experienced body man to work on the Jag. My stall was the closest to the showroom, which I sometimes took advantage of whenever I worked on an engineering student's car. I could immediately spot these cars, as they were filled with engineering textbooks and I could usually see the student sitting in the customer waiting area, busily working on homework. I would look for some excuse to go up front and ask the student a question about what he wanted me to do to his car. In the ensuing conversation I would let it slip that I had a Masters' degree in Mechanical Engineering. "It got me where I am today" I would say with pride. Then I'd wander back into the shop, busily cleaning whatever piece of grimy metal I

135

was carrying, and let the student wonder how far his degree was going to take him.

The body man did a beautiful job on the XK-150. It took him well over a month to finish it, but when he was done it rolled out of the shop resplendent in dark forest green, looking like it had just come off the show room floor.

XK-150 Drophead Coupe

About a month later the owner wrapped it around a tree and literally cut the car in half. The owner was extremely fortunate to escape with nothing more serious than a broken leg and a few bruises, but the body man was not so fortunate. That crash broke his heart. When they towed the two halves of that Jaguar into our back lot he spent most of the day just staring out the window. He never showed up for work the next day, or any day after that. Eventually we learned he'd moved back to West Virginia to work in the coal mines. He'd grown up there, and he decided being a coal miner was better than working on old Jaguars.

There were only two other mechanics at Riccotto's, so I joined an elite group. Well, at any rate we were an unusual group. There was no such thing as a certified mechanic back then, but the other two definitely qualified as professional mechanics. I was professional only in the sense that people who didn't know any better paid me to work on their cars. Umbarti was the lead Jaguar mechanic. Short, heavy set, with glossy black hair and a ready smile, he looked like the epitome of an Italian mechanic. The only thing that didn't fit this stereotype was that he hated working on Fiats. Jaguars and Ramblers were his specialty, although he could fix anything on four

136

wheels. Umbarti was probably in his mid-30's, and he had been working at various jobs since he was 8 years old. He dropped out of third grade to get a job because his family needed money, and as a result he never learned to read. If he was doing something for the first time, like rebuilding a new type of transmission, he would occasionally have to ask someone to read him a paragraph from the shop manual or look up the technical specifications. He only needed to hear it once, though, because he immediately committed it to memory. He had also memorized the part numbers on virtually every part we ever used. When the parts lady took her annual inventory, if she found any part without a readable sticker she simply held it up and shouted "Hey Umbarti. What's this?" Umbarti could usually identify it from half-way across the shop. "That's a generator bracket off a Humber Super Snipe" he'd reply. "The part number is 660-4697."

Although Umbarti didn't like to work on Fiats, he would work on them if Luis asked him nicely. He just complained about it a lot. The only thing he absolutely couldn't tolerate was a snake. One day a customer towed in a 1961 Jaguar E-Type that had sat behind a barn for a few years and asked us to get it running. For some reason, Umbarti took out the seat cushions. There are no mechanical parts under the seats, so I suspect he was looking for loose change or cigarettes. Umbarti was too cheap to buy cigarettes, not surprising considering his childhood, but he enjoyed smoking them if he could get them for free. This time he didn't find any cigarettes, but he did find a snake skin. That was it for Umbarti and that car. He didn't want to have anything to do with it after that. Luis had to sweet talk him for a long time before Umbarti was even willing to stick he head under the hood. Luis told him that snakes shed their skins in the spring, so that skin had been there a long time. Maybe even for several years. The snake was probably long gone, and even if it had still been in the car it would have jumped out as soon as the tow truck driver started hooking his truck up to the car. "Snakes are afraid of people" Luis explained. "It would have gotten as far away from that car as possible." I volunteered the fact that it looked like a garter snake skin to me, and garter snakes are harmless. (If truth be told, I didn't have the slightest idea what kind of a skin it was, but I suspected Luis didn't know what he was talking about either so I was just following his lead.) Umbarti finally calmed down enough to get back to work and he had no more problems with the snake. At least, not while he was working on the car. About a day or two after he got the car running and the owner proudly drove it home Umbarti was sitting on the can when a snake slithered out from behind the toilet, looked up at him, and stuck out its tongue. I'm pretty sure they heard the screams in the next county.

(A few years after I left Riccotto's I heard that Umbarti had gone to night school and finally learned to read. Good for you, Umbarti!)

The other full-time mechanic was called "Wack." I think his full name was "Wachowski" or something like that, but everyone just called him Wack. He was our resident hippie. Tall and thin, he had curly red hair, a full beard, and a ready smile. He'd grown up in Berrytown and spent a year in Vietnam. When he came back he decided to drop out of life for a while and live in a tent in the city park. Apparently the city didn't object to this. I guess life in a tent got boring after a while, so he bought a used MG Midget and started doing a little amateur sports car racing. Racing is an expensive hobby, even if it's amateur racing and you're only doing "a little." Before long he started doing odd jobs for Luis to earn money for parts. Then he started working regularly. It's hard to set an alarm clock and make it to work on time when you're living in a tent, so his unencumbered life style gradually started to crumble. By the time I met him the tent was gone and the Midget was gone. He was married, with kids, living in a house with a mortgage, and driving a pickup truck to work. Only the beard and the carefree attitude remained from his vagabond days.

Wack could also fix anything that rolled into the shop, but MGs and Triumphs were his favorites. Of course, he also got to work on Fiats because Umbarti didn't like them and Umbarti was the senior mechanic. Wack used to say there were more sharp pieces of metal to cut yourself on under the hood of a Fiat than on any 10 British cars combined. Once in a while, someone would bring a Volkswagen into the shop. We didn't usually work on VWs, but we offered a special "first come, first served" service on Thursday nights which attracted a lot of hard luck cases. We scheduled normal appointments from 8:00 AM until 5:00 PM Monday through Friday. On Thursdays the mechanics came back to work from 6:00 PM until 10:00 PM so customers who couldn't take time off from work during normal business hours could have us fix their cars. We were the only shop in town that did this, so sometimes people brought us VWs and other unusual cars on Thursday night. Wack had once owned a

Porsche, which as far as Luis was concerned was the same as a Volkswagen. The only problem was, Wack had gotten rid of his Porsche because he hated working on it, so Luis would have to sweet talk him into working on any VWs that came through our door. Luis would put his arm around Wack's shoulder and explain that he wouldn't have taken the job if the customer hadn't been in a bind. The customer was counting on us to fix the car so he could drive his blind mother to Arizona for an operation. Wack was the only one who knew enough about VWs to get them back on the road before her pain medication ran out, etc. Wack would grumble a bit, but he'd fix the car.

When Wack wasn't working on VWs he always had a smile on his face. He was one of those people who had a knack for making work enjoyable, and cheering up everyone around him at the same time. Whenever oil dripped onto the floor - a daily occurrence when you're working on British sports cars - the rest of us would simply dump some oil drying compound on the spill, grind it into the floor with our boot, and sweep it up. (Oil drying compound is similar to kitty litter.) That wasn't Wack's style. Wack would do a little soft shoe dance routine on the compound, humming to himself and clapping his hands in rhythm as he worked the compound into the oil spill. Even when things went wrong, Wack kept his cheerful, carefree attitude. Of course, sometimes things went wrong because he was a little too carefree.

Bleeding brakes was a fairly common task. Whenever we replaced a wheel cylinder or did similar work to a braking system, air got into the brake lines. We needed to bleed this air out of the system so the brake pedal wouldn't feel "spongy." To bleed the brakes we'd run a small tube from a bleed valve into a glass jar with a little brake fluid in it, open the valve, and have another mechanic step on the brakes. If there was air in the brakes, we could see it bubble up from the end of the tube. When it stopped bubbling, we knew we'd bled out all the air. Wack used an old Pepsi bottle to bleed brakes, and he left this bottle on his work bench between brake jobs. Wack also enjoyed drinking a Pepsi now and then, and he also set those bottles on his workbench. One day the inevitable happened. Wack grabbed the wrong bottle, tipped it up to his lips, and then sprayed brake fluid all over his workbench. When he'd finished washing his mouth out with soap and water he told me he'd learned an important lesson. "You know all those warnings they put on brake fluid cans saying 'Don't take this internally?' They're completely unnecessary. When that stuff touches your lips you just pucker up and blow. You don't even think about it."

The one time when Wack's happy-go-lucky attitude deserted him was in the aftermath of the infamous Fiat Undercoat Incident. No car built during the 70's is revered for the quality of its design and construction, but Fiats had even more problems than most. The Fiat 128 is the only car I ever worked on that was subject to a recall to fix serious frame rust problems that occurred during the first 12 months. (I think a Fiat could have won a rusting contest against my dad's 1957 Plymouth, if the Plymouth had lasted until the 70's.) The recall required us to inspect the frame, tapping at suspicious spots with a little prospector's hammer Fiat gave us, to make certain the car wasn't already rusted so badly it wasn't worth saving. If it was still salvageable, we would undercoat every square inch of the frame with a special "gunk" Fiat supplied. It looked like Hershey's Syrup when you first sprayed it on, but it quickly set up to a rubbery tar-like substance. We didn't just undercoat the outside of the frame. We also had to drill holes at strategic locations and snake a long flexible tube inside the frame, then pull the trigger on the undercoat machine and slowly pull the tube out, undercoating the inside of the frame as we went.

As our lead Fiat mechanic, Wack got to undercoat a lot of Fiats. One day as he was carefully snaking the tube as far into the frame as it would go, it somehow doubled over on itself and began snaking back the way it had come. Unknown to him, it emerged from another hole in the frame. The spray nozzle wound up a few inches from the side of his face. Intently focused on the hole where the tube went into the frame, Wack satisfied himself that it was in as far as it would go and squeezed the trigger on the undercoat machine. A spray of gooey brown undercoating immediately engulfed the beard on the right side of his face. He spent the next half hour hunched over the parts cleaner, trying to scrub the undercoating out of his beard before it set up. He emerged from the ordeal with a clean beard, a cherry red face, and for once in his life, without a smile on his lips or a quip on his tongue.

One thing Wack wasn't casual about was time. He was always first in line at the time clock to punch out for lunch or at the end of the day. Luis and I hung around the shop for a little while longer, taking care of odd jobs while Leto went back to the house to prepare our lunch. One day about 10 minutes after our lunch hour started I was surprised when Wack called out to me as I walked through the shop. "Hey Steve, could you give me a hand with this?" He had a TR-4 up on the lift and he was trying to remove a bolt that was tucked up in a nearly inaccessible position. "Hold this nut, will you, while I turn the other end." He handed me a wrench and started trying to work the bolt loose. "Awfully quiet around here" he muttered to himself. Then he looked around the shop. I could see his eyes widen with shock and disbelief. "What time is it?" he asked.

"About 10 after 12" I replied.

"What? Then it's . . . I mean . . . Why didn't you tell me?" There was a sharp clang as he dropped the wrench right where he was standing. He rushed to the time clock, punched out, and was gone, leaving me still holding the other end of the bolt.

I learned a lot while working at Riccotto's. I learned a lot about cars, of course, but I also learned many valuable "life lessons." One thing working there taught me was to be absolutely fearless about tearing into something I knew nothing about. We had shop manuals and other references to guide us, but they never covered every question you might have. At some point you just had to tear into it and trust that your skill and experience would tell you what to do next. When I first started there I had neither skill nor experience. Many times I would carry some assembly over to Umbarti's stall and ask him how to take it apart. "How do you think it comes apart?" he'd ask.

"Well, it looks to me like you could just pry these two pieces apart, but they're pretty tight. I don't want to break it."

"That's what they've got factories for" Umbarti would reply. "To make more parts for the ones you break. The people who put that together at the factory aren't any smarter than you are. Trust your instincts."

Sometimes my instincts would lead me astray, but they got better as I gained experience. I once worked on an Austin Marina whose left turn signal wouldn't flash. I traced the problem to a faulty turn signal switch, but we didn't have a new one in stock. Rather than just ordering a new one and asking the customer to bring the car back when the new switch came in, I decided to take the old switch apart to see if I could fix it. That's what I would have done if it were my car. I had to pry on the cover a bit and . . . sproing! The cover popped off and tiny little springs and brushes flew all over the driver's compartment. The customer didn't have any turn signals now, and unless I could put the switch back together I'd actually made the problem worse. Putting it back together would have been a whole lot easier if I'd been able to see how the pieces originally fit in there, or even if I just knew how many pieces there were supposed to be. I spent the next hour searching the car for tiny pieces of the switch, trying to piece them together, deciding maybe there should be another piece, and repeating the process. Eventually I got everything back together and I actually fixed it so that both turn signals worked, but I also wasted an hour we couldn't bill the customer for. Working on a customer's car is different from working on your own car.

Another time we had a beautiful gray-green Jaguar XJ-6 sedan with power windows that wouldn't go up or down. After a few minutes studying the wiring diagram and taking voltage readings I decided something called the "thermal overload" was bad. Unfortunately, the manual didn't say were this magical thermal overload switch was located. My first guess was that it was in the center console, near the window switches. I pulled the console out, but no luck. Next I pulled off the door panels to check the window motors, but it wasn't mounted near any of them. I pulled the valence from under the dash to look near the fuse box, but it wasn't there. Luis called the Jaguar service rep on the phone and asked him where it was. He said sometimes it was behind the passenger's kick panel and sometimes it was under the rear seat. I pulled both of those, but no thermal overload. Finally I began tracing wires from the console switches, disassembling the car as I went so I could trace the wires. It turned out to be mounted on the back of the tachometer, a nearly inaccessible spot that necessitated removing the top of the dashboard. I had just finished removing the switch when the lady who owned the car walked into the shop and screamed "My Jaguar! What have you done to my car?" Suddenly, I could visualize the scene from her point of view. She didn't see a clever mechanic who had just won a game of hide-and-seek with the Jaguar factory. She saw her beautiful car gutted - seats, console, door panels, and dash panel strewn about the shop – while some grinning kid in grimy clothes squatted on the floorboards where her seats used to be, triumphantly holding up a tiny metal box. Luis took the customer up front and gave her a cup of coffee to soothe her nerves while I put the car back together.

One of the other lessons I learned was a respect for just how hard people had to work to make a small business successful. The Riccotto family staggered their wake-up times from 6:00 to 7:00 AM so they could take turns using the single bathroom in their house. Breakfast was staggered too, with the kids catching the school bus during the winter or heading for the shop with their dad during the summer. Leto stayed behind to clean up, but the rest of us had to get to the shop before 8:00 to open it up. Leto arrived at the shop around 9:00 so she could take care of the books and manage the office. She went home a little before noon to start making lunch, and the rest of us followed around 12:15 or so. We were back in the shop by 1:00, with Leto following as soon as she cleaned up the kitchen. The mechanics, the parts lady, and the car salesman left at 5:00, but Luis kept the shop open until 8:00. That gave people who worked the day shift a chance to pick up their car and possibly peruse our collection of new and used cars after work. The parts department was officially closed, but if someone was in a bind we would open it up long enough to find the part they needed. It also wasn't unusual for me to do a quick repair job for someone who came limping in after 5:00. Leto usually left around 7:00 to fix dinner, and the rest of us followed at 8:00. After dinner we watched television or read for about an hour, and then it was time for bed. Thursdays the schedule was a little different because the shop re-opened from 6:00 to 10:00 PM. We either had a quick dinner at 5:00 or we ate hamburgers in the shop. (Mr. Happy Burger was just a couple of blocks up the road.)

Saturdays were more relaxed because the mechanics and the parts lady didn't work on Saturday and the salesman went home at noon. We still kept the shop open from 8:00 AM until 8:00 PM, though, as a lot of people shopped for cars on Saturday and there were always a few hard-luck cases who talked us into opening the parts department or doing a quick repair job even though we were "officially" closed. The rules of etiquette were a little different on the

Saturdays, since we were doing these jobs as a favor to the customer. One Saturday a man came in looking for a small metal clip that went on an MGB rear brake cylinder. He was rebuilding the brakes on his car and had lost this clip. He got upset when Luis told him the parts department was closed on Saturday and he raised enough of a ruckus that Luis asked his son AJ to look in the parts department and see if he could find a clip. AJ was about 14 years old then and knew his way around the parts department pretty well, but it still took him close to half an hour to find the right book, look up the part number, look through the index cards to see if we had one, and check the parts bins to make certain the index card was correct. (This was long before computers.) Rather than appreciating this extra service, the customer was growing visibly upset at the fact that this "kid" was taking so long to look up the part, especially when it turned out we didn't have one in stock. That really upset the customer, and he started berating AJ for not stocking the parts people needed to fix their cars.

AJ was trying his best to help, so he dragged a jack into the back lot, jacked up a junk MGB, and crawled underneath it to pull off the clip. He proudly showed it to the customer as he dragged the jack back into the shop, but the customer complained that the clip was rusty. We had a wire brush on an electric motor in one corner of the shop, so AJ carried the clip over to the wire brush and cleaned off all the rust. Then AJ dragged out the price book, looked up the part, and told the customer it would cost him a dollar for the part.

"That's the price for a new one" the customer shouted. "I'm not paying full price for a used one. How the hell do you expect people to buy your cars when you don't have parts in stock and you charge new prices for used parts?"

This was too much for AJ. He held the piece in front of his face and announced "You ain't supposed to lose the damn thing in the first place!" Then he threw the clip back into the bowels of the parts department where it pinged off the shelving and vanished into a pile of mufflers. AJ slammed down the roll-up door over the parts counter and stormed out of the shop. The customer stared at the closed door in shock for a moment, started toward the showroom to complain to Luis, and then thought better of it. That was probably the first intelligent decision he'd made all day. He then stormed out of the shop himself and drove off.

Saturday night, when Luis closed the shop, I drove home to Yodersburg to spend Sundays with my parents and my younger brother. I knew that Luis usually did odd jobs around the shop after church on Sunday, but six days a week was enough for me. On Monday morning I drove back to the shop and we started a new week. This schedule was enough to wear me out, and I only did it for a little over a year. Luis and Leto lived this schedule for their entire lives. After a few months of this schedule I discovered I really had no life outside the shop. Once in a while I'd visit Don or go to a party on Saturday night, but I had nothing to talk about. Everyone else would be talking about sports, politics, TV, current events, or whatever was going on in their lives. All I could say was "I worked on an interesting car the other day." Even I found those stories boring, although that hasn't stopped me from inflicting them on anyone who reads this book. I really take my hat off to Luis and Leto, and to everyone else who runs a small family business.

Another lesson I learned working at Riccotto's was that I never wanted to run a car repair shop. Long hours aside, I wouldn't want to run any kind of a car business because so many customers assume you're a crook from the moment they walk in the door, and nothing you can do will make them happy. The customer who complained to AJ about paying $1.00 for a part AJ had just spent an hour locating was, sadly, not unusual. Not all customers were like this, of course. Most were very nice people. Many customers had been coming to Riccotto's for years. We were their family car dealership, much like their family doctor. They bought a new car from us, we took care of it for years, and when it finally wore out they bought another new car from us. There were some customers, however, who treated us as common thieves. I remember being surprised to learn that some customers put a chalk mark on their oil filter before they brought their car in for an oil change. Wack explained that the customers would look for the chalk mark afterward to see if we really had changed the filter or if we were charging them for work we hadn't done. In this case they were demonstrating their ignorance as well as their distrust, as most of the cars we worked on used replaceable filter elements that fit inside a reusable canister, so the chalk mark was still on the canister even after we'd replaced the filter.

One particularly obnoxious customer brought in a Jaguar E-Type that wasn't running right. Umbarti knew his way around Jaguars pretty well – some customers brought their Jags to Riccotto's from as far away as Chicago because of Umbarti's work - but this customer was convinced from the outset that we didn't know what we were doing. Umbarti fixed several problems with the ignition system and did the best he could with the carburetors, but the car still wasn't running right. Most British cars back then used SU carburetors, a type that was dramatically different from the carburetors on American cars. (SU stands for "Skinners' Union." Another piece of useless trivia I've picked up over the years. Way back when somebody had the wild idea to make a carburetor with leather seals, hence the connection to Skinners. The leather seals never worked out, but the company survived without them.) SU carbs have changed very little since they were first used in the 1920s, but they were a clever design that was remarkably effective. They were a variable venture design, meaning the carburetor opening automatically got bigger or smaller as required to provide the right mixture of gas and air to the engine. They were one of the reasons a car like the Jag could accelerate as fast as cars with engines nearly twice its size, top out at 150 mph, and still get 25 mpg on the highway. (That may not sound very impressive by today's standards, but for a car without electronic ignition or computer controlled fuel injection it was pretty damn good.) SU carbs were also pretty rugged and would work fine for years with no maintenance. Most Americans didn't understand them, though, so they got blamed for anything that went wrong with the car. For example, it was not unusual for Lucas distributor points to burn out after 6,000 miles. When this happened the car would run rough, and some owners would immediately blame the carburetors and start fiddling with them. The owner then had two things wrong with his car, and even if by some lucky coincidence he changed the points it still wouldn't run right until somebody who knew what they were doing readjusted his carburetors. This just convinced the owner that the carbs were "finicky" and had to be adjusted frequently, so the next time the car didn't run right he'd immediately start messing with the carbs again. In the case of the Jag that Umbarti was working on, someone had messed with them big time. Not only had they twiddled everything that was adjustable and a few things that weren't, they'd drilled new holes in the carbs trying to get more gas into the engine. Umbarti adjusted them as well as he could, but the car still wasn't running right and he told Luis he wanted to try replacing the carbs to see if that would fix the problem. The owner wouldn't hear of that and drove his ailing Jag off in search of a mechanic who knew what he was doing.

A few weeks later he was back again, more obnoxious than ever, telling Luis that he'd taken the car to a "real" repair shop where they got it running as good as new. Luis was surprised to hear this, and asked him how they'd fixed it. "They had this little gage thing they put on top of the engine and they said my cams weren't working right. They said any Jaguar shop that was worth a damn should have had one of these gages."

"They checked the cam timing?" Luis asked in astonishment? "What in the hell made them check that? Those cams are driven by a chain. There's no way a Jag camshaft can slip out of time."

"That was one of the first things they checked" the customer replied smugly. "I told them the car hadn't run right since I had the valve job done and they said they'd better check the cam timing."

"You never told us you just had a valve job!" Luis protested. "You have to take that chain off to do a valve job, and if you don't put it back on right the cams won't be timed properly. If you'd have told us about the valve job we would have checked the cam timing."

"Oh. Didn't I . . ." For a brief moment the customer hesitated, poised on the brink of rational thought while he considered the possibility that he might have withheld vital evidence; that he might in some way bear some responsibility for our not having torn the engine apart to check the cam timing. Then he realized where that line of reasoning would take him, and he didn't like the destination. "You should have checked it anyway" was all he said. He never brought his car to us again, but we later heard he was badmouthing us all over town, saying we didn't know the first thing about Jaguars.

New Cars on the Lot at Riccotto's

Of course, the customers didn't always complain without reason. 1974 was the year of the infamous seat belt interlock law. All cars were required to have electronic circuitry that prevented the car from starting if the passengers didn't have their seat belts fastened. You couldn't just leave the belts fastened either, as the car also would not start if the belts weren't unfastened and then refastened between trips. This undoubtedly well-intentioned law doesn't sound too odious today, but this was long before the age of microprocessors, and the relays and transistors of the day just weren't up to the job. Cars often refused to start even if all the passengers were belted in, and frustrated travelers sometimes had to get out of the car so the circuit would reset itself and then get back in and try again. This device nearly caused a couple my parents knew to freeze to death when they got stuck in a snowbank during an Indiana winter. Trying to follow the well-established survival technique of only running the car 10 minutes out of every hour so the gasoline (and heat!) would last longer, they were suddenly faced with a car that refused to start no matter what they did. It simply buzzed at them and flashed the "Fasten Seat Belts" message.

This law proved so unpopular that not only was it repealed the following year, it was replaced by legislation that required car dealers to disable the device for any customer who had been unfortunate enough to buy a car the previous year. It was absurdly simple to disable it on most cars, as there was a weight sensor in each seat to determine if anyone was sitting there. If you unplugged the sensor, the car didn't think there was a passenger so it didn't expect the seat belt to be fastened. Surprisingly, FIAT was the only car we sold that was smart enough to assume there had to be a driver, so they didn't put a sensor in the driver's seat. Or maybe they were the only company that was too cheap to pay for a driver's sensor. In any event, we had to short some wires in a FIAT to disable the interlock.

Before it was legal to disable interlocks I prepared a brand new Triumph Spitfire for delivery to a local businessman. While I was showing him where the overdrive switch was he asked me if I could disable the interlock for him.

"No, I'm sorry but I'm not allowed to do that." I explained. "It's a federal law." I then showed him the rest of the controls and wished him well when he assured me he didn't have any more questions. That night, as I was undressing, I heard a crackling sound in my shirt pocket. I looked, and there was a neatly folded $20 bill. Apparently the customer had tucked it into my pocket as he asked me to disconnect the interlock. Completely oblivious, I just told him "no" and then continued to show him the car. Fortunately it was about this time that we learned the law had been repealed, so when he came in for his first service I was able to give him his $20 back and disconnect the interlock.

A third lesson I learned while working as a mechanic was to maintain professional standards at all times. When I started at Riccotto's I was little more than a "grease monkey." I had experience working on my Model A and my MG, and my engineering background gave me a technical understanding of the design principles underlying the machinery I was working on, but my mechanical skills were amateurish to say the least. I left tools lying all around my work area. I barked my knuckles and otherwise injured myself regularly, and I got grease everywhere. By the end of the day my clothes were filthy, my hands and face were filthy, there were greasy tools lying all around me. Often I was also working frantically to clean greasy handprints off a customer's car. And while I have never been one to throw tools or otherwise stoop to temper tantrums, I was known to mutter a profanity every now and then when things didn't go my way. On rare occasions I muttered rather loudly. Especially if the difficulty at hand involved a loss of blood on my part. It didn't take me long to notice that none of the other mechanics ever behaved that way. They did their jobs without fuss or bother, they kept clean, and they stayed calm when things went wrong. That's not to say they used the vocabulary of a Victorian schoolmarm while discussing the trials and tribulations they encountered.. A technical discussion regarding a difficult service procedure might, for example, include the words "I had to use a #*@& sledgehammer to get the %#!*^ muffler off!" This information would, however only be discussed in a low voice with another professional mechanic. Such phrases were not for the customer's ears.

Nobody had to tell me my behavior made Laurel and Hardy look professional. It was obvious I'd have to change my act if I wanted to gain the respect of my coworkers. Bit by bit I learned to clean things up as I worked, keep my tools in order, and hold my temper. I also learned to pay close attention to whatever I was doing, even if it seemed routine. This lesson was driven home with particular effect when I changed the clutch on an MG Midget. The only way to access the clutch on a Midget is to pull the engine, a trait it shares with many other British sports cars. This is not a technically difficult operation, but it's very time consuming because you have to remove the hood, the radiator, the carburetors, and several miles of wiring and tubing before you can even reach the bolts that hold the engine in place. Changing the clutch is pretty much an all day job. I didn't have any real problems with this particular car, and by late afternoon I was refilling the radiator and getting ready to take it on a test drive. This was a fairly new Midget with a sealed coolant system and it didn't have a traditional radiator cap, just a large steel plug that screwed into the side of the radiator. This made it a little more difficult to add antifreeze, but I soon had the radiator filled, the hood closed, and was taking it for a test drive.

I had a favorite stretch of twisty road by the river that I used whenever I had to test clutches, transmissions, brakes, or steering. Despite the stories you may have heard, all the mechanics I knew were very careful when driving a customer's car. We knew our customers tended to push their cars pretty hard so we felt an obligation to at least push the cars a little bit when we were testing them, but we did it carefully. I mean, if a Jag owner complains that he feels a vibration above 120 mph, how are you going to know if you've fixed the problem? In any event, I took the Midget for a moderately spirited drive along the river, making certain the new clutch didn't slip, the gears shifted smoothly, the throttle didn't stick, and that everything I took apart when I pulled the engine was now working correctly. After a couple of miles the road veered away from the river and made a few switchbacks going up one of the few hills in that part of Indiana. Satisfied with the way the car was driving I turned off the road into a gravel parking lot about 2/3 of the way up the hill and made a tight U-turn to head back to the shop. When I finished the turn I was shocked to discover I could not straighten out the wheels and the car remained locked in a right-hand turn, making doughnuts in the gravel. I stopped the car, looked under the hood, and discovered the plug had fallen out of the radiator and wedged itself between a frame member and the universal joint on the steering column. Apparently I hadn't tightened it sufficiently when I finished refilling the radiator. If it had fallen out a mile or two earlier I would have flown off the road into the river, down the hill, or into some other undesirable landing spot. Even if I'd had the strength to break the steering wheel, there was no way I could have forced that car out of a right-hand turn. If it had fallen out a couple of miles later the customer would have been driving and . . . I didn't even want to think about that. From that day on I have always double-checked my work and gone through a mental checklist after any major mechanical project. I have also always insisted on taking my test drives alone, no matter how much my kids or anyone else might beg for a ride. God may give us a warning now and then, but he doesn't suffer fools who won't learn from their mistakes.

And what was happening to my cars while I was busy learning these lessons? Not much, actually. Just as the cobbler's children go barefoot, so my cars languished while I worked on everyone else's car. The Model A was sitting in my parent's driveway while I worked at Riccotto's, so it at least wasn't getting any worse, but I depended on the MG to drive home every weekend. The steering was getting tight enough that it was verging on becoming unsafe. When I told Luis about this problem he suggested I spend the next Saturday working on my MG, but on Saturday morning a man limped into the shop in a Triumph Spitfire that desperately needed a new clutch. The man and his wife were just passing through town on a vacation trip, and now they were stranded hundreds of miles from home. Luis asked me to put a new clutch in their Spitfire, promising to loan me one of the used cars "off the lot" for the weekend. This turned out to be the pattern we would follow for the better part of a year. It was a long time before I got my MG fixed, but I got to drive a lot of interesting cars in the interim.

My first loaner car was a 1962 MG Midget, a car that had evolved from the Austin Healey "Bugeye" Sprite. In 1962 the Midget hadn't evolved very far. The body looked much more modern than the Bugeye, but the car still had side curtains instead of roll up windows. Or at least, it came from the factory with side curtains. The side curtains had long since disappeared from the Midget I drove, as had the top for that matter. As long as the sun was shining, this Midget was a lot of fun to drive. Later Midgets lost so much space to plush upholstery, padded dashboards, padded door panels, roll-up windows, and other "soft" accessories that they began to feel claustrophobic, but this Midget was still fairly roomy. It did have one minor idiosyncrasy you had to be aware of. The clutch master cylinder had a slow leak so if you held the clutch pedal down for a long time, such as while you were waiting for the light to change at a busy intersection, the clutch would begin to engage and drive the car forward all by itself. This could add a bit of unwanted excitement to an otherwise boring stoplight session. As long as you were careful to always put the car in neutral when you stopped, the car was trouble free.

The most memorable trip I took in the Midget was going home for my high school class's five year reunion. The reunion was scheduled to start at 6:00 PM on a Friday night, so Luis gave me Saturday off. I had planned to leave early Friday afternoon, but a Fiat with a mysterious starter malady delayed my departure. It was after 5:00 PM before I got on the road, so I knew I'd miss the cocktails and hors d'oeuvres. Still, it was a warm June evening, the sun was shining brightly, and I was enjoying the drive. There was only a hint of a cloud on the western horizon. As I drove on, this hint began to grow larger and darker. By the time I got to Warsaw, the last major town before Yodersburg, it looked like I was about to get hit by a major thunderstorm, probably the leading edge of a cold front. Black clouds obliterated all traces of the sun, lightning danced across the clouds, and I could hear an almost continuous rumble of thunder. I only hoped I'd be able to make it through Warsaw before it hit. If you can keep moving at, say 30 or 40 mph, driving through rain with your top down isn't too bad. Your windshield blocks a lot of it, and the wind coming off the windshield carries the rest over the top of your head. If you get stopped at a traffic light, however, or held up in traffic, you get wet. There were at least a half-dozen traffic lights and a whole lot of traffic in Warsaw, so I wanted to make it to the other side before the rain hit. I probably would have, too, if I hadn't had a flat tire on the outskirts of the city. The first drops of rain started to fall as I was lowering the car off the jack. By the time I got to the first traffic light it was pouring. By the time I got to the other side of town, it was hailing! It was a warm evening when I left so I was just wearing a T-shirt, and now the hail was bouncing off my bare arms. I was soaked to the bone, the windshield fogged up, my glasses fogged up, and I was leaning out over the door so I could look around the windshield to see where I was going. The cars ahead of me slowed to 15 mph, and for once I didn't want to drive any faster. The rain didn't slack off until I reached the Yodersburg city limits, but by the time I got to my parents' house the sun was beginning to peek through the clouds.

I knew I'd missed the dinner, but I could still make it in time for dessert and coffee. I poured myself out of the Midget, sloshed into my folks' house, and gave myself a quick, hot shower. In no time at all I was dressed and headed for the VFW hall in the Model A. When I got there, I was surprised by the lack of cars in the parking lot. Surely I hadn't gotten the location wrong? Inside, a few vets were sitting at the bar, but there was no sign of the reunion. The bartender checked the special events calendar in the business office. I had come to the right place all right, just a day too early. The reunion was on Saturday night, not Friday night.

After the Midget, I drove a Fiat 850 coupe one weekend, but one weekend was enough with that car. The cars I was borrowing were not the pick of the lot, mind you. They weren't even ready to sell. I drove cars that Luis had just taken in on trade, and as I drove them I would check them out to see what needed to be done to get them ready to sell. The 850's acceleration would really push me back in the seat, but not because it was a fast car. Fiat 850's did not have a reputation for neck snapping performance, and this car was no exception to the rule. What was different about this car was that the latch that held the driver's seat in place was broken, so when you stepped on the gas the seat slid all the way back to the end of its adjustment. That would have been bad enough, but the bolts that held down the front part of the seat were rusted away, so when you reached the end of the adjustment the seat tried to tip over backwards and dump you into the back seat. I never actually got dumped because I always kept a good grip on the steering wheel, but the first couple of times I stepped on the gas I did slide back far enough that my foot lifted off the gas pedal. That made the car slow down, of course, so I slid back forward into the gas pedal again. My first several starts in that car were rather jerky, until I learned to properly brace myself before stepping on the gas. Stepping on the brake produced the opposite effect. When the car slowed down the seat slid forward and, if you weren't expecting it, that made you step on the brake even harder. Basically it was a new and entirely unwanted form of power brakes.

I ditched the 850 as soon as possible and switched to a Fiat 124 coupe. This was a much nicer car. I always enjoyed driving Fiat 124 convertibles (or spyders, as the Italians called them) but not as much as I enjoyed driving an MG or a Triumph so I never really lusted after a Fiat. Somehow, though, the coupe version felt like an entirely different car. An MGB GT was a great car, but it just felt like an MGB with a tin top. The Fiat 124 coupe, on the other hand, felt much more solid and comfortable than the convertible. In many ways, it reminded me of a Datsun 240-Z. Neither one could compare to an MG with the top down, but when the weather turned nasty they made a great winter car. Of course, Datsuns had a reputation of running forever, and they often lasted so long that owners grew tired of them long before they wore out. Fiat owners never had that problem. While MGs tended to mark their territory by leaving a puddle of oil wherever they were parked, Fiats marked their territory by leaving small piles of rust in their parking spots. At the time I borrowed this Fiat, we were also having problems with the windshield wiper motors overheating and melting key parts of the motor housing. Sometimes this even happened to brand new cars that were under warranty, but we were having a hard time convincing the factory service rep that this was actually a factory problem and that our customers weren't abusing their windshield wipers. The warranty had long since expired on the Fiat I was driving, but I was still pretty disgusted when the wiper motor burned out as I was driving to Riccotto's one rainy Monday morning. It was almost impossible to see without the wipers, so I took off my boot laces, tied one to each wiper blade, and ran them in through the vent windows. I then took off my belt and tied it between them, so when I pulled my belt from side to side it made the wiper blades go back and forth across the windshield. As luck would have it, the Fiat factory service rep was paying his monthly visit to the shop that day. He was talking to Luis in the showroom,

154

trying to convince him that Fiats didn't have a problem with their windshield wipers, when I drove into the lot. He took one look at my hand operated windshield wipers and conceded defeat.

Probably the most fun car I borrowed was a 1961 Triumph TR-3. This car was a little larger than my MG and the handling didn't feel as precise, but that may have been because this car had seen a lot of hard miles. The engine still ran strong, though. At just a shade over 2 liters it was significantly larger than my MG engine, and it had tons of low end torque. Let up the clutch on this beast and it would leap forward. As an engineer I knew the difference between torque and power from an intellectual standpoint, but this car dramatically illustrated the difference through the seat of your pants. The modifications I'd done to my MG gave it more power than this car, but my car's power built steadily as you wound the engine up into higher RPMs. It got you moving at least as fast as the Triumph did, but because it was a smooth acceleration you didn't feel it as much. The TR-3 engine kicked you in the butt when you took off, and you didn't notice or care that the power fell off as you speeded up. Legend has it the TR-3 engine evolved from a British tractor engine. Wherever it came from, it was fun. The doors were cut down low, like Viktor's MG TC, so I got a lot more wind in my face than I got with my MGA. That added to the fun and sensation of speed – as long as it was warm out. Of course, this car was far from perfect. (Luis wouldn't have needed me to check it out if it was.) Among other things, I had trouble getting the tail lights and turn signals to work consistently. Eventually I traced the problem down to the fact that the fenders were so badly rusted they were no longer making good electrical contact with the rest of the car. Once I installed ground straps on each fender, the lights worked perfectly.

The TR-3 next to Don's MGB which, sadly, was near the end of its days.

One of the most memorable cars I got to drive was a Ferrari 250 GTE Coupe. OK. I didn't get to drive it around for a couple of weeks as my personal transport. I got to drive it into the shop from the parking lot. It still counts. The car was Luis's personal car, one which he only drove on special occasions. It had a silver 2+2 body and a V-12 engine that made the most beautiful music a sinner will ever hear. When Nick and I were still in the dorm at Purdue, Luis would occasionally call Nick from the house and say "I'm driving the Ferrari to visit you. Time me." He once *averaged* over 100 mph on that trip, a record which I'm sure still stands today. Considering how many turns, stop signs, and small towns with cops and stoplights force you to slow down along that route, he must have been approaching the sound barrier when he was out among the cornfields.

Ferrari 250 GTE

On the day he let me drive the car, his brother Guido arrived at the shop about an hour before closing. Guido lived in New York, so his visit was a special occasion. Luis pulled a bottle of Lambrusco from his office and the three of us began celebrating. (I, of course, didn't know Guido from Adam, but I wasn't about to refuse the wine Luis was pouring.) I suspect maybe Luis may have pulled out another bottle or two, as the next thing we knew Leto was calling because she had dinner ready and we weren't there. Actually, the call was just a "heads-up" that she was coming to pick us up. She knew Luis well enough to know that after an hour or two of welcoming his brother he wouldn't be in any shape to drive the few blocks it took to get to the house. As we were hurriedly locking up the shop, Luis suddenly remembered his beloved Ferrari was parked outside. He had pulled it out to make room for Whack to work on a customer's car, but he wasn't about to leave it out all night. He didn't trust himself to drive it after drinking all that wine, and he was so far gone that he somehow thought that I was in better shape than he was.

"Steve – Drive my Ferrari into this stall" he said as he tossed me the keys. He didn't have to ask me twice. I grabbed the keys and ran to the Ferrari. As I slid into the red leather seats and stared at the wood-rimmed steering wheel, the enormity of what I was about to do suddenly struck me. I was about to thread a priceless piece of automotive art through the eye of a cinder block needle, at night, with the volatile Italian owner of this masterpiece scrutinizing my every move. A single scratch would mean I'd be in debt until doomsday. OK. So the eye of the needle was really a 10 ft wide garage door. When you've had a few glasses of Lambrusco it looks like the eye of a needle. Not only that, I didn't have a clue how to drive this thing. Steering wheel, pedals, gearshift – all the key elements seemed to be in the normal location. I had no idea what the shift pattern was, but I figured I could find a gear that would work by trial and error. I found the ignition switch, put in the key, and turned it to the first click. The ignition light came on but I hesitated before I turned it any further. On my car when you turned on the key the fuel pump began ticking madly behind the seats, and you had to let it build up fuel pressure before you started the car. I was pretty sure I remembered hearing a fuel pump when Luis started the Ferrari. It was a much more sophisticated sound than the wild chattering of my MG pump, but a sound nonetheless. Tonight I was sitting in silence. I knew I would invoke the wrath of Luis if I made a single error while starting his precious Ferrari, and worse yet he might lose confidence in me and drive it in himself. Frantically I scanned the dazzling array of gauges and switches on the instrument panel. Suddenly I saw a switch labeled "Pompa." That sounded a lot like "pump." I flipped the switch and was relieved to hear the fuel pump kick in. Now I could start the car. The starter ground through a few revolutions and the engine roared to life.

I carefully waited until the oil pressure built up and all the gauges looked normal before I stepped on the clutch and searched for something that felt like first gear. I'm not certain what gear I found, but I found something that worked well enough for me to ease the car forward. Slowly and carefully, I inched the car out of the parking lot and into the garage. I stopped every foot or two to twist my head around and make certain there was nothing on either side that could possibly touch the Ferrari. Finally I got it through the door and into the parking spot. I took it out of gear, set the parking brake, and was about to switch it off. Suddenly I couldn't control myself any longer. I mashed the gas pedal down toward the carpet.

"Vroooooooo-**Pah**! Vroooooooo-**Pah**! Vroooooooo-**Pah**!"

The thundering exhaust note of that magnificent V-12 echoed off the concrete walls and reverberated throughout the shop as I blipped the throttle. Satisfied, I switched off the engine. I sat there for a moment listening to the silence that abruptly followed the booming symphony of the exhaust, hearing only an occasional tick from the cooling engine. I stared at the gleaming gauges and breathed in the heady aroma of Italian leather tinged with exhaust. Reluctantly, I opened the car door and stepped out. I wondered what Luis would say about me revving his Ferrari, but all he said was "Let's go eat some spaghet." For a moment I was puzzled, but then it dawned on me. That's exactly what he would have done if he was in my place.

As much fun as these cars were to drive, I missed my MGA. It was obvious I was never going to get time during the day to work on it, so I reverted to my schedule of going back to the shop after dinner to spend an hour or two working on my car. We didn't have any organ donors in the back lot with the suspension pieces I needed, but fortunately a customer's car urgently needed a part that was only available in a junkyard just north of Indianapolis. The junkyard also had an MGB with suspension pieces which could be modified to fit my MGA, so I volunteered to make the trip. People who don't work on old cars don't realize how serene and peaceful a junkyard can be, especially on a warm spring day. There's always a lot of noise and activity up front, near the office, because that's where the new cars are. That's where the people who run the junkyard congregate, as they're busy extracting high-dollar parts for the well-heeled customers who can afford to just walk up to the counter and buy a part someone else has pulled off a car. If you need something old, though, you need something off a car that's way off in the back corner. It's also not worth the junk man's time to pull your part, so they'll just point you in the general direction and let you carry your tools back into their "secret garden." Back there you can commune with nature and become one with the rusting derelicts of yesterday's highways. Birds sing, crickets chirp, and lush green grass grows up between the cars. In the years since I worked at Riccotto's I've lived many different parts of the country, and I've often wished I could get the grass in my lawn to look as healthy as the grass in those Indiana junk yards.

In addition to rebuilding my front suspension, I also decided to do another rebuild on my gearbox. I had to re-use several questionable parts when I rebuilt it the first time, because British Leyland listed the parts I needed as "NLS – No Longer Supplied." Since then I'd learned a lot about MGs, and about British Leyland, and I'd discovered that while the MGA parts book listed them as NLS, early MGBs used many of the same parts and if you ordered them through the MGB parts book British Leyland would be happy to sell them to you. The parts were the same and the part numbers were the same, you just had to know which book to look in. Go figure. So, I pulled my engine once again and dissected my gearbox. It was at this point that I finally heard from the Air Force. After ignoring my letters and phone calls for nearly a year and a half, they waited until I had my suspension and gearbox scattered all over the shop to tell me I had three weeks to report to Griffiss AFB in upstate New York.

Chapter 14 – Off We Go!

In the years to come I would get used to the idea of packing all my worldly possessions on a moment's notice and moving to a place I'd never heard of before, but this first move was a novel experience. And it wasn't the kind of novel you expect will a happy ending, either. It was the kind where you expect a lunatic with a chain saw and a hockey mask will jump out of the closet. To begin with, there was the fact that I had just disemboweled my MG and scattered its innards throughout Riccotto's. Except, of course, for the vital bits that were being reworked at a local machine shop. Then there was the fact that I had to find a home for my Model A. My father was a patient and understanding man, but he was also very wise. He knew that if he let me park the A in his garage "for the time being," it would stay there until time ceased to be. And, of course, I had to gather all my clothes, my tools, my stereo, my scuba gear, my Victrola, and all the potentially useful household items that my mother wasn't guarding and ship them to upstate New York.

The Air Force would hire a moving company to take care of this last task so I focused on my cars. After a lot of late night garage sessions and a few pleading calls to the machine shop I got my MGA back on the road again. I said a fond farewell to Riccotto's, drove to Yodersburg, and began searching for a place to store the Model A. I soon found a farmer who was willing to let me park it in his barn for $100 a year. That seemed like a lot of money, but I was running out of time so I parted with the bills, scattered moth balls throughout the interior, and pickled the engine. Then, following instructions which I dimly remembered a sergeant had given me in ROTC, I set off for the nearest military base to find something called the "Transportation Management Office." I was naïve enough not to even think of calling ahead to make an appointment, but fortunately I caught them on a quiet day. I filled out a lot of forms, estimated the weight and volume of every item I owned, and stapled copies of my orders to everything in sight. It all went very smoothly until a middle aged woman with half-height reading glasses perched on her nose asked me when I wanted to have my household goods picked up.

"Well," I replied. "I'm supposed to be there on Wednesday, so I'll probably leave on Tuesday. Could you pick up my stuff on Monday?"

"You mean this Monday?" the lady asked in horror. She rifled through my paperwork, and for the first time she actually looked at the reporting date on my orders. "They can't do that!" she exclaimed. "We're supposed to give the movers at least a month's advance notice!" I tried to explain that I wasn't given a month's advance notice, and I had to rebuild my car before I could even drive to her office, but it didn't matter. She was already on the phone to a moving company and before I knew what had happened everything was arranged. It was my first experience with someone who quickly and efficiently worked a miracle, all the while protesting that it couldn't be done. I was to run into a lot of people like that in the Air Force.

On the following Monday two men who said little more than "sign here" jammed all my priceless belongings into series of cardboard boxes, slid the boxes into a truck, and headed for the horizon. I spent one last evening with my friends, tossed and turned through a final night in the room I'd grown up in, and enjoyed a long leisurely breakfast with my parents. Finally, much later than I'd planned, I gave my mom a final hug, shook hands with my dad, hopped into the MG, and headed east.

I seemed to be making good time. In about seven hours I crossed into New York State and merged onto the New York State Thruway. This was not a road that was designed for sports cars. In addition to the fact that it was laser straight, and therefore very boring, it was a concrete highway with regularly spaced expansion joints. These joints had been enthusiastically filled with a sealant that bulged above the surface. The net effect of this was that every 30 seconds my tires went "thump-thump" while the seat kicked me in the butt. MGA seats could never be described as "plush," even when they were new, and over the years mine had deteriorated to the point where it was little more than a leather covered hunk of plywood. After getting my butt kicked for five hours I was happy to arrive at a little motel just outside the base gate in Rome New York.

The next morning I spread my uniform out on my bed and tried to remember how it all went together. I had very carefully kept everything assembled in the years since my last ROTC class, but in a burst of exuberance I took it to a dry cleaners in Yodersburg shortly before I left home. When I picked it up they said "Oh, here" and handed me a bag filled with all the insignia, name tags, and other removable items which I had so carefully left untouched. Now I was vainly struggling to remember where everything went. I gave it my best shot, and figured I'd take a good look at the guard's uniform when I got to the gate to see if I'd guessed correctly. I hoped he wouldn't chew me out if I had my name tag on the wrong side. It seemed like I'd gotten chewed out a lot in ROTC. Adding to my anxiety, Griffiss was a SAC base – a part of the Strategic Air Command. During the cold war SAC was king, and they had a reputation for being a stickler for details. I guess when you're fooling around with nuclear weapons you don't want people making up the rules as they go along. (While it was Air Force policy to neither confirm nor deny the presence of nuclear weapons on any installation, I could see B-52 bombers parked behind a double barbed wire fence, and that was a strong clue that just maybe there were some sensitive materials on this base.) I didn't know what to expect when I got to the gate, but I had my orders clutched in my hand and was prepared to salute and say "yes sir" a lot. That seemed to be about the only thing I could remember from ROTC.

When I got to the gate, I was surprised to see that the guard was a civilian. He looked just like an ordinary cop from my home town. Worse yet, he wasn't wearing a military uniform so I still didn't know if I had my name tag on the correct side. He didn't interrogate me, he didn't search my car, and he didn't even ask to see my orders. He just waved me through the gate. He seemed surprised and a little upset that I stopped anyway. The truth was I didn't have a clue as to where I was supposed to go next. As it turned out, neither did he. He gave me a base map and suggested I go to the VOQ – the Visiting Officer's Quarters.

The people at the VOQ didn't really know what I was supposed to do either, but they were a lot friendlier than the guard. It turned out the VOQ was basically a motel for officers who were visiting the base. Nobody seemed to know what I was supposed to be doing at Griffiss, but they assigned me to a room since that's what they normally did when a customer wandered up to their desk. Then they helped me decipher my orders. I was assigned to something called the 416th Civil Engineering Squadron, so they looked in the phone book and found a number for this squadron. I called the number they gave me, but that turned out to be the number to call if your toilet was broken or your roof had collapsed. The dispatcher who answered the phone gave me another number to call. The people at that number in turn gave me a third number to call, something they called the Orderly Room. When I called that number I was connected to someone with a very perky female voice.

"416th Civil Engineering Squadron Orderly Room, Airman Dickerson speaking."

"This is Lieutenant Tom, reporting for duty." I'd heard people use that line in old war movies. It seemed like the correct thing to say at the moment. There was a long pause at the other end of the line.

"Lieutenant who?"

"Lieutenant Tom. Steve Tom." There was an even longer pause. I could hear the sounds of shuffling paper in the background.

"Are you supposed to be assigned to us?"

I read her the information from my orders that described my duty location and unit of assignment.

"Oh my gosh! Where are you?"

All traces of calm professionalism had disappeared from her voice. She sounded like she was on the verge of panic. I told her I was at the VOQ.

"Stay there. I'll get back to you in a day or two."

There didn't seem to be much more to discuss, so I said good-bye and hung up. I was beginning to worry that somehow I'd screwed something up. Was I really supposed to be at Griffiss? Could it be that I was supposed to go to Grissom AFB instead? How much trouble would I be in if I was at the wrong base? I re-read my orders, and they very clearly said Griffiss AFB, Rome NY. Not knowing what else to do, I went out to my car to get my luggage. As I was untying it from the luggage rack, a Captain Hyde showed up and introduced himself as the executive officer for the 416'th Civil Engineering Squadron, or "CES" for short. He welcomed me to the squadron and sounded much calmer than the Airman on the phone. He apologized for the confusion, and explained that the Air Force personnel center had told them my orders were cancelled so they weren't expecting me. Eventually he tracked down the source of this bureaucratic snafu. Apparently there was a minor mistake on my original orders, so the Air Force had cancelled those orders and issued new orders with the error corrected. Somehow they had notified Griffiss of the cancellation without sending them the new orders.

Despite this rather shaky start to my Air Force career, everything turned out OK. Capt Hyde introduced me to a Lieutenant Kelly who helped me find an apartment and get settled. Lt Kelly was the proud owner of a 1974 Chevrolet Corvette with a 454 cubic inch V8 engine, the last year this big block engine was available in a Corvette. Actually, "proud owner" is an understatement. Lt Kelly worshipped that car. He never drove it in the rain, or in the snow, or on days where the sun was bright enough to fade the paint, or if there was a chance that a passing bird might disgrace itself on the coachwork. He had a 1964 Rambler American with a flathead 6 cylinder engine which he used for daily transportation, while the Corvette sat in his garage. He had a block heater in the Corvette which he kept plugged in during the winter, so it wouldn't get cold. His Rambler, on the other hand, sat outside in the cold and snow with no heater. It wasn't unusual for him to call me on cold winter mornings, asking for a ride to work because his Rambler wouldn't start. One morning I asked him if his Corvette would start and he proudly told me he started it every week and it always fired up immediately. I then asked him why he didn't drive that car to work and his horrified gasp almost sucked the phone out of my hand. Lt Kelly was a southerner, born and raised in Tuscaloosa Alabama. He'd never been north of Birmingham until the Air Force assigned him to Griffiss, and the idea that anyone would actually drive a Corvette in such weather was rank heresy in his eyes. His goal for life after the Air Force was to put snow tires on his car and drive south until somebody said "What are those?" When he reached a land where people didn't know what snow tires were, he'd know he was far enough south.

Civil Engineering turned out to be an interesting place to work. I was concerned when I first got my orders because Civil Engineering had been used by my ROTC instructors to illustrate one end of the spectrum of possible Air Force careers. The instructors, mostly ex-pilots, said that as an Air Force Officer we could do anything from flying F-4 jets to helping CE haul the garbage off base. Once I was assigned to CE I learned that CE did a lot more than just haul garbage. CE was responsible for the design, construction, operation, and maintenance of all the buildings and utility systems on base. Yes, we did haul the garbage off base (actually we were working with local EPA officials to develop a regional program to turn solid waste into a coal substitute) but we also built new buildings, kept the power on, plowed snow off the airfield, operated a central heating plant, and basically took care of everything on the base that didn't move. We also provided the pilots with such niceties as a runway, runway lighting, and a place to sleep when they got tired of all that flying and fighting.

Setting up an apartment was also an interesting challenge. I had shared an apartment with Viktor and Tony in grad school, of course, but that was a furnished apartment. Since it was an apartment for college students, "furnished" meant it had a few pieces of broken down furniture scavenged from second-hand shops and garage sales. My apartment in New York was unfurnished. That gave me an opportunity to furnish it to my own tastes, which meant I began scavenging second-hand shops and garage sales for my own broken down furniture. One of the first garage sales I went to had an incredible deal on three Victrolas so I was able to fill my apartment with music – as long as I kept cranking the phonographs. Two of the Victrolas were table top models, which more or less fit in the passenger seat of my MG. The third was a large floor model which was a little trickier. Eventually I managed to balance it on the luggage rack and tie it down, but it dwarfed the back of my car. One passer-by pointed out the fact that the Victrola had casters on its legs and suggested it might be easier to tie my car on top of the phonograph and push it home. Over the next several weeks I used that luggage rack to transport a bed, a chest of drawers, several chairs, lamps, and all the other furniture I needed to set up housekeeping.

When I first joined the CE squadron they were getting ready for the "Commander's Annual Facility Inspection," or CAFI in military jargon. The unofficial motto of CAFI was "Don't fix it – paint it!" While we did fix a few things during our CAFI preparations, mostly we just made things look nice, and that meant we did a lot of painting. Buildings, curbs, guardrails, fire hydrants – if it didn't move fast enough we painted it.   And we painted it in a hurry. I had never before given much thought to the question of why softball backstops were silver, but I soon learned they were silver because new ones were zinc plated. After a few years, though, the backstops began to look a little the worse for wear, so we painted them with bright silver paint. The sheet metal shop made giant paint trays for us, we poured a couple gallons of silver paint into each tray, and used push brooms on long extension poles as paint brushes. That was messy enough by itself, but as the inspection date drew near and we realized we were running out of time, we started painting both sides of the backstop at the same time. By the end of the day we looked as though we had showered in silver paint, which was exactly what we had done. Of course, as an officer I was entitled to special privileges. I had my own paint tray. The enlisted troops had to share trays. In the final weeks before the inspection we worked 12 hour days, 7 days a week. Suddenly, working 6 days a week at Riccotto's didn't look so bad.

Once the inspection was over the squadron dropped back to a normal 5 day work week and for the first time in years I found myself with time on my hands. It was about this time that I saw a notice in the base newspaper that the Griffiss Sports Car Club was having its monthly meeting at a local restaurant. I had never been active in any kind of a car club before, but this sounded like it might be fun so I went to the meeting. It turned out the club members were a great group of people and I was soon participating in autocrosses and rallies and helping with the club newsletter.

An autocross is basically a race in a parking lot. We would use rubber traffic cones to set up a twisting course with tight corners and slalom sections and drive the course one car at a time. An electronic timer measured our lap time, and the driver with the shortest elapsed time won. The course was too short to build up much speed – I seldom got out of second gear in my MG – so good handling and smooth driving were crucial to a low elapsed time. There were a wide variety of cars competing – MGs, Triumphs, Porsches, Corvettes, Mustangs, Opels, Hondas, Toyotas, Volkswagens, etc. – so we divided the competitors into classes based upon the size and power of the cars. Because the courses we drove were short and twisty the small cars were generally faster than the big cars. After I gained a bit of experience I had no trouble beating the Corvettes and Mustangs. The club president drove a Porsche 911s which was a very fast car on the highway, but I could often beat him on a tight autocross circuit. Or at least, I could beat him if I focused on my driving. I had never been interested in sports, and the idea of focusing on anything that required hand/eye/foot coordination was entirely foreign to me. Throughout my school years I detested PhysEd class, and the feeling was mutual. I was the classic, last-one-picked, standing out in left field, praying nobody would hit the ball my way so I wouldn't screw up. While driving a car in an autocross isn't exactly the most strenuous sport in the world, for the first time in my life I was actually engaging in a competition that I enjoyed. While I soon realized I was never going to be a world famous race driver, I still felt I had at least some chance of winning a local autocross. Going into a competition with a goal of winning is a completely different feeling than going in with a goal of not screwing up. The key was to find the right line through the course, stay on the line, and drive as fast and as smoothly as possible. That required me to put all other thoughts out of my mind and focus on the physical act of driving. I only had to maintain this focus for a couple of minutes, but it was the most intense focus I had ever experienced. If I let my mind wander for a second, to worry about the effects of being a little wide on the last turn or to doubt my ability to make the next turn, I was lost. When my run was over and I came off the track I felt like I was in a daze, as if I had to reprogram my brain to think about something other than driving.

Many times my downfall was the idea of driving "as smoothly as possible." The fastest line through a corner is not the most fun. The fastest line does not involve squealing tires and skidding. My MG was perfectly balanced and eminently controllable. If I focused on taking a corner in exactly the right manner, it was more than willing to comply. If I entered the turn a little too fast, it would slide through the curve in an ecstasy of controlled exhilaration. And if I entered a turn a little too fast and goosed the throttle, the rear end would slide around as I fought the steering wheel, then snap back with a breathtaking "fishtail" as I exited the turn. The first method was the fastest. The second method was slower but more fun, and the third method was a dog-slow bundle of joy. To me, driving in an autocross was a constant battle between my desire to win and my desire to have fun. Sometimes other drivers tried to give me tips on how to slow down and drive faster. A Midget driver was particularly persistent in this regard, until I let him drive my car during an autocross so he could show me how it should be done. His first run was pretty tight, and pretty quick. His next run was a little looser, and not quite as fast. On his third run he was hanging the tail out even more than I did. He came off the course grinning from ear to ear. "God that was fun!!" he yelled as he pulled off his helmet. I gave him the bad news that his third run was his slowest time yet. "I don't care!" he shouted. "It was fun!"

167

Autocrossing my MGA

The fact that I let the Midget owner drive my car was not unusual. We often "traded rides" during an autocross. In general I preferred my MG to any other car I drove, but there was one exception. One day a club member showed up with a car he normally kept tucked safely away in his garage – a 1962 Shelby Cobra. This car was based on the AC Ace, an obscure British sports car that looked a little like a larger version of my MGA. In England the AC Ace was sold with a six cylinder engine, but the legendary Carol Shelby imported these cars into the US without engines, installed a Ford V8, and sold them as Shelby Cobras. The earliest Cobras had a 260 cubic inch engine, but that was soon replaced with a 289. Later, to keep up with the Ferraris on fast tracks like Daytona and Le Mans, Shelby crammed a 427 into the Cobra, but that was so overpowered that driving one on the street bordered on silliness. The 289 had more than enough power to keep things exciting, and it looked sleeker too. Luis had owned a 289 Cobra before I met him. He complained that it was nose-heavy and steered like a pig, but Luis complained about every car except his Ferrari. It was obvious from the gleam in his eye that he had enjoyed driving that Cobra. His son Nick told me about a day he followed his dad and a friend when they took the Cobra for a Sunday drive. Nick was driving an MGB from the shop, a car that was hopelessly outclassed by the Cobra. When his dad turned onto a short stretch of four-lane highway near the shop, Nick saw his chance. No one ever knew why the State had decided to expand that particular stretch of highway to four lanes, as there was almost never any traffic on it. You entered the highway at the peak of a hill, with a clear view of the road for several miles in either direction. There was a stop sign where the access road joined the highway, but you could easily see whether or not there was any traffic long before you reached the stop sign. On this particular day there was no traffic, so when Luis stopped for the sign Nick flew around him and floored the MGB on the downhill section of highway. He got that B up to 110 mph, which is flying in an MG. He knew he wasn't going to stay ahead of his dad for long, and in fact when he looked up from the speedometer he saw his dad was cruising effortlessly beside him in the Cobra. His dad casually flicked the ash off his cigar, shifted the Cobra into 4th gear, and disappeared over the horizon. Nick was devastated. "It's bad enough getting shut down like that" he told me, "but by your own father?"

Shelby Cobra 289

Needless to say, the Cobra that showed up to our autocross immediately became the center of attention. I was astonished when the owner of this car asked me if I'd like to drive it in the autocross. I have no idea what motivated him to make such a foolish offer, but I immediately accepted. The Cobra was a little heavier than my MG, and the V8 made it nose heavy, but the power more than made up for the extra weight. This was the first car I had ever driven that I felt had "enough" power. When you came out of a curve you stepped on the gas and tried to keep the front wheels ahead of the rear wheels until you came to the next corner. This was a fairly early Cobra which didn't have rack and pinion steering, but it really didn't matter. You only needed the steering wheel to start the car turning in the right direction. After that, you steered with your right foot. Give it a little gas and the rear wheels would snap around until the car was pointing where you wanted to go. To quote my Midget driving friend, "God that was fun!!" I don't know what ever became of that Cobra or its owner, but all I can say is "Thank you for giving me the ride of a lifetime."

Of course, autocrossing was a special event that occupied one Sunday a month, and then only during good weather. Most of the time I just used the MGA as my daily driver. It was surprisingly reliable for a $50 car, although I did have a bit of bad luck one day while driving home from work. I was about a mile outside the base gate, humming along on a nice spring evening, when the engine sputtered and died. I coasted off to the side of the road with my fuel pump chattering madly behind the passenger's seat. "TICK TICK TICK TICK TICK!" The MG has an SU electric fuel pump that, under normal circumstances, gives a friendly little tick every now and then while you're driving, just to let you know it's working. It also helps you start the car in the morning. Turn the ignition switch to the "run" position and listen to the pump. "Tick tick tick tick . tick . . tick . . . . . tick . . . . tick . . . ." The ticking slows down as the fuel pressure builds up, and when it stops ticking you're ready to start the car. When you run out of gas, however, the pump gets angry and begins shouting at you. "TICK TICK TICK THERE'S NOTHING WRONG WITH THIS CAR YOU IDIOT! YOU JUST RAN IT OUT OF GAS! TICK TICK TICK!"

The problem was, the gas gauge said I still had over a quarter of a tank. The MGA has an instantaneous gas gauge that always gives you an immediate indication of how much gas is in the tank. Unlike modern gas gauges which slowly creep up when you turn the key on, the MGA gas gauge springs into life instantaneously when you turn on the key. The needle jumps into position and quivers with excitement, like a caffeinated Chihuahua. The needle also sways back and forth as you drive around curves to let you know the gas is sloshing around in the tank, in case you wanted to know that. It may be spastic, but it's never wrong and in this case it insisted I had gas in the tank. I turned off the key, and the needle stayed between ¼ and ½. That had never happened before. The needle is supposed to jump to zero when you turn off the key. I switched the key on and off a couple of times and the needle twitched a little, but stayed put. Then I noticed the gas gauge looked hazy compared to my other gauges. I bent down and peered intently into the gauge. It was filled with the tiny gossamer threads of a spider's web, and those threads had immobilized the needle. Crouched in the dark recesses of the gauge was a tiny colorless spider, smiling with anticipation. I have no idea what kind of a fly he anticipated catching in there, but he had very effectively caught the needle of my gas gauge.

Fortunately it was only a short hike to the nearest gas station, and once I gave them my watch, my driver's license, and a first round draft pick for collateral they let me borrow a gas can to carry fuel to my car. When I got back to my apartment I disassembled the gas gauge, shook the spider out, and freed up the needle. Well, that's the Reader's Digest condensed version of what I did. Actually, when I took the back off the gauge a lot of tiny little parts fell onto the table and a miniature electromagnet spun its way down to the floor, unwinding a hair-like copper wire as it fell. I had hours of fun winding the wire back onto the coil and figuring out how all the little pieces fit together. Once I got the gauge back in the car I discovered the little screws I thought held the back on were really calibration adjustments. I spent a lot of time under the dash over the ensuing weeks making minute adjustments to the position of those screws until the gauge read full when the tank was full and empty when the tank was empty. Other than that, it was a simple repair and the spider did no lasting damage.

One of the great things about living in upstate New York was being able to attend the US Grand Prix race at Watkins Glen. This was held in October, and if the weather was good it was absolutely beautiful. The racetrack was located in the Finger Lakes region, and in the fall the trees were stunning. Watching the Formula 1 cars thunder around the track against a backdrop of red and gold trees was unforgettable. Combine that with unbelievable driving by Nikki Lauda in a Ferrari, James Hunt in a McLaren, Jody Scheckter in the six-wheeled Tyrrell, and other Formula 1 legends and I enjoyed a great race weekend. One of the interesting features of the Watkins Glen track was that to reach the infield you had to drive across the track. Obviously you could only do this when the track wasn't being used for racing. One year I was leaving the infield after a practice session, stuck in bumper to bumper traffic, and I happened to be crossing the track when the policeman directing traffic stopped us dead to allow one car to cross into the oncoming lane and pass everyone who was waiting in line. I looked to see why this car was being given special treatment and recognized the driver as Emerson Fittipaldi, the legendary Brazilian driver and former World Champion. OK. Maybe I was just stuck in traffic, but I can honestly say that I was passed by Emerson Fittipaldi while driving on the track during the 1976 US Grand Prix.

1975 US Grand Prix at Watkin's Glen

Griffiss was close enough to Indiana that I could drive home when I took leave and I made that trip in the MGA many times. One year when I was getting ready to drive home for Thanksgiving it was raining a cold, steady drizzle. I checked the weather forecast and the prediction was for "occasional showers." That didn't sound too bad and I had my dad's World War II leather flight jacket to keep me warm so I decided not to put the top up for the trip. It occasioned to shower all the way through New York, Pennsylvania, and half of Ohio but I still enjoyed the drive. The rain hit the windshield and went over my head so I was relatively warm and dry. I didn't have a radio in the MGA (and couldn't have heard it over all the other noises anyway) so I sang songs, munched on sandwiches, and otherwise whiled away the hours. After an hour or two, I began to notice that I was the only driver who was truly enjoying the drive. I passed car after car driven by grim-faced men and women, peering through their windshield wipers at the leaden skies. They had tin roofs over their heads, roll-up windows, stereo sound systems, and all the comforts of home, but they weren't having nearly as much fun as I was having in my battered MGA. There was one exception. About half-way through Pennsylvania I saw a TR-3 headed east. Like me he had his top down, and like me he had a smile on his face. We flashed our headlights at each other and waved madly across the median as we passed. Then we disappeared on our separate journeys. Two kindred spirits, enjoying the pleasures of driving British sports cars on a cold, rainy day.

Chapter 15 – The Ballad of Old Number 12

I began my tour at Griffiss AFB in July, at the height of a glorious, and as I was soon to learn, short summer. This was followed by an equally glorious fall. The fall colors were absolutely magnificent. Everywhere I looked, the trees were resplendent with red, orange, and yellow foliage. On weekends I enjoyed taking trips through the countryside in my MG. I never realized how flat Indiana was until I drove through the hills of upstate New York. Whereas Indiana featured mile after mile of well-manicured farmland, upstate New York had thousands of acres of undeveloped forests, rivers and streams flowing through scenic valleys, and bucolic pastures where cattle grazed on rocky hillsides. The mornings were a little nippy, but the heater in my MG put out enough warm air that I could thoroughly enjoy top down driving in the crisp fall air. There were, however, ominous signs that this happy state of affairs wouldn't last forever. On base, we started fastening tall orange flags to the fire hydrants, so the snowplows could tell where they were. Some people fastened similar tall flags to the bumpers of their cars, with orange flags fluttering at least six feet above the pavement. When I asked about these I was told they were there so other cars could see them as they approached an intersection. Apparently the snow banks created by the snowplows grew to the point where you couldn't see over them, but an orange flag would warn you of approaching traffic.

One of the other things I noticed was how quickly the cars rusted. Cars that were only a few years old were visibly dissolving from the ground up. Even though I hadn't yet experienced a New York winter, I recognized the symptoms and knew the cause – road salt. Apparently New York put even more salt on the road than Indiana did. My MG already had serious frame damage from the Indiana salt, and I didn't relish the thought of it getting even worse. What I needed was a "winter rat." A car I didn't care about to drive through the winter salt so I could save my MG. Since any car I drove in the winter was soon going to rust away anyway I wasn't looking for a good car, just something I could drive for at least one winter. The trend toward disposable items was becoming popular in the 70s – disposable razors, disposable diapers, disposable lighters, etc. What I needed was a disposable car.

My friend Lt Kelly came to my rescue. He knew a man who had a car which exactly suited my needs: a 1966 Chevrolet Impala convertible! Today many people consider a '66 Impala to be a classic, but believe me, this particular Impala was no classic. Rust had already eaten away the fenders to the point where the chrome trim was falling off, the red plastic interior was coming apart at the seams, and the engine barely ran. There was battle damage on the passenger door and the right rear fender, evidence that at some point in its life this car had come into contact with other vehicles. Or maybe a previous owner had simply kicked it out of frustration. On the plus side, the owner only wanted $40 for it. Actually, I felt I wasn't so much buying a car as I was betting the current owner $40 that I could get it to run better than he had. At that price it didn't take long to count out the cash, so in no time at all the car was mine. Ironically, it was not only the cheapest car I'd ever bought, it was also the newest. This was 1975, so the car was only 9 years old when I bought it. That will give you some idea of how bad the rust was.

I spent the next Saturday giving the car a tune-up, changing the oil, and otherwise trying to make up for years of neglect. It actually ran fairly well after that. The tune up parts cost nearly as much as the car had, and I'd like to meet the sadist who decided to put Chevy distributors at the far back end of the engine. For years I'd heard people complain about how hard it was to work on foreign cars because they were so cramped, but those complaints lost all credibility as I stretched my body across the acres of fenders and engine, trying to set the points and adjust the timing of my Chevy.

Despite its obvious faults, it wasn't a bad car. The 283 cubic inch V-8 engine seemed huge, and in fact it was over 2-1/2 times as big as my MG engine. Despite that, the car didn't feel particularly fast. I suspect it was because the car weighed one or two tons more than my MG. It certainly didn't handle like the MG. The combination of a heavy car with a 1960's American suspension and worn out shocks made the car drive like a barge. The power steering gave almost no feedback to let the driver know what the wheels were doing, and the steering ratio was so low you had to start spinning the steering wheel long before the car would begin to wallow its way into a curve. I've never captained an oil tanker, but based on the descriptions I've read it's a lot like driving that Chevy. I needed to plan my maneuvers well in advance, spin the steering wheel in the correct direction, and wait for the car to respond. It would list hard to the port or starboard, depending on which way I was turning, and then gradually plow its way around the curve. Once I had completed the turn I'd spin the wheel to straighten it and ring up the engine room for "ahead full." Still, the engine started on the coldest mornings, it had a great heater, and it got me to work and back. With a couple of studded snow tires (retreads) it made a perfect winter car.

One problem I did have with this car was that for some reason my insurance company seemed to think I needed comprehensive coverage. I asked for liability insurance only, but they argued that since it was a convertible I really should get comprehensive coverage as well. "Someone might slit the top to break into it" they said. I promised to leave the car unlocked, adding that there was nothing in the car worth stealing and no self-respecting auto thief would dream of stealing the car itself. "You can add comprehensive coverage for only $50 a year," they argued. When I pointed out that I'd only paid $40 for the entire car they grudgingly admitted that I might have a point. Nevertheless, when the bill came it included full comprehensive coverage with no deductible. When I called to complain that I didn't want the comprehensive they said it would be best if I just paid the bill and included a note saying I didn't want the comprehensive. They promised to send me a refund. I included the note, but the next bill still included comprehensive. This went on for several months, well into the winter.

The question of comprehensive insurance came to a head in early January, when a freak warm front swept through Rome. In Alaska they call this weather a Chinook, a sudden warm wind that brings a quick thaw followed by another cold snap. In New York they just call it a warm front. Whatever it was called, the temperature shot up to the high 40's and the wind howled around the corners of my apartment. My apartment was a converted attic on a three story house, and I could hear a scraping noise on the roof as the winter's accumulation of snow and ice slid off the eaves and went crashing to the ground.

The next morning was trash day, and I had to carefully pick my way through the blocks of ice that had slid off the roof as I carried bags of trash to the curb. I guess I must have been focused on my footing because I never even noticed my car until I set the trash down and turned back toward the house. Then I saw it. It looked like a giant had stomped on the convertible top and squashed it like a bug. The top bows were touching the back seat. The windshield was smashed on the passenger side. The hood looked like someone had beaten it with a sledge hammer, and there was a 50 pound block of ice sticking out of a hole where the rear window had been. I guess the ice picked up a bit of momentum before it came into contact with my car. If I'd lived in a four-story house the car would have looked like a pancake. As it was, I suspected the resale value of the car had been adversely affected. I hoisted most of the ice boulders off my car and swept off the snow, but I decided not to touch the ice in the rear window since it would help block the wind. Then I drove to work.

Old Number 12 – Back View

Old Number 12 - Front View

I called my insurance company from work and asked whether or not I was covered for ice damage. They checked their records and said I had full comprehensive – no deductible. "In that case I'd like to put in a claim" I said. They said they'd send an adjuster out to look at the car that very afternoon.

"Where can he find the car?" they asked.

"It's parked outside the Civil Engineering Building on Griffiss Air Force Base" I replied.

"You can still drive it with a cracked windshield?" they asked.

"That's the least of my problems" I replied. Then they asked for directions to the parking lot, what color the car was, and what was the license plate number. I didn't remember the plate number.

"The adjuster will need the plate number to identify the car" they said.

"Tell him it will be the only 1966 Chevy in the parking lot with the roof smashed down to the back seat and a 50 pound block of ice sticking out of a hole where the rear window used to be."

They weren't completely satisfied with this, but agreed to send the adjuster out to look for the car. That afternoon I happened to see a man with a clipboard walking through the parking lot looking at cars. Thinking he might want to talk to me I put on my parka and went outside. I was walking toward him when he found my car. He stopped dead in his tracks, stared at the car, and dropped his clipboard in the snow.

"The ice did quite a number on it, didn't it?" I said as I walked up.

Still staring at the car, he simply said "It's totaled. Even if we used junk parts, it's totaled."

A few days later I got a short note from my insurance company explaining that they'd found a note from me requesting they cancel the comprehensive coverage on my vehicle. Since that note predated the accident, they regretted to inform me that they could not pay for the damages to my car. I wasn't surprised. The next weekend I wrestled a car jack into the back seat and managed to jack the top bows back up until they were more or less where they should be. I hauled the ice out of the rear window, picked out the broken remnants of the rear window, and used some fish line to sew a plastic "convertible window repair kit" over the hole. The car would never again look as nice as it did when I bought it, which wasn't saying much, but at least it was warm and dry inside and I could see out my rear view mirror again.

The sports car club didn't hold autocrosses during the winter, but they did hold rallies. A rally is an event where the contestants are given a rather cryptic set of directions for a meandering drive through the countryside. The directions are given in terms of clues and puzzles rather than specific road signs, and each leg of the rally is assigned an average speed which must be maintained. (The speeds are well within the legal limits for the roads.) Checkpoints are set up at undisclosed locations along the route and the cars are timed between checkpoints, so the challenge is to follow the directions without getting lost and maintain the specified average speed for each leg of the rally. Penalty points are assessed for every second too early or too late a car arrives at each checkpoint. Since I didn't want to drive my MG when there was salt on the roads, I used the Chevy for rallying.

At my first rally I drew the 12'th starting position. The club member who had volunteered to set up this rally took white shoe polish and wrote a "12" on the passenger's side of my windshield. This was standard practice in rallies, so the checkpoint workers could immediately identify the car when they clocked it into the checkpoint. The small number 12 on my windshield didn't look very impressive on such a large car, so I started looking for a way to make a bolder statement that this was no ordinary Chevy Impala. This was a rally car! If you've ever driven a car through winter road salt you know how much dirt and grime gets thrown up on the side of your car. My Impala was white, so this grime showed up exceptionally well, and since it was a $40 winter rat I didn't wash it very often. Or ever, for that matter. I therefore had a pretty thick layer of grime on the side of my car. I took a damp paper napkin and drew a large circle on each door with a number 12 in the middle. Now it looked more like a true race car. I don't remember where I finished in that rally, but I do remember the driver behind me complained that he had to use his wipers to clear the falling rust off his windshield.

At the next month's rally the number 12 was still faintly visible on my door, so the organizers agreed to assign me the number 12 again. When I'd finished freshening up the "12" on each door, one of the other club members asked if I'd mind if he added an STP logo. That started a tradition. After that, I was always assigned the number 12, and the club members would line up to decorate my car with race logos, "this side up" signs, flames behind the wheel wells, a Mercedes emblem on the trunk lid, etc. By the following month's rally a new layer of grime would have obliterated the previous month's artwork so we could start with a clean slate. I never won a rally in that car, but I doubt that any of the winning cars is as fondly remembered as is "Old Number 12."

Needless to say, the appearance of Old Number 12 didn't exactly appeal to people who were concerned about what kind of an impression their car made on others. I suppose in some perverse way I found that appealing in itself. Having grown up during the Age of Aquarius I was infected by a certain amount of anti-materialisitc snobbery. I may not have worn love beads and driven a clapped-out VW Microbus, but blue jeans and Old Number 12 suited me just fine. That feeling was reinforced by some of the customers I had seen at Riccotto's. There were customers who loved to drive sports cars, and customers who loved to be seen in sports cars. As a rule the former were fun to talk to, brought their cars in for legitimate service, and drove cars that were well maintained but which showed a patina of hard use. The latter were a pain to work for, brought their cars in for nitpicking problems, and drove cars that were polished daily. The ratio of customer types also seemed to vary with the price of the car. Lots of fun customers drove MG Midgets, but only a few Jaguar owners fell into the "fun" category. To this day I feel slightly self-conscious whenever I drive an expensive car, especially if it's shiny, for fear people will mistake me for one of "those" owners. I'm much more comfortable in a slightly battered MG.

It was clear when I drove Old Number 12 that no one was ever going to mistake me for one of "those" customers. Mechanically it was in good shape. It wasn't noisy and it didn't belch clouds of blue smoke, but it didn't look like an expensive toy either. When I drove onto the base the civilian guards at the gate weren't quite sure what to make of it. They'd stare at the car as I was driving up. Then they'd look at the base sticker which identified me as an officer, stare at the car some more, and finally wave me in with a salute and a barely concealed sneer of contempt. One morning I picked up an Airman who was hitchhiking to work. We were chatting away about our squadrons and what kind of work we did when we came to the gate.

179

The guard saluted, I returned the salute, and the Airman got very quiet. "Oh I'm sorry, sir." He said. "I didn't see any stripes on your sleeve so I thought you were an Airman Basic like me." I tried to assure him that there was nothing to apologize about, that officers were people too, and he didn't need to "yes sir" me to death on the way in to work, but he remained quiet. He slowly looked around the interior of the car. We were in the midst of another base clean-up and Air Force vehicles were in short supply (maintenance funds were very scarce between Vietnam and Reagan) so I'd been using Old Number 12 to ferry my work crew around the base. Time was short, we were painting everything in sight, and we didn't always have time to clean up before moving on to the next job. As a result, there were fire hydrant yellow handprints on the passenger door, softball backstop silver fingerprints on the steering wheel, guardrail white footprints on the floor mats, and a half-dozen empty spray cans and old paint brushes rattling around in the back seat. And, of course, the windshield still had a spider web of cracks on the passenger side where the ice had hit it. The Airman silently took all this in and then very quietly said "Gee. I never rode in an officer's car before."

All good things come to an end, and eventually it came to pass that Old Number 12's days of carefree motoring were over. The crack in the windshield never interfered with my vision, but I knew the car would never pass New York's annual safety inspection unless I replaced the glass. A new windshield would cost considerably more than the car was worth, so essentially the car was what the medical profession calls a "no code." I was willing to invest in gasoline and oil, but if the car ever needed anything more expensive it would be the end of Old Number 12.

The end came in the form of a collapsed lifter. She began billowing blue smoke out the tailpipe, although she gamely ran on using the remaining seven cylinders. I appreciated her spirit, but even I didn't want to drive around in a "bug sprayer." An Airman in my squadron needed a replacement engine for his pickup truck, so I gave him Old Number 12. She gave her engine so that another vehicle might live. He replaced the lifter, and the engine purred like a kitten in its new home. Sadly, he had no use for the rest of the car. I bowed my head in respect as he towed the engineless body off to an auto graveyard. Ashes to ashes, rust to rust.

Chapter 16 – Here Today, Guam Tomorrow

During my Air Force career I had the opportunity to see a lot of different management styles. Although I didn't realize it at the time, the management style at my first base was about as "different" as they come. The squadron was led by Colonel Thompson, a big, burly commander whose bulldozer personality permeated everything the squadron did. Whatever he wanted done, was done. Sometimes he simply waded in with a "damn the torpedoes" attitude and forced the action, leaving his staff scrambling to catch up with all the paperwork that was supposed to have been done first. Other times he sat back and pulled strings behind the scenes, with a devious cunning that would have made The Godfather envious. "You owe your Colonel a favor" was a favorite phrase in the squadron, although admittedly one that was only whispered when The Colonel wasn't around.

Early in his career, then Lieutenant Thompson had found himself in charge of the engineering team at a neglected radar site in Alaska. Mission changes and subsequent funding cuts had left the site with many empty or half-empty dilapidated buildings, most of them adorned with a red "X" which meant they were slated for demolition. Lt. Thompson's predecessor had ignored these buildings, claiming he lacked the funding and the manpower to dispose of them properly. A few weeks after Lt. Thompson took command of the engineering crew a no-notice inspection team arrived, ominously threatening dire consequences if any of the condemned buildings were still standing. Lt. Thompson escorted the team to the Visiting Officers' Quarters, where they were going to rest up from their long flight before beginning their inspection the following morning. Lt. Thompson then took advantage of Alaska's 24 hours of summer daylight, keeping his team up all night bulldozing any building that had a red "X" on it. If a condemned building still housed a critical operation, they painted over the red "X," swapped building numbers with a less critical facility, and tore down that building. By the time the inspection team woke up there wasn't a single condemned building standing, at least, not according to the building numbers.

Colonel Thompson told me that story himself, as we were relaxing on his patio after a huge "farm spaghetti" dinner. Colonel Thompson had grown up on a farm in Michigan, and he proudly dumped a variety of leftover meats and vegetables into what he called his farm spaghetti sauce. He often invited junior officers from the squadron to join him for these dinners, as he took a personal interest in developing our leadership skills. Sometimes he taught us skills more appropriate to Mafia Lieutenants than to Air Force Lieutenants, but they were leadership skills nonetheless. He was a keen observer of human nature and he always stressed that leadership involved working with people, while management involved working with papers. Both were important, but it was clear that leadership took priority in his mind.

Col. Thompson had his fingers in a lot of pies off-base as well as on-base, so I wasn't surprised one day when I got a call to meet him at a house out in the country. The call itself was typical of Col. Thompson. He almost never phoned anyone himself. Instead he called the 24 hour Civil Engineering Service Desk and let them track down whoever he wanted. In the days before cell phones the service desk kept a list of everyone's home phone number, plus the numbers of various friends and other alternate contacts. In this case it was a Saturday and I was at home when they called.

"Colonel Thompson wants you to come take a look at a Model A, if you're not busy." This last phrase was a diplomatic courtesy. No one was ever too busy to heed a call from Col. Thompson. He then relayed the driving directions Col. Thompson had given him.

As I drove through the rolling farmland I wondered how Col. Thompson had gotten involved with a Model A, especially so far from the base. He wasn't a car collector, and although he had expressed a mild interest in my car when I mentioned it after dinner one evening he had never asked me about it since. Apparently that was just one of the tidbits of information he had filed away, in case it ever became useful. Following the directions I turned into the driveway of a large, modern ranch-style house with a beautiful view of the surrounding fields and forests. Scattered outbuildings and an in-ground pool adorned the back yard. A flatbed truck carrying a Model A coupe sat next to one of the buildings, and I recognized Col. Thompson in a group of people next to the truck. I parked my MG and headed toward the truck.

"Oh my God, it's a wreck! I bought a pig in a poke!" A short, genial-looking Italian man was holding his head with both hands as he made this announcement. "Look at that! The tires are flat" he added as two men used a winch to ease it off the truck and down a ramp. Col. Thompson stepped in and introduced me to Paulie Pellegrino, the man who had just bought this Model A.

"Steve knows all about Model A's" the Colonel said reassuringly. "He's got one himself."

"I'm sorry you had to drive all the way out here to see this," Paulie replied. "Is that a piece of junk or what?"

The Model A was now resting on the ground where I could see it clearly. It was a 1931 Deluxe Coupe. Although the tires were indeed flat and the car was covered with years of accumulated barn dust, it appeared to be in excellent condition. The car was complete, with no parts missing. There were no dents or rust showing anywhere. The top appeared to be intact. The upholstery was dusty and soiled here and there, but with no tears or worn spots. I pulled the crank out from under the seat and turned over the engine. It turned freely and smoothly. The odometer showed about 20,000 miles, and a dusty 1936 license plate hanging on the rear gave credibility to that number. The car had obviously been stored for a long, long time, but there appeared to be nothing wrong with it.

"This is a beautiful car" I told Paulie. "It's in excellent shape. I wish my car were in such good condition."

"But the tires are flat!" Paulie protested.

"You can get new tires," I replied. "They're not that expensive."

"It looks like a wreck!"

I noticed a bucket of water with a sponge in it sitting next to one of the outbuildings. I carefully sponged away the dirt on a section of the passenger door. The original Ford Maroon paint shone through clearly, with a Vermillion pin stripe along the belt line. "Look at that!" I proclaimed. "The original paint is still good. You don't even need to do any bodywork. With a little bit of polish, this car will look brand new."

"Does it even run?" Paulie asked, with a small glimmer of hope.

"I'm sure the battery's dead." I replied. I tried the horn and the dash light, but there was no sign of any current. The engine looked fine, although the oil could stand to be changed and I suspected the points were corroded. I made a half-hearted attempt to crank start it, but as I expected the engine didn't even cough.

"It needs a new battery." I told Paulie. "It would be a good idea to change the oil before you start it, and you should probably put in a new fan belt for safety's sake. It will need some fresh gas, and it wouldn't hurt to give it an electrical tune-up, too. New points, plugs, possibly a new coil. That sort of thing."

"Can you take care of that?" Paulie asked. "I don't know anything about cars."

I assured him I would enjoy working on his Model A. Paulie, Col. Thompson, and I then retired to the porch on Paulie's house and enjoyed the rural scenery while we sipped red wine and socialized. It turned out Paulie had heard about this car from a friend, and on a whim he had offered to buy it. The owner wasn't interested in selling it at the time, and Paulie forgot all about the car. A few years later the owner finally realized he was never going to restore the car himself, and he let Paulie know he was ready to sell the car. Paulie bought it, sight unseen.

As the afternoon waned, Paulie had to leave but insisted Col. Thompson and I stay and finish our wine. His wife and a man who apparently worked around the house would be home all day. We finished our wine quickly after Paulie left. Then Col. Thompson left, and I washed the Model A and pushed it into one of the outbuildings. The next day I came back with a jack and a couple of jack stands so I could take the wheels off the car. Paulie planned to take them to a local tire shop to get new tires put on them. I also took out the battery so he could get a replacement for that. I ordered the rest of the parts we needed from a Model A parts supplier that had given me good service in the past.

Over the next few weeks I drove out to Paulie's whenever I had a couple of hours to kill on a weekend. I cleaned the interior, polished the paint, and put on a good coat of wax. When the parts came in I gave it a tune up. With the tires and battery that Paulie had gotten we soon had the car in running condition. I showed Paulie how to drive it, and he was eagerly looking forward to taking his grandkids for a ride. Suddenly a look of concern crossed his face. Even though it was just the two of us in his garage, he took me aside and whispered "I paid $500 for the car. Do you think that's too much?"

He seemed relieved when I assured him that was a steal. He was also surprised and delighted when I refused to take any money for the work I'd done on his car. I just asked him to reimburse me for the parts I'd bought. The truth was, I'd had a lot of fun fooling around with his Model A. It was good to get 40 year old grease under my fingernails again.

I drove out to see Paulie a few times that summer. Sometimes my girlfriend and I would swim and relax in his pool. He had some sort of a job in the liquor wholesale business, and he gave us sets of bar glasses emblazoned with various distillery logos and other advertising "giveaways" when we visited. Then cooler weather set in and I just never had occasion to visit Paulie again. A couple of years later I was having dinner at the Officers' Club when somehow we got to talking about the fact that people never helped motorists in distress any more. I told the group about a dark night when I was struggling to push start my MG by myself, only to have a police car with two able-bodied patrolmen watch, laugh, and then drive away.

"Why didn't you just tell your friend Paulie about it?" one of the older, more experienced officers asked. I was surprised he had even heard of Paulie, let alone that he somehow knew that I knew Paulie.

"Does Paulie have any influence with the police?" I asked in surprise.

The officer looked at me in astonishment, as if he couldn't believe anyone could be so naive. "You don't control liquor distribution for half of New York State without having a little influence" was all he said.

Now it was my turn to be astonished. I had heard rumors that Rome had a low crime rate because the Mafia dons lived there and they kept the city "clean." We heard news reports of gangland slayings in nearby cities, but never in Rome. I had always dismissed those rumors. That kind of thing only happened in the movies. Paulie was just a really nice guy who happened to have a Model A Ford, wasn't he?

In the military, people move frequently. After I'd been at Griffis for about two years Colonel Thompson got orders to become the chief engineer at the Alaskan Air Command. His going away party was attended by the Wing and Base commanders, the only two officers on base who officially outranked him. On an air base, the Wing Commander is God, and the Base Commander is the Right Hand of God. At the party, the Wing Commander told of a time when he decided to ignore Colonel Thompson's advice and push ahead with his own ideas for changing a few buildings. He called the Base Commander into his office, outlined his plan, and told the Base Commander to go inform Colonel Thompson. After some hemming and hawing, the Base Commander finally came to the point.

"Could you do it, sir?" He asked. "To tell you the truth, I'm scared of the man."

"I'm scared of him too," the Wing Commander confessed. "That's why I'm sending you to do it."

After the demise of Old Number 12, I had to look for another winter rat. Once again, Lt. Kelly provided the solution. For some reason he had retired his Rambler. I don't remember exactly why he stopped driving it, but I'm sure it wasn't because we'd dropped a valve keeper into the bowels of the engine when we did a valve job on it. The car ran fine after that, and there was more than enough sludge in that engine to swallow up a valve keeper and prevent it from bouncing into something vital. Whatever the reason, he'd retired his Rambler and bought a 1968 Chevy Impala 4-door sedan. Then, shortly after Col Thompson went to the Headquarters of the Alaskan Air Command, Lt. Kelly mysteriously got orders to report to Ft Yukon Alaska. Since he couldn't take a car to Ft Yukon (he actually made part of the journey there by dogsled) he offered to sell me his Chevy for $80. His only stipulation was that when it was my turn to move on I not make a profit on the car but instead sell it to some other starving Lieutenant for no more than I'd paid for it.

The '68 Impala cost twice as much as Old Number 12 did, but it was in at least twice as good condition. Warm and dry in the winter, it ran fine and was excellent transportation. It came with two studded snow tires mounted on a spare set of rims, and with the two I had left over from Old Number 12 I could put studded snow tires on all four wheels in the winter. While it was customary to only put snow tires on the back, with studded tires on all four wheels I found I could not only get the car moving through snow and ice, I could also steer and brake! Sometimes these last two maneuvers came in handy. The only work I had to do to the car, other than routine tune-ups and oil changes, was to install an AM/FM stereo radio and a couple of decent speakers in place of the factory AM unit. The car was comfortable, dependable, and, well, boring. Old Number 12 may have been a piece of crap, but it was crap with character. This car had no endearing vices, no noteworthy handling characteristics, and nothing distinguishing in its physical appearance.

That's not to say my new winter rat was a perfect car. I couldn't have bought it for $80 if it was. The old demon rust was slowly eating it from the bottom up and it had a bit of battle damage here and there. Its main claim to fame was that it started whenever I asked it to, got me where I was going, and turned off when I was through with it. I couldn't make that same claim about most of the other cars I'd owned. This was the first car I'd ever owned that let me watch the odometer roll over 100,000 miles. While I suspect the Model A and the MG might have already passed that milestone, their odometers didn't work so I had no way of knowing. In any event, this was the first time I'd been able to see that happen on a car. It happened while I was driving the car home for Thanksgiving, which also happened to be the only time this car provided me with even a mild adventure. This was the first long trip I'd taken in it, and the first time I ever filled the tank all the way up. I was astonished to discover it held 24 gallons! I was used to the 10 gallon tank in the Model A, or the 12 gallon tank in my MG. (Actually, the MG held 10 Imperial gallons, which amounted to 12 US gallons. Why the US and England couldn't agree on the size of a gallon is something I've never understood.) I don't believe I ever filled the tank in Old Number 12 because I was never confident the car would last long enough to use that much gasoline. In any event, I definitely wasn't used to putting that much gas into one car.

At the time I was dating a girl who drove a white 1971 Triumph GT-6. (That's not why I was dating her. I liked her for who she was. The car was an added bonus.) She was driving to Virginia to spend Thanksgiving with her parents. We decided to convoy as far as the New York State Thruway and then go our separate ways.

We had just gotten out of town and were beginning to pick up speed when I heard the unmistakable sound of dragging metal. "Oh great" I thought. "My exhaust system." I had just entered a ramp up to an overpass and there were guard rails on both sides of the road, so I couldn't pull over. I had to go over the overpass, down the other side, and around a shallow curve before I found a place to pull off the road. I got out of the car, walked around to the back, and saw to my horror that it wasn't the exhaust system that was dragging – it was the gas tank! A full tank proved to be too much of a strain for the rusted straps that held the tank to the car and they had given way, allowing the tank to drop down and be dragged across the pavement by the fuel lines. My girlfriend pulled in behind my car.

"What happened?" she gasped. "It looked like the whole back end fell out of your car. There sure were a lot of sparks!" That was not something I needed to hear.

It soon became obvious that with the tools I had in my trunk there was no way I was going to lift 24 gallons of gas and fasten the tank back into place. Fortunately a friendly New York State Trooper stopped to help, and he called for a tow truck. Together we dug a hole under my tank (I was getting good at digging holes under my cars) and used his hydraulic jack to lift the tank into place. I had a couple rolls of wire in my trunk, left over from installing the new speakers, and I was able to wire the tank into place securely enough to get me to a garage in the next town. They put in a new set of mounting straps, and I was on my way, good as new.

As time went by, the squadron began to change. Col Thompson and Lt Kelly weren't the only officer who left. When I first arrived, we had 10 lieutenants. We were a close-knit group and we had a lot of fun together. Then, one by one, they got orders to report to other bases and they disappeared. I began to feel like a character in a bad horror movie, the kind where a group of people are trapped in a strange house by a terrific storm and begin disappearing one by one. After I'd had more experience in the Air Force I realized this was normal, as most officers moved to a new base every two or three years, but at the time it seemed eerie. Seemingly overnight I'd gone from being the new kid on the block to being the old timer, the one who was showing the ropes to all the newcomers. Then it was my turn. I got a call from an airman in the personnel office who could barely contain a chortle when he said "Can you spell Guam?"

Sure enough, he had a set of orders for me to report to the Island of Guam to be the Squadron Environmental Officer. (Actually, my orders said I would be the Squadron Invironmental Officer. Environmental Awareness was still pretty new back then, and the administrative bureaucracy hadn't learned how to spell it yet.) The first thing I had to do was find a globe so I could figure where Guam was. It turned out to be an island in the Pacific Ocean, about 2/3 of the way from Hawaii to Japan, not too far north of the equator. I noticed the island was about 45 miles long, but only 4 or 5 miles wide.

At the time, Guam didn't have a particularly good reputation within the Air Force. This wasn't because there was anything bad about the island itself, but because it had been unpopular with the ground crews and aviators who flew B-52s out of Guam on missions over Vietnam. Normally the Air Force personnel system tried to treat people fairly. They recognized that sending people off to remote locations far from their family and friends caused hardships. For this reason they had a policy that if you were stationed anywhere without your family for more than 180 days you got credit for a "short tour." Theoretically, you wouldn't get assigned to another short tour until everyone else with your qualifications had also been on a short tour. I don't know if it was because SAC was short of people to fly and maintain B-52s or if it was because they were just plain ornery, but their policy during the war had been to send people to Guam in a "TDY" (temporary duty) status for 179 days and then rotate them back to the US. This meant they didn't get credit for a short tour, and in a month or two SAC could send them back to Guam for another 179 days. The aircrews were flying long, nerve wracking combat missions under some of the most screwed-up circumstances imaginable. (Rumor had it SAC was filing international flight plans for these missions, giving the enemy anti-aircraft gunners plenty of advance warning as to when and where the bombers would arrive.) The ground support personnel were living in tents and working 12 hour days, 7 days a week. Given these conditions, it's not surprising that many of these people didn't have fond memories of Guam.

I would learn much more about Guam in the coming year, but my immediate priority was to get everything packed or stored so I could leave New York. I thought it would be great to have a sports car on a tropical island, but people who had lived on Guam told me horror stories about maniacal drivers, typhoons, and rust caused by the sea spray. It turned out these stories were wildly exaggerated, but of course I didn't know that at the time. I worried about taking my MG there. What I wanted was the island equivalent of a winter rat. I needed a Guam Bomb. I didn't want just any Guam Bomb, though. I wanted a British sports car Guam Bomb. Somehow I suspected British sports cars would be hard to find on Guam, so I decided to look for one I could take with me. I didn't have to look far. A lieutenant in my squadron had a 1958 MGA which he'd bought shortly before his first child was born. His wife gave him 10 points for style, but deducted a couple of hundred points for bad timing. She was "encouraging" him to sell the MG and buy something they could take the baby in. He offered to sell it to me for $350. OK. There was a reason he only wanted $350 for it. In addition to the fact that the engine and drive train were in a questionable state of repair and the interior was shot, there was some custom bodywork on the front end. Someone, obviously not a craftsman, had tried to give the car a Cobra-style nose. The bodywork had been done with tin snips, bondo, and what appeared to be an upside-down hood from a Ford pickup truck. Rather than looking like a Cobra, the nose resembled a dying carp sucking air in the bottom of a boat. Adding to the overall appearance was the fact that the car was mostly chalky blue, with patches of black primer and bondo scattered across the body like scabs on a mangy camel.

As luck would have it, the Airman I had given Old Number 12 to was taking a course in auto bodywork and he needed a cadaver to experiment on. He offered to sand the car and paint it red for $100 plus materials. It wouldn't be beautiful, but at least it would be all one color. Actually, when he was finished it didn't look half bad – as long as you only looked at the half behind that carp nose. After giving the car a quick tune-up I packed the trunk with all the spare parts I expected to need over the coming year and drove it to the dockyards in Bayonne New Jersey. People in Rome warned me the New Jersey dock workers would be rude and dishonest, but when I got there I found them to be friendly and surprisingly candid. The Air Force had told me it would take from 6 to 12 weeks for my car to arrive on Guam, and I asked the man filling out the paperwork at the dock why it took so long. "Well" he said, "when you strip a car, if you do it right, it takes time." It's always nice to meet people who take pride in their work.

Now that I had my Guam Bomb, I had to make arrangements for the cars I was leaving behind. Riccotto's agreed to store my MGA for me. The car needed some minor touch-up bodywork so the next time I went home on leave I dropped the car off to have the bodywork done, with the understanding that it would be over a year until I could pick it up. They planned on keeping it in a back corner of the shop, and promised to start it every month or two just to keep things limber. While I was in Indiana I also paid a year's storage on the Model A in advance.

Now the only car left to take care of was my Chevy. I posted a notice about it on the squadron bulletin board:

For Sale

Four studded snow tires on Chevrolet rims.
AM/FM stereo car radio, with speakers.
$75 for all.

Free Bonus: Attached to the above, and at no additional charge, is a running, street legal, 1968 Chevrolet Impala 4-door sedan.

I sold the car within hours of posting the notice. I now had all my automotive affairs in order, so I boarded the plane for Guam with a clear conscience. About 24 hours and several plane changes later I arrived on the island of Guam. I was unshaved, disheveled, and jet-lagged, but I was there. My luggage had gotten lost somewhere near San Francisco so all I had with me was a briefcase containing a camera and my orders. Oh, and I had a car, too. Despite all the warnings and horror stories, my car had beaten me to the island. It arrived without a scratch, and all the tools and spare parts I'd packed in the trunk arrived intact. Shipping an MG from New Jersey to Guam turned out to be much easier than forwarding my luggage from California.

Carp-nosed MGA on Guam

After I got over my jet lag I started exploring the island. I found it to be absolutely beautiful. The northern part of the island, where the Air Force base was located, was a high limestone plateau, with cliffs dropping straight down into the sea in some places. Other places had a narrow strip of jungle ("the boonies" in local slang) between the cliffs and the ocean, with gorgeous strips of palm trees and sand beaches at the water's edge. The southern part of the island was hilly volcanic terrain, coming to a peak in Mt. Lamlam. Mt Lamlam doesn't look like much, as it only rises about 1300 feet above sea level, but some people claim it's the tallest mountain on Earth because it has its roots in the Marianas trench and rises almost 38,000 feet above that point. I found the scuba diving on Guam to be fantastic, with coral reefs, a dazzling variety of fish, and sunken ships and aircraft from World War II. I'd been snorkeling since I was a little kid (the result of watching "Sea Hunt" on television) and I got my diver's certificate when I was 14, but the cold mud lakes in Indiana couldn't hold a candle to Guam. On top of everything else, the water was so warm I didn't need a wet suit, or the multiple layers of jeans and sweatshirts I wore as a kid in Indiana because I couldn't afford a wet suit. A pair of cut-offs and a tee-shirt kept me warm for hours when diving around Guam.

As near as I could tell, I had the only running MGA on the island. For that matter, I never saw another running MG of any kind on Guam. There was a "shop" that advertised itself as a sports car center and they had a battered MGA carcass rusting away behind the shed that served as their garage, but they weren't aware of any running MGs on the island either. Fortunately, my car ran fine the whole time I was there. I did have to replace the battery once, and that was enough of an adventure. A previous owner had replaced the two six-volt batteries with a single 12-volt battery, which made it easier to find a replacement. The Navy exchange on the south end of the island had one in stock, as a matter of fact. When I was picking up the battery they asked if I'd like them to install it for a $3.00 installation fee. That sounded like a good deal to me, so I drove my car around to a carport in back of the store that served as their garage. Their "mechanic" was looking for a way to open my hood when I showed him the battery was located behind the driver's seat. I lifted the top out of the way, tilted the seat forward, and removed the access panel that covered the battery. He stared into the dark recesses where the battery lived and whined "It's all dirty down there." I said nothing, but thought of all the greasy, grimy jobs I'd done at Riccotto's. Changing an MGA battery wasn't fun, but it was a picnic compared to some of those other jobs.

The mechanic horsed around with the battery cables for a few minutes, and when I saw he was trying to remove them with a pair of pliers I got my tool box out of the trunk and loaned him a wrench. Eventually he was able to wrestle the old battery out of my car. Then he looked at his watch and simply said "I think this is too much work, and it's already after 5:00." He walked around the corner of the building and disappeared. Shocked, I tried to go back in to the store to complain to the service manager but I discovered the store was locked and everyone else had gone home as well. The mechanic had done just enough work to disable my car and then left me alone in an empty "shop." Fortunately, the new battery was sitting beside my car and I had my own tools, so I was able to install the battery myself and get back on the road. I couldn't ask for a refund of my $3.00 installation fee because there was no one left to complain to.

My other transactions on Guam were much more pleasant. I met some very helpful people when I shopped for a replacement TV. The black & white portable I'd bought in a New York secondhand shop died shortly before I left Rome. I had heard tales of fabulous deals to be had at overseas BX's (Army/Air Force Base Exchange Stores) so I decided to wait until I got overseas to buy a replacement. The tales of fabulous deals turned out to be wild exaggerations. Prices at the Guam BX turned out to be roughly equivalent to prices at stateside chain stores, but the inventory was much more limited at the BX. Tales of BX shortages were a running joke at the office. People would buy a camera that was on sale, only to discover the BX had no film that would fit it. The store carried razors and replacement blades, but the blades couldn't be used with the razors and vice versa. Sure enough, when I looked for a television they only sold one model within my price range (I wanted to upgrade to a color TV) but they were all out of that model. They were, however, nice enough to call around to the other military bases on the island and they discovered the Naval Air Station had one of these sets left in stock, and it was actually $10 cheaper than the Air Force price. I'd have to hurry, though, as the store closed in less than an hour and it was at least a 45 minute drive away. I'd only been on the island for about a week and had no idea where the Naval Air Station was, but the directions were simple and the people in the BX assured me I could make it if I hurried.

I hopped into my MG, hurried out the back gate, and rushed along the back road toward the Naval Air Station. (There were only two roads that led to the Air Force Base – the front road and the back road.) It was a beautiful tropical evening – as usual - and a beautiful night for a drive. The directions from the people in the BX were perfect, and I rushed into the Navy Exchange shouting "I'll buy that TV!" a few minutes before they closed. The people at the Navy Exchange were also very helpful. They carted the TV out to my MG and helped me figure out a way to shoehorn it into the passenger seat. (The box was at least twice as big as the TV it contained.) I set my course for the Air Force base and headed up the back road at a much more relaxed pace than I'd used on my way down. The moon was rising, the wind was blowing clouds past the stars, the warm tropical air was filled with the scents of exotic flowers, . . and my gas gauge read empty! I hadn't paid much attention during my drive to the Naval Air Station but I was pretty sure there were no gas stations along the back road. While I suspected there was a gas station somewhere on the Naval Air Station, I also suspected it closed the same time the main exchange closed. That's just the way the military did things. To make matters worse, it was Saturday night and BX gas stations weren't open on Sundays. Again, that's just the way things were done. I had little choice but to keep motoring on and hope for the best. I didn't have enough experience with this MG to know how accurate the gauge was, but I knew from having worked on the gauge on my other MG that there were any number of factors that could cause the accuracy to range from "right on" to "dead wrong."

As I drove up the back road, even more gently than before, I spent a lot of time trying to figure out what I should do if the car did run out of gas. I was alone on an unfamiliar island, driving down a nearly deserted road, top down, with a giant box in the passenger seat with the words "Color TV" boldly emblazoned across every available surface. Did I dare leave the car and the TV by the side of the road and walk? I couldn't even attempt to hide the TV by putting the top up, as the box was too big. If I did walk, where would I walk to? I didn't recall seeing any stores or phone booths along the back road, and even if I found a phone I didn't know who to call. I'd only been on the island a few days and I barely knew anyone's name, let alone their phone number. I finally decided that if the car did run out of gas I'd have to stay with it, all night if necessary, and offer to buy a can of gas from anyone who might stop to help.

Fortunately the car did not run out of gas and I managed to limp back onto the Air Force base. I was running on fumes by the time I got there, but I made it. I didn't dare drive the car on Sunday, but I was able to make it to the gas station and fill it up on Monday morning. I resolved to keep a closer eye on my gas gauge from then on, or at least for as long as I was on Guam, and I enjoyed watching that TV for the next 20 years.

Typhoons and tropical storms were a serious threat on Guam. The island was located near the area where many Pacific storms were born. Storms could form, grow to typhoon strength, and hit the island within 72 hours, which meant that Guam was always in Typhoon Condition 4 or higher. It was amazing how powerful these storms could become in a short time. When I was there Guam was still recovering from Typhoon Pamela, which devastated the island in 1976 with winds up to 200 mph. I was lucky not to see any storms anywhere near that strong while I was there, but we were hit by a few tropical storms and narrowly escaped a typhoon or two during my tour. I tried to keep a close eye on the weather forecast, but when storms arose that quickly they sometimes caught me by surprise. One Saturday my dive partner and I spent the day exploring reefs near the south end of the island. As evening drew near, I rushed back to the base, cleaned up, and headed down the back road for a dinner party at a friend's apartment. I had a tail wind that kept getting stronger and stronger, until it finally matched my car's speed. I had the eerie experience of driving top down, 55 mph, without the slightest trace of wind or wind noise. I could stick my hand straight up over the windshield or straight out the side and feel nothing. The air was moving at the same speed I was and only my speedometer and the pavement whipping by beneath my wheels gave any hint that I wasn't standing still. Fortunately, there was no rain, just wind. When I slowed down to turn into my friend's apartment complex I suddenly felt the full force of the wind behind me. As I pulled into the parking lot outside his building the entire apartment complex erupted in cheering. Flattered though I was, the cheering turned out to have nothing to do with my arrival. People in the apartments were cheering because they had been without electricity for the last 20 minutes and the power had suddenly come back on. It turned out the island was being buffeted by a tropical storm, but since I had been outdoors all day instead of listening to weather forecasts I was totally unaware of it. I was simply the fool driving an MG with the top down in the middle of a tropical storm. There was no hint of this storm in the morning forecast, it had grown from nothing to tropical storm strength while I was out diving. Fortunately I made it into my friend's apartment before the rain hit, rode out the storm, and was able to drive back to the base after it passed.

Although tropical storms were rare, rain was an almost daily occurrence on Guam. Guam actually had a rainy season and a dry season, but to a boy from the Midwest it was hard to tell the difference. The only time we had a dull, horizon to horizon overcast like those that were typical in Indiana (and even more typical in New York) was when we were in the middle of a tropical storm. The rest of the time we had clear blue skies, scattered fleecy clouds, and trade winds. During the rainy season we had a couple of showers every day, and during the dry season we had a shower every two or three days. Even while it was raining, though, the sun was often shining as the trade winds meant the rain was coming from one of the clouds off to the East. This was ideal sports car weather, as the tonneau cover protected the car when I wasn't driving and if it happened to be raining when I wanted to drive I could usually wait a few minutes and the shower would pass. The only time I put the top up was when I was battening down the hatches for a tropical storm. I didn't really need a rain car, but I wound up with a couple of them anyway.

My first rain car wasn't really mine. An architect who worked in the squadron was due to spend a month back in the states taking an Air Force engineering class and visiting family. For some reason, she was concerned about leaving her car sit while she was gone and she asked me if I would keep it and drive it regularly. Since her car was a brand new Datsun 280Z I quickly agreed. I had driven a few 240Z's while I worked at Riccotto's and I was really looking forward to seeing what the 280Z could do. I must say, I was disappointed. Where the 240Z felt light and nimble, like a sports car, the 280Z felt heavy and stolid, like my parent's sedans. I joked to a friend that it felt like the best car Buick ever made. Some of this feeling could be attributed to the fact that her car had an automatic transmission, which took much of the fun out of driving. The car was roomy, comfortable, air conditioned, and boring. I dutifully drove it once a week while the owner was stateside, thanked her profusely when she returned, and silently crossed it off my list of cars I might like to own someday. This seems to be a common trait for sports cars. Early models are light and nimble, but as the years go by they put on weight, gain additional padding, and waddle around corners. Sadly, the same is often true of their owners.

My other rain car was a 1971 Dodge Colt which I got from a fellow officer in the Squadron. This car definitely fit the definition of a "Guam Bomb." Rusty, "rattley," and grossly under-powered it was a car perfectly suited for bouncing around base, running through the gears in a vain attempt to make the most of the little four-banger under the hood. That is, it was perfectly suited on the days when it would start. The problem first surfaced before I bought the car. Some mornings the engine would lock up solid when my friend hit the starter. A few minutes troubleshooting soon revealed the problem. Either the head or the head gasket was bad, and the number 4 cylinder would fill with water overnight and keep the engine from turning. The quick fix was to remove the number 4 spark plug, crank the engine over, and watch the water squirt out the spark plug hole. When it stopped squirting, you could put the spark plug back in and start it. This wasn't a very satisfactory solution, but the car wasn't worth a major repair so we tried pouring some "magic radiator repair pellets" into the cooling system. Surprisingly, this worked. The cylinder never filled with water again and the car started reliably ever after.

The other major problem was the overall appearance of the car. Like most cars on Guam this one was rusting from the top down. The sun and salt spray had liberally spotted the roof, hood, and trunk lid with rust. My friend had a solution for this – he decided to repaint the car with spray cans. He was overseeing major repairs to buildings on base that had been damaged by Typhoon Pamela, and he knew of a hangar that was going to be turned over to his construction management team on a Friday. They weren't scheduled to turn it over to the repair contractor until the following Monday, so for that weekend the hangar would be empty and would be the perfect place to paint his Colt. This happened to be a weekend when there was an air show on base and the flight line was going to be open to the public anyway, so we wouldn't have any problem driving the car to the hangar.

On Saturday morning we drove the car into the hangar. Actually, we were just using a small side room off the main hangar. We immediately began wet sanding the car to get it ready for painting. We'd been working an hour or two when my friend wandered off with the buckets we'd been using, looking for some fresh water to finish the job. He looked a bit pale and shaken when he returned, as he'd seen tool boxes in the main hangar marked "For SR-71 Use Only." The SR-71 was an incredibly high performance Air Force/CIA spy plane, and at the time most details about it were still a closely guarded secret. Everyone on base was astonished when it was announced we would have one on display at our air show, because up to that time we'd never heard of the Air Force allowing people to even look at one. Obviously they intended to service the plane in this hangar after the air show and we didn't think the guards who protected the plane would be very enthusiastic about having two junior officers painting a rusted out car in the next stall. We also didn't think our argument of "you're not supposed to be in this hangar – it was turned over for renovation" would carry much weight.

We finished the sanding as quickly as we could, slapped masking tape over the windows and bumpers, and broke out the spray cans. My friend had picked up a couple cases of white spray paint at the BX. I'd never before tried to empty one can of spray paint after another as quickly as possible, and I was surprised at how tired my finger got pushing down on the nozzle. Actually, "tired" is an understatement. In no time at all I had searing pain along the whole length of my forearm and my finger started twitching so badly I couldn't hold the nozzle down. I switched to my left hand and continued to empty cans until that finger gave out. My friend was having a similar experience. By the time we finished painting that damn car we were holding the cans with both hands and pressing the nozzle with our thumbs – one thumb on top of the other to gain more strength. Our arms ached up to our shoulders and they were twitching so much we couldn't do much more than aim the paint in the general direction of the car, but we did succeed in covering the entire car with paint. We ripped off the masking tape, threw the trash in the trunk, and drove the car out of there as quickly as possible, with the paint drying as we drove. Surprisingly, the overall effect wasn't too bad. It didn't stand up to a close inspection, of course, and it would have looked better if we'd rubbed it out afterwards but neither one of us felt like putting that much work into it. This was, after all, still a 1971 Dodge Colt.

A few months later my friend got orders to return to the states, so I bought the Colt. As I recall, I paid $350 for it, which was the same price he'd paid. He didn't charge me anything extra for the new paint job or for the can of radiator sealant. I had about six months left of my 15 month assignment to Guam, but I'd already applied for an extension to spend a full two years on the island because I was enjoying my tour. Apparently someone in the Air Force personnel system decided I'd gone "island happy," because instead of granting my extension they cut my assignment back to 12 months. The official reason was that they wanted me to attend an upcoming offering of Squadron Officer's School in Montgomery Alabama. Attending this school was supposed to be an honor, although most officers wound up going to it, and neither I nor my boss were very happy about my leaving Guam before my normal tour was up. We tried to get my orders changed, but we had no luck with that endeavor so I packed up my MG and shipped it back to the states. It had been a dependable and fun car during the year I spent on Guam, but it was obvious that it was going to need a clutch soon. I had brought a spare clutch with me, but there was no good place to pull the engine on Guam so I limped into the Navy shipyards on the old one. I was hoping it would rest up on the cruise home, and maybe I'd find a good place to change it on my next assignment. I had no trouble finding a buyer for the Colt, as there was a batch of female officers who had just arrived on the island and they were looking for a car they could share. None of them wanted to put much money into this venture, so the Colt suited them just perfectly. They didn't blink an eye when I told them the head was repaired with radiator sealant. They handed me $350, I handed them the keys, and I caught the midnight plane to California.

Chapter 17 – A Horse of a Different Color

It was December 22nd, 1978 when I left Guam. I hadn't seen my folks for a year so my bags were stuffed with Christmas presents and I was eagerly looking forward to spending the holidays at home. I had about two weeks leave to burn through before I reported to Squadron Officer's School (SOS) in Alabama. After having spent a year on a tropical island where it never got cold enough to wear a long sleeve shirt I suspected I might not be prepared for an Indiana winter. I didn't realize just how bad it would be, though, until we landed in Hawaii to refuel. I was cold in Hawaii. I was wearing a lightweight Air Force jacket, which I had zipped up as high as it would go and I was trying to pull my hands up inside the sleeves. It was 68 °F at the Honolulu Airport, and I hadn't experienced weather anywhere near that cold for 12 months!

The plane was supposed to land at San Francisco International but it was fogged in so they diverted us to Travis AFB and bussed us to San Francisco. Apparently the fog lifted during this diversion, as my connecting flight left long before I arrived at the airport. I spent a few tense hours going from one airline counter to another looking for a standby seat, as all flights were booked solid until after Christmas. I did my best to play the part of a lonely GI trying to get home for Christmas. In truth, it didn't require much acting. Fortunately somebody failed to show, and I took their place. I arrived home on Christmas Eve. I was tired, jet-lagged, unwashed, and suffering from the onset of the worst winter cold I'd had in years, but I was home. It was great.

After Christmas I called Riccotto's to arrange a time to pick up my MG. Their answer of "Are you back already?" didn't surprise me a bit. After all, I'd worked there, and I knew how time just flew by when this customer wanted to pick up his car at noon and that customer's car had to be finished by 3:30 because that's when her mother-in-law was going to drop her off to pick it up on their way back from the beauty shop. Long term projects, like my car, weren't even on the radar screen. I knew even when I dropped it off that the talk of starting it once a month was a pipe dream, despite Luis's best intentions. My expectation was that while I was gone the car would sit in a corner of the shop, covered with Visqueen, and it would gradually acquire a protective padding of dust reinforced by an armored surface of mufflers, door panels, and other relatively lightweight car parts. I also expected that my call saying I was ready to pick it up would be the signal for the mechanics to try to remember which mound of car parts contained my MG, while Leto would search through stacks of old work orders trying to find out just what it was they were supposed to do to my car while they had it. In these expectations I was not disappointed, but when I actually arrived at the shop to pick up my beauty Luis took me aside and told me of a development I had not expected. It seems that just that morning Whack had tried to start it and discovered the head gasket had leaked anti-freeze into the cylinders and the engine was stuck tight. They would fix it, of course, since this unfortunate incident had occurred while they were storing the car, but it would not be ready in time for me to drive it to Alabama.

This put me in a bit of a predicament. The school in Alabama was going to start on schedule, and leaking head gaskets would not justify my being AWOL. I could get the Model A out of storage, but there was at least an outside chance that it might not make it to Alabama without suffering some sort of mechanical malady, and that would leave me with two dead cars between Yodersburg and Alabama and still no way to get to the school on time. I had the $350 I'd gotten for selling the Colt, and I could afford to kick in a little extra so I turned to Luis and said "I would like the best transportation $500 will buy."

Luis had just the car. It was a 1971 Ford Pinto hatchback with blue over rust coachwork. The Indiana road salt had done its customary work on the fenders, in fact there was about a three inch gap on the left rear fender between the point where the body ended and a stainless steel trim strip that marked the point where it had originally ended.   On the plus side, it had the optional 2-litre overhead cam engine. This ran great and provided enough oomph so that the car didn't feel horribly underpowered. The tires and suspension were good, and the manual gearbox made it almost fun to drive. It also had a pair of "eyeball" vents on the dash that provided fresh, cool air even when the heat was on – a feature I wish I could get on modern cars. All in all, I could have done a lot worse. I was about to drive it out of the shop when Luis waved me to stop.

"Look at that fender" he said, pointing to the giant gap between the body and the trim strip. "I can't let you go out looking like that!" Luis grabbed a roll of metal tape from the body shop, the kind that's generally used to seal furnace ductwork. In about two minutes he had neatly filled the gap with metal tape, masked the trim strip, and sprayed the tape with blue Rust-Oleum paint. He peeled off the masking and - I'll be damned if that fender didn't look a whole lot better than it did before. It wasn't going to win a trophy at the Pebble Beach Concours d'Elegance, mind you, but it was better than a gaping hole. I thanked Louis and proudly drove off in my new winter rat. Over the next few years that Pinto would prove to be excellent transportation. It looked like an escapee from a demolition derby, but it always started in the morning, it got good gas mileage, and it was economical to maintain. Late in its life it would develop an annoying habit of popping its headliner down against my head whenever I drove it over 50 mph – I assume some inner panel had rusted away and was allowing air to rush up into the space above the headliner – but once I slowed down again I could pop the headliner back into place.

After a quick side trip to spend New Year's Eve with Don I drove to Maxwell Air Force Base in Montgomery Alabama. Montgomery turned out to be a much nicer town than I'd expected. (Growing up in Indiana I had a lot of mistaken stereotypes about the Deep South. The mayor of Montgomery didn't help matters much when he gave the keynote address to our class. He reminded us that Montgomery was in a different time zone so we all needed to set our watches back. "About a hundred years ought to do it" he suggested.) Squadron Officers' School was about as interesting as any school that alternates sitting in lectures with running laps can be. I've never been much for organized calisthenics – too many bad memories of boredom, sweat, and foul smells in my high school Phys-Ed class – so I really appreciated having the Pinto. It provided me with a means of escape on weekends so I didn't go stark, raving mad in the SOS barracks. I couldn't afford to leave every weekend, as there was too much homework for that, but the ability to get away every once in a while helped me stay on an even keel. When the SOS class was over I pointed my Pinto north and took off for Rome NY. On the way, I stopped in South Carolina and spent the night with Nick Riccotto and his wife Kerri. We reminisced about old times, bored Kerri to tears with car stories and, true to form, made a service call to help a friend of Nick's whose car wouldn't start. Nick had an ancient Jeep Wagoneer with two tool boxes and a mountain of junk parts in the back, so we left my Pinto in the driveway and took his Jeep to rescue his friend. While we were out, Kerri decided to make a quick run to the grocery store.

Kerri was one of those drivers who has trouble backing up. The week before she had backed into an oak tree that had somehow moved closer to the driveway than she expected. The tree didn't seem bothered by the impact and the damage to the car was minimal, but Nick had given her a hard time about it so this time she was focused on missing the oak tree. Predictably, she missed the tree and backed into my Pinto instead. Actually, she barely grazed the rear fender, but since that was the fender Luis had put together with tape the damage looked catastrophic. From her perspective, the entire fender crumpled and fell onto the driveway. A lone strip of chrome hung in mid-air, marking the spot where the fender had once lived. When Nick and I got back Kerri was on the verge of hysterics. We calmed her down as best we could. I let her examine the tape to prove she hadn't hit a real fender, and I even straightened the tape out as much as possible and patted it back into place. She didn't seem totally convinced by my assurances that it was "as good as new," but at least she stopped sobbing. I'm not sure she ever backed a car again, though. The next day I resumed my trip to New York. After a few days reliving old times at Griffiss I headed to my next assignment at Hurlburt Field, Florida.

Hurlburt Field is located near Ft Walton Beach, on the Florida panhandle. Originally it was an auxiliary field for the huge Eglin Air Force Base complex. During World War Two Jimmy Doolittle used Hurlburt Field to practice launching B-25s off a strip of pavement the size of an aircraft carrier. That stretch of pavement was named "Doolittle Strip" and had been proudly maintained ever since. Hurlburt had always hosted unusual missions like this, and when I was there it housed several Special Operations helicopter and C-130 Gunship squadrons. I didn't know or ask much about what those folks did, as most Special Operations were classified. One mission did, sadly, become all too public. The entire base went into mourning in 1980 when a mid-air collision at Desert One scuttled the attempt to rescue the hostages in Iran. The aircraft and aircrew that were lost came from Hurlburt.

I worked on the other side of the base, far away from the Special Operations squadrons, in an unrelated unit called RED HORSE. RED HORSE was a mobile engineering construction and repair team organized to go anywhere in the world and set up an emergency airfield on 24 hour notice. There were only a few RED HORSE squadrons left. They were formed during Vietnam, when the Air Force needed construction teams with heavier equipment and more construction skills than a standard Civil Engineering squadron could supply. The reason these skills weren't available in normal CE units dated back to 1947, when Congress split the Air Force off from the US Army and made it a separate branch of the military. Depending on your point of view, there was either a rational attempt at consolidating services or successful lobbying by the Army and the Navy, but the net result was that the Air Force was not given its own engineering corps. The Army and the Navy already had engineering corps capable of managing large construction projects, so Congress dictated that these existing corps would handle all major Air Force construction. The Air Force would only have a small maintenance force to take care of the buildings the Army and the Navy built for it. The Air Force was never entirely happy with this arrangement, but they made do with it until Vietnam. Suddenly, the Air Force was faced with the need to quickly turn jungle into airfields and repair those airfields when they got damaged by enemy attacks. Unfortunately, the Army and the Navy were faced with similar requirements, and after they committed troops to their projects there never seemed to be enough engineers left over to help the Air Force. The Air Force responded by creating RED HORSE – Rapid Engineering Deployable Heavy Operations Repair Squadron Engineers. I strongly suspect this was an acronym that someone made up first, and then figured out what the letters stood for. Note that while the second "Engineers" may be redundant, it's not unimportant as otherwise the units would have been known as the RED HORS. In any event, RED HORSE units were designed to provide the Air Force with a mobile engineering capability to meet its wartime needs. Sometimes they managed to stretch the Congressional intent of "maintenance and repair" as far as it could go, to the point of repairing buildings that hadn't existed before the repair, but they got the job done. After Vietnam a few RED HORSE units were retained to be ready for the next contingency. We could martial a pretty impressive amount of equipment in a very short time. I was assigned to an engineering survey team that could be airborne with weapons, vehicles, tents, food, and engineering supplies within 12 hours of notification. To keep our construction skills sharp we traveled all over the Eastern half of the US and occasionally overseas to repair airfields, build roads, erect temporary buildings, and do other construction projects that were similar to the type of work we might be involved in during a war. As a young, single officer I thought RED HORSE was just about the best assignment I could imagine.

From an Engineering standpoint, RED HORSE gave me an opportunity to design and execute several small construction projects in the southeastern US. From an automotive standpoint, RED HORSE gave me an opportunity to drive to these construction sites, as well as to training courses in nearby states. I didn't want to be stuck driving my Pinto on all these road trips, so I needed to find a place to live that had room for my other cars. Ideally, I wanted a one bedroom apartment with a three car garage. Better make that a five car garage. It's nice to have a little working space.

I discovered early in my apartment hunting that I probably wasn't going to find a place that met all of my expectations. There were a few closed gas stations on the market which I briefly considered. Lots of parking space. A spacious two-bay garage with hydraulic lifts. Two bathrooms, and a panoramic view out the front window. But, there were no kitchen facilities and privacy was only available in the store room. Besides, I was a bachelor and had fantasies of perhaps occasionally inviting a young lady over for dinner. I didn't know for certain, but I suspected they might have reservations about dining beneath a Texaco sign. I decided perhaps it was best to look for a more conventional abode, even if it did mean sacrificing garage space.

At that time housing prices in the Florida panhandle were pretty low, and I eventually found a small two bedroom ranch house which I could afford to rent. It looked pretty sparse with my furniture (visualize a spacious dining room and eat-in kitchen with a single chair and a TV tray) but that didn't matter because it had an attached garage and enough driveway space to park the cars I wasn't working on. As it turned out, the time I had to work on cars was severely limited by my work schedule. RED HORSE kept me hopping. One year I celebrated the Fourth of July in a tent in the Sahara desert, about 40 miles west of Cairo. Looking back, I realized that since Christmas I had spent 5 weeks in my house in Florida. The rest of the time I had been deployed on training exercises, emergency construction of a tent city for Cuban refugees, attending Air Force training courses, and overseeing RED HORSE construction projects.

As an example of the types of projects RED HORSE got involved in, I had an opportunity to "repair" an abandoned SAC Alert Facility at MacDill AFB (near Tampa Florida) and turn it into a headquarters facility for the newly created Rapid Deployment Joint Task Force. This new force was being formed at the direction of the President (or, in military jargon, the POTUS – President of the United States.) The Secretary of Defense toured MacDill AFB with dozens of generals from all three services to approve the site. I received orders to travel to MacDill overnight to participate in a preliminary planning conference. At the conference I got a rough idea of the scope of work – how much carpentry work, how much electrical work, etc. – and then I flew back to Hurlburt to begin assembling a team while the base frantically began to design the project. We would wind up building it while they were still working on the design.

The RDJTF headquarters also gave me an opportunity to observe how a bureaucracy functions. The President had ordered the headquarters to be built ASAP and the Secretary of Defense (SecDef in military jargon) and dozens of generals were scrambling to make this happen. Unfortunately, somewhere deep in the bowels of the Pentagon the clerk who was supposed to give us the account number we needed to charge our expenses hadn't been told this was an urgent project. Or maybe he just didn't care. In any event, he stuffed our paperwork into his "to do" pile along with hundreds of other projects which needed to be pondered, prioritized, scrutinized, Simonized, and otherwise processed in the fullness of time. My crew sat with their bags packed for over two weeks waiting for the funding to be approved. Finally a three star general managed to break through the logjam and give us the clearance we needed to deploy. (Actually, he didn't really break the logjam in the Pentagon. He just told the Accounting folks at our base "I don't care what account you charge it to, just get that team to MacDill! We'll figure out how to pay for it later!!)

I had similar experiences with the base personnel at MacDill. Most people bent over backwards to help us. We were given all the materials we needed, tools, vehicles – all on the basis of "take it now and we'll figure out how to pay for it later." Then there was the sergeant at the Base Photo Lab. I had a camera with me on the project and I took pictures to document the work we were doing. When I finished the first roll of film I asked my NCOIC (Non-Commissioned Officer in Charge – the senior sergeant who served as my right-hand man) to drop it off to be developed at the Base Photo Lab while he was coordinating supply issues in the same building. He came back in a foul mood. He had no problem obtaining the thousands of dollars' worth of materials we needed. That was mere child's play to a good NCOIC. His foul mood was due to the fact that the sergeant who ran the Base Photo Lab refused to develop the film because he didn't have the correct paperwork. I had to write a letter appointing my NCOIC to be the "Unit Audio-Visual Coordinator" and we both had to sign a "signature verification card" – he signed it at the top to supply them with a copy of his signature and I signed it at the bottom to verify that his signature was authentic. Once we had the paperwork filled out, they developed my pictures.

Overall, the project was a success. We turned what had essentially been a dormitory into a headquarters facility in three weeks, complete with high security vaults, briefing rooms, and offices for three generals and a bevy of lesser beings. It wasn't the finest craftsmanship I have ever seen, but it was functional. (When you're working seven days a week to meet a deadline, sometimes you have to settle for functional.) Late in the project my NCOIC asked for an afternoon off to help hang a drop ceiling in a local church. How he had found time to even locate a local church was beyond me, but apparently he had spent what little off-duty time he had helping them fix up their church. Naturally I gave him the afternoon off, and after he left I walked to the Base Photo Lab to drop off my last roll of film. To my consternation, the sergeant behind the counter wouldn't accept it because I wasn't the Unit Audio-Visual Coordinator. I pointed out that I was the one who had signed the letter appointing my NCOIC to that position. To me it seemed only logical that if I had the authority to do that, I should have the authority to drop off film myself, but it was no use. I had apparently run into a twin brother of the troglodyte in the Pentagon who had held up our funding. I realized that logic and common sense were not going to win this argument. Suddenly it dawned on me that if I ignored common sense I could use his own bureaucratic rules against him. It was almost as though I could hear the voice of Obi-wan Kenobe saying "The Farce, Steve. Use The Farce!" I looked at the sergeant and asked "Can I borrow a typewriter?"

The sergeant pointed to a typewriter so I sat down and typed out a letter appointing myself as the Assistant Unit Audio-Visual

Coordinator. I then signed the letter as the deployed unit commander. I asked for a blank signature card, and when he gave it to me I signed the top line to give him a copy of my signature and I signed the bottom line to verify that the top signature was authentic. I handed the letter and the signature card to the sergeant. He studied them to make certain everything was in order, and then he carefully filed them in the correct folder and accepted my film. The Farce can have a strong influence on the bureaucratic minded.

In between construction projects I slowly managed to reassemble my fleet. The first car to join the Pinto in Florida was my MGA. Riccotto's had given it a "ring job" and it was ready for me to pick it up. By chance the Air Force sent me to a three week school in Ohio, and I was able to pick up my MG during that school and drive it back to Florida.

By the time I got back from that trip, my Guam MG had arrived at the port in New Orleans. Chris, my boyhood friend from the lake, lived nearby in Pensacola Florida and he offered to drive me to New Orleans to pick it up. I don't think he knew what he was getting into. The trip there was pleasant enough. Chris had a Datsun 510 that provided reliable, if not elegant, transportation and it quickly chewed up the miles. The docks in New Orleans weren't quite as picturesque as the French Quarter, but we found my car without any trouble. I was happy to see the car had survived the trip unscathed. (That imitation Cobra nose was scathing enough for any vehicle.) We were on the road headed back to Florida by lunchtime. Unfortunately, a few months rest hadn't done my clutch any good whatsoever. It was slipping as bad as it had on Guam, and as we baked in the afternoon sun the slipping got worse and worse. Eventually, 55 mph was the top speed of my MG. I could press on the gas and rev the engine faster, but the clutch was just barely strong enough to push the car against the wind resistance at 55. Giving the car more gas only served to make the clutch slip more, the speed stayed at 55 mph. Worse still, there were long stretches where I-10 was not yet finished and we were forced to drive on secondary roads with lots of stoplights. The clutch didn't like to get the car moving from a dead stop. I soon learned to watch the lights on the cross street. When the cross street light turned yellow, it was time to let up on the clutch and very gently try to give the car a little gas. Nothing happened at first, but by the time the light turned red for the cross traffic, our light turned green, and the cars ahead of me moved out of the way the

MG would begin to roll forward. With luck I could make it through the intersection before the light turned red again. Needless to say, I was not very popular with the drivers behind me.

The afternoon dragged by as we inched across Louisiana, Mississippi, and a corner of Alabama, but at least we were moving. Then, when we were back in Florida and just about 30 miles from the end of our odyssey, the tailpipe started belching blue oil smoke. The engine was still running so I hadn't thrown another rod, but I figured as a minimum I had burned a hole through the top of one of the pistons. This was definitely not the type of malady that heals itself, and for once I decided discretion was the better part of valor. I let Chris tow the MG the rest of the way.

Once I got the MG back in my garage, I pulled the engine and gearbox out and began a major rebuild. At this point, though, I wasn't rebuilding it for myself. As much as I liked my MGA, I really didn't need two of them. On the other hand, this "Guam Bomb" MG was actually in pretty good shape – the distorted nose job notwithstanding. What if I sold it and then something happened to my '57 MG? All it would take would be an inattentive moment by an idiot driver (not me, of course) and I could find myself without an MG. I knew I'd never find a better deal on another MGA than the one I had sitting in my garage. My solution was to put it into "rolling storage" with my younger brother Jack. He had recently turned 16 and I was pretty sure he'd be thrilled to drive this car to high school if I could get it fixed up. I could loan the car to him until he was through college, found a job, and spent a couple of years getting settled financially. Then, if he still liked the car and my MG was still hanging in there, I could sell it to him. Until then, he'd have free transportation and I'd have a backup.

I had planned on discussing this idea with my parents the next time I was home on leave, but Jack pre-empted me. I barely had time to set down my bags before he started asking me what I was going to do with the MG. That speeded up my timetable a bit, but I was able to fend off his questions until I'd had a chance to discuss it in private with my folks. They thought it was a great idea, he was excited about it, and everybody was happy. There was one detail I didn't tell him about, however. I wanted it to be a surprise. I got the idea for this surprise while I was working on his MG engine on a hot summer day in Florida. I was carrying the engine block across the garage when I stepped in something slippery and nearly threw my back out trying to catch my balance. I looked to see what I had slipped on and was disgusted to see it was a puddle of my own sweat. Florida gets pretty hot during the summer, and working in a non-air conditioned garage isn't as much fun as you might think. I had the garage door opened all the way trying to get some air, and that's how a traveling MGA parts salesman saw I might be interested in his wares. I'd never met a traveling MGA parts salesman before. Never met one since, for that matter. But on this particular day a man stopped his car at the end of my driveway, rolled down his window, and shouted "How'd you like to buy some MGA parts?"

It turned out he had once planned on buying an MGA himself, and had given a man a $100 deposit on an MGA and assorted spare parts. He picked up the spare parts when he made the deposit, but when went back to pick up the vehicle he discovered a minor discrepancy on the title. Neither the vehicle ID number nor the engine serial number matched the numbers on the title. The seller claimed this was just an irrelevant detail. He said most old cars didn't match the numbers on their title, but this buyer was smart enough not to fall for that. He refused to buy the car. This made the seller mad, and he refused to give back the deposit. The buyer then refused to give back the spare parts and they parted company, not exactly on the best of terms. I believe their good-byes may have been punctuated with irrelevant references to ancestry and matriarchal incest. In any event, the gentleman in my driveway now had a garage full of spare MGA parts which he was willing to part with for the amazingly low price of $100. I followed him to his garage and discovered he had fenders, doors, a hood, a trunk lid, a nose section, a spare engine and transmission, and numerous other parts, all in good condition. It was easily worth $100, and as he helped me haul it back to my house I realized I now had all the body pieces I needed to get rid of that damned imitation Cobra nose and make my spare MG look like an MGA again. All that I needed was a body shop.

Finding the right body shop isn't easy. There are lots of body shops that specialize in accident repairs. If somebody crumples a fender on a new car, they can bolt on a new fender and paint it so it looks as good as new. What's more, they can do the work in less time than the insurance companies think it should take, which is how they make their money. They're not interested in working on old cars, though. Dealing with rust, unavailable parts, and unknown paint colors takes time, and their focus is on getting a car in and out in as little time as possible. There are also repaint shops that offer $99.99 specials. They can spray a car in no time and when they're finished the car is incredibly shiny. Fenders, hood, bumpers, dents, rust, and bugs – everything's shiny when they get through with it. I didn't want that kind of a body shop.

If you look hard enough, you can still find a true craftsman. Someone who takes pride in his work. Someone who truly understands old cars and will lovingly hand sand every square inch of the bodywork, weld in new metal to get rid of all the rust, use lead instead of bondo, and slowly build up layer after layer of hand-rubbed lacquer until the car looks like it's been poured from a vat of liquid color. These craftsmen do incredible work, and they charge incredible prices. I didn't want a craftsman, either. What I wanted was a hole-in-the-wall body shop with piles of dust in every corner and a body man who was good at everything except estimating how long a job would take. The kind of place that will promise to finish your car in a week and then devote the next two months to swearing about how much money they're losing on that @#%$# MG you dragged into their shop. Fortunately I found such a shop.

Tucked away in a remote corner of the industrial part of town was "Florida Sports Cars," a used car dealer/garage/parts supplier/body shop run by a tall, slightly dishonest looking man named Jerry. I'm not certain exactly what it was about Jerry that made me suspicious of him. He was exceedingly polite, with a soft patrician southern accent, and a style of speech that smoothed away any potential problem. Maybe it was his speech that aroused suspicion. It was a little too smooth. It didn't help that he cast these elegant airs while wearing greasy blue jeans and a torn gray t-shirt. Something about him reminded me of "Honest John," the fox who sweet talks Pinocchio into skipping school and going to Pleasure Island instead. I instinctively knew I'd have to watch him like a hawk, but I also knew he was just about perfect in terms of fitting my needs – if he was any better I wouldn't have been able to afford him, and if he was any worse I wouldn't have wanted him to touch my car.

There were perhaps three or four other people who worked in the shop. It was hard to tell exactly how many, because except for the proprietor I never saw the same person in the shop twice. There was absolutely nothing about this shop that gave me confidence in their ability to repaint my MG except that (a) I'd seen some of the body work they'd done and it looked pretty good, and (b) they promised that for $500 they could have the car done in a week. We shook hands on the deal, and I spent the next two months pestering them about the car while listening to them swearing about how they were losing money hand over fist on that @#%$# MG I dragged into their shop. When they were finished, though, the car was a thing of beauty. Not a concours restoration, of course, but infinitely better than the Cobra-nosed abomination I'd dragged into the shop. I had to redo all the wiring when they were finished, but that wasn't a surprise. For some reason body men always wire the tail lights into the windshield wiper switch and take other novel approaches to electricity. A few nights cursing over a wiring diagram put things right. My younger brother was thrilled with the results, especially so since I'd sent him pictures of the Cobra-nosed MG on Guam and he thought that's what the car would look like when he got it.

I delivered the car to Jack the next time I went home on leave, and my plan for the return trip was to rent a car and a trailer to tow the Model A back to Florida. The only problem was that nobody would allow me to use a rental car to tow a trailer. They all insisted I needed something capable of pulling more than 4,000 pounds. I tried to explain to them that the Model A weighed less than 3,000 pounds when it was brand new, and that much of that weight had already rusted away. Unless I was accelerating at 1-1/2 G's I would be well under the 4,000 pound limit, but they were unconvinced. I guess they never studied physics. The problem wouldn't have been so frustrating except that the cost of renting a truck one-way to Florida was more than the Model A was worth. Once again, Riccotto's came to my rescue. I called Luis and asked him if he had any tow cars on the lot, and he fixed me up with a 1970 Ford LTD station wagon for $500. It was green, with fake wood paneling on the sides, and a monster V-8 that could have towed five Model A's with ease. I thought it looked and drove like a barge, but my mom claimed it was the nicest car I'd ever owned. I guess fake wood paneling is more attractive than I thought, because as soon as I got the Model A to Florida a co-worker paid me $500 for the LTD. I never even got a chance to wax that car, let alone put a "for sale" sign in the window.

My brother's car had looked so nice when Florida Sports Cars got through with it that I decided to take my MGA to them for some paint

212

& body work. I was about to leave for Egypt to set up an encampment for the first joint US/Egyptian air exercise since Sadat had kicked the Russians out of Egypt. (The deployment was originally supposed to be a secret, but somebody forgot to tell that to the Base Public Affairs Office and he publicized it in the newspaper and the local TV station.) I would be gone for about a month, which they assured me would be plenty of time to paint my car. It turned out they needed much more time than that, of course, but that didn't surprise me. I didn't expect they'd finish it in a week. What did surprise me was that it was plenty of time to steal my engine. Perhaps "steal" is too strong a word. It was plenty of time to "exchange" my engine. I got a heads-up that something was amiss even before I returned from Egypt because Chris had stopped by the shop while I was gone and he noticed the car was sitting in a suspiciously nose high attitude. He opened the hood and the engine bay was empty. Jerry quickly explained that one of the body men had started it up to move it one day, revved it before the oil pressure built up, and spun a bearing. They, of course, accepted full responsibility for this unfortunate incident and were rebuilding the engine for me.

When I returned from Egypt and visited the shop Jerry hastened up to me and told me the same story. I had never heard of an MGB engine spinning a bearing before, but I held my tongue. It was only when I opened the hood and looked into the engine compartment that I felt I ought to say something. "That's not my engine" was what I said.

"Are you sure?" Jerry replied hopefully. "All MG engines look pretty much alike."

"Look" I said. "I've owned this car for 10 years. I rebuilt the engine myself. It was a five main bearing engine. This is a three. I repainted the engine MG red. This engine hasn't been painted since it left the factory. I rebuilt the carbs and they were spotless. These are so filthy I'm surprised the car even runs."

By this time a man who appeared to be a mechanic had walked up to us and was standing beside the Jerry. They looked at each other for a long moment, and then Jerry spoke. "You know, we were rebuilding two MGB engines at the same time, weren't we Mike?"

Mike nodded "yes" enthusiastically.

Jerry continued in his 'conversation' with Mike. "Remember how we sent them both to the machine shop at the same time? I guess we must have just gotten them mixed up when they came back."

Mike continued to do his bobble-head impersonation while Jerry turned to me and continued speaking. "I'm afraid Mike put your engine into an MGB we sold to a lady from Alabama." Mike slowly stopped nodding when he realized he was being blamed for the 'mistake.' Jerry tried a more positive approach. "This is a real good engine, though, isn't it Mike?"

Jerry shifted his focus back to me. "Everything checked out fine on this engine. You know, the only reason they went to five main bearings was for the factory race cars. The three bearing engines rev quicker."

Mike resumed his enthusiastic nodding. By this time I was pretty sure I knew what had happened. They had an MGB they were trying to sell, but the engine was bad. Then somebody wanted to buy the car, maybe it really was a lady from Alabama, but they wanted it right away. It takes time to rebuild an engine, so they pulled my engine, put it in the MGB, and sold it. Then they rebuilt the engine that had been in the MGB and put it in my car, hoping I'd never notice the difference. My engine was long gone, probably out of state. I could see that this engine had new gaskets throughout, so probably they were telling the truth about rebuilding it.

"I had 10:1 pistons in my car," I said, "and a factory half-race cam. I also had ported and polished the head, shot peened the rods, balanced everything, and generally fixed it up pretty nice."

Jerry and Mike exchanged another long look, this time with an "Aha!" expression. Jerry then uttered what was probably the first 100% truthful thing he had said all day. "I guess that's why we never could get it to idle right." There was just a moment's hesitation while he processed this new information and tried to find a way to turn it to his advantage. "This engine will get better gas mileage" he said hopefully.

The gas mileage was a smoke screen, but he had touched upon one point in favor of the substitute engine. When the MGB was new, the owner's manual cautioned the driver to always use a good grade of petrol of octane 98 or better. That was overstating things a bit, but when I put the high compression pistons and the hot cam in my car I discovered the engine would ping like mad if I didn't use premium gasoline. ("Pinging" is a slang term for premature detonation. Hot spots on the cylinder head can ignite the gas/air mixture before the spark plug fires, causing a loss of power and a noise that sounds like someone is dropping loose nuts and bolts into your engine. High compression engines are especially prone to pinging, and if allowed to continue it can burn holes in the pistons.) A few months after I rebuilt my engine the Arab oil embargo began, and the quality of gasoline began to plummet. I soon found I had to use "super-premium" gasoline to keep my engine from pinging. Then stations stopped carrying super premium, and for a while Sunoco 260 was the only gas that would work in my car. When Sunoco stopped selling 260 I couldn't find any gas that my car liked. I tried octane boosters, but they didn't seem to help. The only thing I could do was to back off the throttle whenever the engine started pinging. This sort of defeated the whole purpose of having a high performance engine. To make matters worse, new cars required unleaded gas and more and more gas stations were dropping leaded gas altogether. My MG really didn't like unleaded gas. I had been wrestling with this problem for years, with my rational side knowing I really needed to rebuild the engine again and go back to stock pistons while my emotional side refused to give up those beautiful forged aluminum wedge top racing pistons. Now the decision had been made for me. I began to feel sorry for that lady in Alabama, who never would know why her engine pinged so badly.

I didn't let Florida Sports Cars off the hook completely, of course. To make up for "losing" my engine they gave me all kinds of new and used parts to spruce up my MG, and they knocked a bit off the bill for the paint job. I checked the engine out very carefully, and every test I did convinced me they really had rebuilt the engine, and had done a good job of it. Actually, that engine is still in the MG today, and after 25 years of hard driving it's still going strong. The shop may have been run by a sleaze ball, but he gave me a good engine and a good paint job.

Now that I had my "family" back together again, life was pretty good. I used the MGA as my daily driver whenever the weather was nice, which in Florida was most of the time, and drove the Pinto when the weather turned crummy. I saved the Model A for special occasions, dates, or just taking a drive in the country. My job with

RED HORSE gave me plenty of opportunities to take the MG on long drives. Ohio, Tennessee, North Carolina, South Florida – we covered a lot of territory together. Sometimes we baked under the cloudless skies, sometimes we drove through rain so heavy I was afraid it would rip the top to shreds, and occasionally we froze. Growing up in the North, it never occurred to me that it could get cold down South. I was surprised to discover that the temperature really did drop down into the teens, or colder, below the Mason-Dixon line. It wasn't as cold as upstate New York of course, but it was cold enough. Especially if you weren't dressed for it. And most especially if you had the top down. I particularly remember a drive to Goldsboro North Carolina one cold November day. It was sunny and moderately pleasant when I set out, but as day passed into night it got colder and colder. By nightfall I was climbing into the mountains of North Carolina, which didn't help things a bit. I had been on the road for about 12 hours, I still had several hours to go, and I was freezing my butt off. I was actually starting to contemplate the unthinkable – pulling off to the side of the road and putting up the top. It wasn't raining, which was my standard criteria for putting up the top, but it was damned cold. Then I rounded a curve and beheld a scene of exquisite beauty. I saw a grassy meadow, with a pond, and an old broken down barn. Everything was covered with frost that glinted silver in the moonlight. A full moon hung low over the mountaintops, and its mirror image shown up at me from the pond. Beyond the barn lay endless hills and valleys, all bathed in silver moonlight. I forgot the cold, I forgot the hours of monotonous driving, and just stared at this beautiful landscape. Somehow, this made the whole trip worthwhile. I felt at one with this scene, in a way I never could have had I been cooped up in a tintop car. I could have peered out the window at it, but the window would have been a barrier and I never would have seen the full 360 degree majesty of it. I wouldn't have seen the stars overhead, shining brightly amid a jet black sky. I wouldn't have "felt" the awesome silence of the hills. For that matter, I might not have noticed the scene at all. I might have just sat hunched over the steering wheel, radio blaring, heater blasting warm air in my face, and cursed at the number of miles I still had to go while I swished past an old dilapidated barn. With the top down, however, I experienced a scene of such breathtaking beauty that it has remained with me ever since. I drove the rest of the way to Goldsboro feeling warm and contented with life.

Chapter 18 – A Different Breed of Cat

Life was good in Florida. I had my MG and my Model A together again, and I had a rusted out Pinto for my foul weather car. I was getting great experience working construction projects with RED HORSE, and my good friend Chris lived nearby in Pensacola. It seemed like I had everything I could ever want. Then one day while I was home on leave my younger brother Jack told me he'd found a man who had an E-Type Jaguar for sale.

It's nice to have a younger brother who's looking out for you. Maybe someday I can return the favor and help him spend lots of money. I wasn't actively looking to buy another car, let alone a Jaguar, and I certainly didn't need another car. On the other hand, how could I resist an E-Type? Even as a kid with no concept of automobiles I had lusted over Chris's dad's E-Type. Since then I had been given the opportunity to work on them at Riccotto's, and of course if you worked on a car you had to take it out for a test drive afterwards. Imagine a car that weighed about 400 pounds more than my MG, roughly the equivalent of two passengers of mother-in-law proportions, but with three times the horsepower. Now wrap that car in a body that was so sexy that even pictures of it came with a parental advisory. I had to take a look at the car Jack had found.

The car turned out to be a 1964 OTS (Open Two-Seater, a convertible to anyone on this side of the Atlantic) in moderately shabby condition. On the plus side, the car was complete and original, and I particularly liked E-Types from the early sixties. This was a Series One car, with a triple-carbureted 3.8 liter six cylinder engine. Later, as emission controls became more strict, Jaguar would bore the engine out to 4.2 liters. Later still they would replace the six with a V-12, but these later engines were never quite as fast or as responsive as the early sixes. The car had covered headlights, chrome plated wire wheels, and an intimidating array of gauges and toggle switches across the dashboard. It had the Moss gearbox, a somewhat brutal racing transmission that was virtually indestructible but which required careful double-clutching if you wanted to drive it smoothly. It had true bucket seats – shaped like each seat had been individually carved out of a leather hogshead. And of course, it had the low, sleek E-Type body, a car so beautiful that one was put on display at the New York Museum of Modern Art.

On the negative side, this particular Jaguar had evidently led a hard life. The odometer only showed a little over 60,000 miles, but the blue smoke pouring out the tailpipe showed it was time for a rebuild. This engine didn't purr, it clanked. I don't think the car had 160,000 miles on it, but I wouldn't have been surprised to learn the speedometer had been broken for an extended period of time. The body showed typical Indiana rust damage and one of the rear axle traction bars had pulled loose from its rusted mounting, causing some squirrelly handling and an unsettling "thump" just below the driver's seat. The top and the upholstery were worn, the carpet was shot (and wet), and someone had run the windshield wipers with no blades, leaving a deep scratch across the width of the windshield. I believe I may have mentioned one or two of these shortcomings to the owner while we were haggling over the price. I must have played my part pretty well, because at one point Jack took me aside and quietly offered to loan me some money if I needed it to buy the car. That was a very thoughtful offer, especially so because Jack was still in high school and didn't have a whole lot of spare cash. I've never forgotten it. In any event, I gradually convinced the owner that my offer was a more realistic representation of the car's true worth than his asking price, and I bought the car for $2500. Later I got to thinking back about all the other cars I'd owned in my life and I realized this was the 9'th car I'd ever bought, and it cost more than the first 8 put together.

Even in 1979, $2500 wouldn't buy a perfectly restored Jaguar E-Type. I certainly didn't have a car that I could cruise down to Florida. I had a ratty Jaguar that barely clattered its way to Riccotto's for an engine rebuild. I knew this was going to be required when I bought it, but still it really drove home the fact that Jaguar parts prices aren't quite as gentle as MG parts prices. When I dropped the car off at Riccotto's I suspected the rebuild would cost as much as a small battleship. If I was extremely lucky, I could maybe even get by for the cost of a frigate. I knew Umbarti would do a good job, though, and I wasn't disappointed. In a few months he rebuilt the engine and transmission, welded new repair sections into the floor pan to replace the metal lost to the demon rust, and fitted an enormously strong if not aesthetically pleasing new mounting point for the traction bar. Now the car drove like a Jaguar! I picked it up on my way to a training class in Ohio, and when the class was over it purred all the way to Florida. I watched the tachometer and the odometer religiously, just itching for the day when I would be finished with the break-in period and I could make it snarl once in a while. My common sense as a mechanic and the memory of the rebuild price helped me keep my right foot in check. I was also keenly aware of the fact that this car was capable of speeds that far exceeded any reasonable bounds of safety. According to contemporary road tests the car would see 150 mph, but only a total idiot would see that speed on a public highway. I may have been a cocksure young Air Force officer, but I wasn't an idiot. Or at least, not a total idiot. I felt that I was a pretty good driver, but I had enough experience with old cars to know that being a good driver wouldn't prevent a blowout, or a locked wheel bearing, or any one of a hundred other malfunctions that could ruin your day if you were driving too fast. I also had no way of knowing how talented the driver of the pickup truck just ahead of me was, the one who was thinking about changing lanes without signaling. Or the driver I couldn't see who was about to pull out of a blind side street into my lane. Those drivers had no reason whatsoever to suspect a vehicle might rush up from behind at two or three times the posted speed limit. James Dean was just one of many drivers who proved that point, and I had no wish to wind up dead or responsible for the deaths of others. That's not to say that I was a choir boy who constantly drove at 55 mph, but I recognized the fact that there is a difference between spirited driving and stupidity.

Once I got the car down to Florida, I began to use it as my daily driver. I've never felt I really knew a car until I had driven it on a daily basis, through good times and bad, for a year or two. Part of that time is spent just "sorting out" the car. Fixing all the niggling rattles, erratic instruments, and other minor irritants while fine tuning the engine and suspension until the car feels "right." Part of that time is spent learning the car's character, finding out what its strengths and weakness are. And of course part of that time is spent simply fixing things that break. In the Jag's case what broke was the back window on the convertible top. It was a standard clear vinyl convertible top window – OK maybe it was more crinkly brown than clear – and it cracked lengthwise when I put the top down one morning to drive to work. It was a little chilly that morning, maybe 20 °F, but not cold enough to keep the top up and certainly not so cold that the vinyl should have cracked. I guess it got brittle with age. I checked with a couple of convertible top shops and was astounded to find they wanted over $75 to replace the back window. That was roughly half the price of a complete new top, and it seemed particularly outrageous because it only cost me $15 to buy the clear vinyl I'd used to fix the top on Old Number 12. Actually, $15 bought me more than enough to fix that window. Was it possible there was enough left to fix the Jag top?

It took me a while to find it, but there was indeed enough left over to fix the Jag. Maybe I'm a cheapskate, but I just couldn't see spending $75 to have someone else repair the top when I could do the job myself for free. The only problem was, how could I attach the vinyl to the top? On Old Number 12 I'd sewn the new window in with fish line, but I didn't think that would look appropriate on a Jaguar. I finally decided I'd have to take the top off the car so I could spread it flat on the floor, cut out the old window, glue in the new one, and use weights to hold it down until the glue dried.

My plan worked OK as far as the top was concerned, but when I took the top off the car I discovered the metal top bows were rusted and grungy looking. So, as long as I had the top off anyway, I decided it was a good time to take off the top bows, clean the crud off, and put a nice new coat of shiny black paint on them. That plan worked too, as far as the bows were concerned, but I had to take off several interior trim pieces to get the bows off. That's when I discovered the trim pieces were shot. They were originally made of thin metal and covered with vinyl that matched the leather seats. Over the years the metal had rusted to the point where several of the trim pieces fell apart in my hands as I took out the bows. So, I had to make new trim pieces. To do that I needed vinyl that matched the leather seats, and the more I looked at those seats the more I noticed how worn the leather was. So I took out the seats and found an upholstery shop that was able to replace the leather and rebuild the seats to match the originals. (Finding an upholstery shop that was willing to do that was tougher than it sounds.) That shop was also able to provide me with vinyl that matched the new leather exactly. Of course, while I had the seats out was a good time to replace the carpeting so I ripped out the carpeting too.

As I stared at my gutted Jaguar, I realized this was an ideal time to have it painted. I really wanted to find a craftsman to do the bodywork, but once again craftsmen wanted just a little more than I could spare from my salary as a junior officer. OK, they wanted a lot more than I could spare. When I ruled out the craftsmen, I really, really, REALLY wanted to find a reputable paint and body shop to do the work. None of them would touch it. Finally, in desperation, I turned once again to Florida Sports Cars. Jerry was more than willing to paint my car, and he absolutely double-dog dare promised not to steal the engine while it was in the shop. Reluctantly, I agreed to let him do the work with the warning that I would be stopping by on a daily basis to see how things were going. Of course, you can't do a decent job painting a car with the chrome on, so I took off the bumpers and other trim before I took the car in to the body shop. There was no point in letting these pieces just lie around my garage gathering dust while the car was being painted, so I took them into an electroplating shop to have all the chrome redone.

For a brief period of time my garage was empty and my wallet was full. Then my "stone soup" method of restoration began to catch up with me. The parts started trickling back from the sandblaster, the upholsterer, and the electroplater. My garage began to fill and my wallet began to shrink. In the end, it required a quantity of cash that would have overflowed the Jag's trunk to get all my parts back. But, the results did look nice. Finally the day came when Florida Sports Cars was finished painting my Jag and it looked sharp! Now I could begin the tedious process of putting my car back together again. I'd saved all the carpet and crumbling trim pieces I'd ripped out of the car to use as patterns so I wasn't starting from scratch, but it still took me several months to get everything put back together. Finally the day arrived when all the carpeting was in, all the trim pieces were in, the chrome was bolted back into place, and I had new rubber seals on the doors, windows, hood, trunk, and top. In short, it looked like a brand new car. Except for the top, and that shabby homemade back window. They stood out like a sore thumb. So, I bought a new top and installed it. Now the car looked brand new. As I stood back and admired my handiwork I thought about how much money I'd saved by replacing the back window myself.

Now the car looked and drove like a brand new Jaguar, and my driving impressions were beginning to gel. I had expected the car to drive like a super-MG. After all, it had 2-1/2 times the power of my MG but only weighed about 400 pounds more. It also had fully independent torsion bar suspension, 4-wheel disk brakes with inboard disks on the rear, a limited slip differential, and other refinements to make it handle even better than my MG. After all, this was basically a street version of the racing D-Types that had dominated Le Mans and other high speed circuits in the late 50s and early 60s. To my surprise, however, it didn't drive like the MG. It truly was a different breed of cat. It was much more refined, gliding over pavement imperfections that would have sent the MG bouncing from one pothole to the next. To say it out-accelerated the MG would be a gross understatement, and it also cruised effortlessly at speeds that would leave the MG gasping for air. It had a wide power band so I didn't have to constantly change gears, upshifting or downshifting to keep the engine in a narrow range between "no power" and "shift dammit!" It would stick like glue on a long, high speed sweeper that would have the live-axle MG skidding sideways toward the weeds.

On the other hand, the Jag wasn't as much fun as the MG on a tight, twisting road. It didn't turn as tightly and the gearshift didn't "snick" effortlessly from one gear to the next. It was faster on these roads, but it felt like I was manhandling a big car around a tiny circuit. It also wasn't as much fun as the MG when I was just "bombing around town." I couldn't just toss it into a right angle turn to veer off onto a side street, and it wasn't as adept as the MG at weaving in and out of traffic. I also felt a little self-conscious driving it. Maybe there was a little "reverse snobbery" involved. After all, I grew up in the generation that rejected the materialistic views of our parents and mined the resale shops for torn jeans and faded tops, what my father-in-law referred to as "fake poor people clothes." I may have also been influenced by the time I spent working as a mechanic for Riccotto's, cringing at the doctors and bank presidents who bought brand new Jaguars and then fouled the plugs by puttering around town in fourth gear. Whatever the reason, I felt a little uncomfortable driving a car that people automatically associated with money.

As a kid, I was astounded one day when I referred to a Jag as a "sports car" and Chris corrected me. A Jaguar wasn't a sports car, he informed me, it was a "gran tourisimo" or "grand touring" car. At the time I didn't understand the difference, but now that I had some experience with the Jag I began to understand what he meant. The Jaguar is a grand automobile for touring. Take it out in the country, rocket through a set of sweeping turns along a river bank, or just cruise effortlessly for mile after mile of scenic highways. I absolutely love to drive the Jaguar on roads like that. On the other hand, if I'm going to be driving a narrow mountain road with lots of switchbacks and right-angle turns, or just zig-zagging through city streets to make a Wal-Mart run, I'd rather drive the MG. And if I was going to be driving in an auto-cross I'd pick the MG hands down. The Jaguar is a touring car, not a sports car.

This of course begs the question "what is a sports car?" If you base your answer on car ads, the correct answer is "anything a car manufacturer wants to sell to younger drivers." Certainly the term "sports car" has great marketing appeal. In many ways the concept of a sports car is much more appealing than the reality. Autoweek probably said it best in a review published when Nissan first unveiled the legendary Datsun 240-Z. They said (and I'm paraphrasing from memory because I don't have ready access to 40 year old weekly newspapers) "According to the last census, in the entire world there are exactly 347 honest-to-God, bugs in their teeth, drive it at ten-tenths of capacity sports car freaks. Great Britain has aimed their entire car production for the last 20 years at these 347 buyers. On the other hand, the last census also showed there were over 2 million people in Tulsa Oklahoma alone who wanted a sporty car that was fun to drive at seven or eight-tenths of capacity. Datsun aimed the 240-Z at these buyers." With such a huge market of potential buyers, it's no wonder everything from a 26 hp Crosley Hot Shot to a 5,000 pound Oldsmobile Toronado has been advertised as a sports car. Adding to the confusion, car companies have called their products sport coupes, sport sedans, sports economy, and sports luxury cars in one ad, and then called them a sports car in another ad. Sometimes they don't go quite so far as to call them a sports car, but they will say they have "sports car handling" or a "sports car suspension." Volvo, Porsche, and possibly others have built "sports station wagons." And of course when the car companies discovered male buyers wouldn't be caught dead in a minivan, they made a minivan that was even boxier, added a few "power bulges," and created the Strikingly Ugly Van or "SUV." The marketing folks liked the car but not the name, so they called it a "Sports" Utility Vehicle and sold millions.

So, since anyone can define the term "sports car" to mean whatever they want it to, I feel free to offer my own definition. This definition is based in part on definitions in books like "The Modern Sports Car" written during the "golden age" of sports cars, and in part on my own experience driving sports cars and sports car wannabes. To me, a sports car is a small, open, two-seat automobile designed to be agile and quick. If you don't like this definition, feel free to write your own.

The "small" term in my definition is part of the heritage of sports cars. Most authors agree the sports car originated in England, but they quickly became popular in France, and Italy as well. All of these countries had narrow, winding roads that could only be driven quickly if the car was small. They also tended to have high fuel prices, so buyers appreciated a performance car that would get 35 or 40 mpg. Making the cars small also kept the weight low, and if you want to change directions in a hurry, or change speeds in a hurry, weight is the enemy. Try driving an MG through a tight slalom course and then drive, say, a 1970's Dodge Charger through the same slalom. The Charger is a wonderful car and it handles great on a long sweeping turn, but if you take it through a tight zig-zag course you'll feel the weight fighting you at every turn. How light is lightweight? My own experience is that 2,000 lbs is about the limit for a sports car. This is not an absolute limit, a 2400 lb TR6 definitely feels like a sports car, but as cars get heavier than 2000 lbs they tend to drive more and more like a touring car and less like a sports car. (This is just one of many areas in which I find myself at odds with the majority of car buyers, as modern cars tend to be much heavier than older cars. It seems amazing to me that I have a 50 year old MG with a cast iron engine, a massive steel box frame, heavy gauge steel body panels, and other ancient materials that tips the scales at just under 2,000 lbs, while modern cars with aluminum blocks, unibody construction, plastic body panels, and all the other modern developments weigh hundreds or thousands of pounds more than my MG. Wouldn't you expect them to weigh less? I suspect the answer is not that there's a technical reason for modern cars to weigh more, but that most buyers don't like light cars. I guess I'm just one of the 347 people who actually prefer a sports car to a sporty car, and we're not the ones who are driving the market.)

To me, the fact that a sports car is an open car is a "self-evident truth." Closed cars just don't have the same feel to them, the same devil-may-care freedom of an open car. That's not to say closed cars are not fun. I've driven some really great sport coupes and sport sedans that are a ball to drive, but it's a different feeling. Even my MG feels significantly different when I put the top up. It's fun to drive, but I don't feel the speed like I do with the top down. Plus, if you ever drive in a "sporting event" like an autocross, hill climb, or road race – the kinds of events that gave "sports" cars their name, you'll quickly discover the importance of the extra visibility provided by an open car. Some of the classic books on sports cars go even further in this regard than I do, insisting that only roadsters (front engine cars with side curtains rather than roll-up windows) qualify as sports cars. Side curtains are lighter in weight than roll-up windows, and they don't take up so much space so the doors can be thinner and cut lower, providing the driver with more "elbow room" than a convertible. While I must admit to a preference for roadsters, I don't think the driving experience is different enough to exclude convertibles from the sports car classification. Plus, if you ever get caught in the rain and have to drive with the top up, you'll discover that roll-up windows do offer certain advantages over side curtains. (They don't rattle and they don't leak, or at least, not as much as side curtains do.)

Like the requirement for a sports car to be open, the requirement to be a two-seater is a self-evident truth. This is probably as much a psychological requirement as it is a technical requirement. Yes, cars with a back seat tend to be bigger, heavier, and not as nimble as a two-seater, but that's only part of the story. Let's face it folks. When we fantasize about driving a sports car the fantasy doesn't include dropping the kids off at the orthodontist while you and your spouse shop for a new washing machine. Sports cars are for fast solo drives down a twisting country road, or a romantic drive in the moonlight with your significant other. If the drive is romantic enough you may eventually wind up shopping for an orthodontist, a washing machine, and a car with a back seat, but that's not part of the fantasy.

"Agile and quick" describe the essence of sports car performance. To be agile, a car must not only be capable of impressive cornering performance on a skid pad, it must be able to switch back and forth, changing directions instantly in response to a quick flick of the steering wheel. Sports car drivers live for switchbacks, slaloms, and right-angle turns. Excellent braking is another agility requirement for sports cars. Success in road racing required drivers to be able to wait until the last possible moment before standing on the brakes, reducing the cars speed as quickly as possible, and then diving into a corner. It's no coincidence that disk brakes became standard on sports cars long before they even became options on other cars. Quickness goes hand in hand with agility. A quick car isn't necessarily a fast car, but it's not a sluggard either. Although some sports cars are fast, most of the classic sports cars from the 50's and 60's would barely top 100 mph. (Not that there are many places where you can legally or morally drive over

100 mph.) Although the classic sports cars may not have been fast, they did have very quick throttle response and gear ratios that let you keep the engine operating near its peak power output while accelerating up to, say, 60 or 70 mph. This isn't a particularly desirable trait for cruising down the Interstate, as the classic sports cars will be whining away at an uncomfortably high RPM under these conditions. They're not designed for this. That's what touring cars are designed for. On the other hand, if you're driving a road race, standing on the brake with your toe while your heel "blips" the throttle as you double clutch into a lower gear for a hairpin turn, and then standing on the gas pedal as you accelerate out of the turn, you'll appreciate the quicker gear ratios and throttle response of a sports car.

One attribute I almost included in my definition of a sports car is "inexpensive." While most sports cars are not cheap, they're not megabuck exotic cars either. After careful consideration, however, I decided this was a consequence and not a requirement of a sports car. There's no reason why you couldn't build an exotic, state-of-the-art, astronomically priced sports car. Indeed, there are specialty car builders who do just that. Some Lotus models in particular would seem to fall into this category. The economic reality, however, is that very few of the 347 sports car enthusiasts can afford to buy a machine like that. People who can afford to buy exotic cars want a combination of luxury and speed. In short, they want a gran tourisimo car, but they want to call it a sports car.

OK. That's a very long explanation of why I consider the Jaguar to be a different breed of cat than the MG. Perhaps the ultimate question is, which car do I like best – the Jaguar or the MG? That's a little like asking a parent which child they like best. I like them both. They both have different strengths, different weaknesses, and different personalities. I wouldn't want to give up either one. If you held a gun to my head and presented me with a choice, I could keep one car but you'd take the other, I'd keep the Jaguar. Then after you left I'd sell the Jag, buy another MG, and keep the change.

My 1964 E-Type

E-Type Fascia

Chapter 19 – Piled Higher and Drier

There's an old saying that "Those who can, do. Those who can't, teach." In RED HORSE we definitely fell into the "doers" set. (This is not to be confused with the "Dewar's" set, although we were known to tip a glass from time to time.) I was therefore surprised when, a little over a year into my assignment, I got a call from the Military Personnel Center asking if I would be interested in taking a teaching assignment at the Air Force Institute of Technology (AFIT) at Wright-Patterson AFB Ohio. The Air Force had a continuing education school there for engineers, and they were short of mechanical engineering instructors. I was very familiar with AFIT, as I had been to several of their courses. When I got my engineering degree at Purdue I had a lot of theoretical knowledge about engineering in general, but no practical knowledge. To make matters worse, I had focused on machine design – gears, cams, and levers. I left Purdue feeling I was ready to design race cars, but the Air Force didn't need race cars. They needed mechanical engineers who could design heating and air conditioning systems for buildings. I didn't have a clue what was required to do that. I had never even thought of heating and air conditioning as a "system." Heating was a clanking radiator that lived under a window. Air conditioning was a big box that lived in the window.

I was not alone in my ignorance. (Ignorance causes many problems, but loneliness is not one of them.) Most new engineers didn't have any experience in the kind of practical applications the Air Force needed, especially in the Civil Engineering career field. Electrical engineers, for example, typically studied electronics and microcircuits in college. When they joined a Civil Engineering squadron they would be taken into an electrical substation and shown the giant transformers and copper bus bars carrying, say, 115,000 volts. The bars would literally be humming with the energy that passed through them. "What's that?" they would ask, pointing at one of the bus bars.

"Don't point" their guide would warn them. "Pointed objects, even your finger, concentrate the field lines and can draw an arc. It's best to keep your hands in your pockets." The new engineer would shuffle through the rest of the tour with their hands thrust deep into their pockets, eyes wide open in horror, as they realized none of their courses in digital circuit design were going to help them in this situation. AFIT provided intense post-graduate courses which would give them the education they really needed in a matter of weeks.

I was particularly surprised that the Personnel folks called me about AFIT because, if they followed their own rules, I wasn't even eligible for a new assignment. RED HORSE had such an unusual mission and required so much specialized training that once you were assigned to the Horse you were supposed to stay there for at least three years. Like all bureaucracies the Air Force had rules for everything, and the Personnel system often had two or three rules covering the same thing. When I asked the folks at the personnel center about the three year tour they just laughed. "Oh we can get that waived," they assured me. "The three year tour just means you can't ask to be moved for three years. If we want to move you we have ways to get it done." Somehow that didn't surprise me. The rules were very strict in terms of what I could do, but they were more like guidelines when it came to determining what the Air Force could do to me.

Their offer put me in a quandary. I had a lot of respect for the courses at AFIT and I knew that teaching there was a once in a lifetime experience. On the other hand, so was RED HORSE. I really enjoyed working in the Horse and I wasn't anxious to leave. In the end, I told the personnel center that teaching at AFIT would be a great job and I really wanted them to keep me in mind for that when my RED HORSE tour was up, but I didn't want to leave the Horse early. We hung up, and I thought that was the end of it.

About six months later I got another call from the personnel center. AFIT had created a new faculty position that required an instructor with experience in the Civil Engineering career field and a PhD in Mechanical Engineering. The problem was, nobody in the Air Force had those credentials. There were only a few officers in the CE career field who had Master's degrees in Mechanical Engineering, and I happened to be one of them. Would I be interested in going back to school to earn a PhD in Mechanical Engineering and then teaching at AFIT? As much as I liked the Horse, this was an opportunity I couldn't turn down. I knew that getting the Air Force to pay for a PhD normally involved going through a very competitive selection process, so I asked what I needed to do to submit an application. "Leave that to us," was their reply. "You just find a school that will accept you and we'll take care of getting you into the program." Sure enough, a few weeks later I received an official Air Force letter congratulating me on having been selected for a PhD program, "from among a very competitive field of applicants." I decided I never wanted to get the folks at the Military Personnel Center mad at me.

Now that I'd been accepted into the program, I had to find a school that was willing to accept me into a PhD program. ("Piled Higher and Drier" in academic slang.) Deciding on a school turned out to be fairly simple. I knew the classes I would be teaching involved the design of heating, ventilating, and air conditioning systems, and when I checked the reputations of schools that offered those courses Purdue was at the top of the list. The fact that it was a state school and I was an Indiana resident made the Air Force happy, as that made the tuition very reasonable. The Admissions office was pretty confident I would be accepted based on my existing Purdue grades, which made me happy since it had been almost 10 years since I took my last college class and I had no desire to take entrance exams. And of course I liked the fact that it was close to home. As an added bonus, Don and his soon-to-be-bride Desiree lived in nearby Attica Indiana.

I started to wrap things up in Florida and took a house hunting trip to Indiana. Once again, I was looking for a one bedroom house with a five car garage. This time, however, I was willing to actually consider buying a house, and not just renting. I knew I'd be at Purdue for three years working on my PhD, and the way housing prices were going up I figured I'd better buy my first house soon or I could never afford to enter the market. Alas, whether I was buying or renting, small houses just didn't come with large garages. The houses that had reasonable sized garages were way out of my price range, so I finally settled on a very small two-bedroom house with a one car garage. The house was priced at $35,000, which was a typical price for a small house in 1984. It had a driveway that was long enough to hold all my cars, and wide enough so that I could back any one of the cars out of the driveway without having to move the others. I could put one car in the garage and use car covers on the rest.

Now that I had a place to put them, I began the tedious process of ferrying my cars from Florida to Indiana. I was able to borrow a pickup truck from a friend to tow the Model A, so this time I didn't have to buy yet another car just to transport the "A." Just when I thought I had everything in order, Jerry at Florida Sports Cars dangled a new temptation in front of me.

If you talk to anyone who plays with old cars, they've always got a story or two about "the one that got away." The super good deal they passed up on some exotic machine that is now worth a maximillion dollars. (A variation on this theme is the car they sold for peanuts which now is a fabulous collector's piece.) The part they usually leave out of their story is that, at the time, the price that seems so low today was a perfectly reasonable price for the car. I have lots of similar stories. In 1973 I stood by and watched without bidding at an auction where a beautiful 289 Shelby Cobra sold for $6,000. Later, the new owner changed his mind and tried to re-sell the car, but couldn't even get an opening bid. Today that car would bring hundreds of thousands of dollars, but in 1973 $6,000 was no bargain, which is why the car failed to get a bid the second time through the auction. Also, in 1973 I was a starving grad student and there was no way I could afford to spend $6,000 for a car, no matter how fabulous it was. Back then, my Dad was only paying $2,000 for brand new cars.

The situation with Florida Sports cars was different, however, because this time I had the money, I wanted the car, and the price was a bargain. When I stopped by their shop to collect the final installment of parts they owed me for having stolen my MG engine, they had a beautiful 1953 Jaguar XK 120 roadster sitting on the showroom floor. The showroom lights sparkled off the flawless Old English White bodywork of the Jag, and the gleaming chrome was like a mirror into another world. I don't know whether or not I gasped when I saw it, but in an instant Jerry was standing beside me. "Wouldn't that look nice in your driveway" he said.

"I've already got a Jaguar" I replied, with as much conviction as I could muster.

"That you do" he agreed. "And it's an absolutely beautiful car. An E-type is probably the most desirable Jaguar in the world. Except, of course, for an XK 120."

Jerry was right. The XK 120 was originally designed as a "show car," a one-off dream machine and test bed intended to showcase Jaguar's new "XK" engine. (The same engine that would later, in uprated form, power the E-Type.) The "120" portion of the name came from the car's top speed of 120 mph. It its day, that was faster than any standard production car in the world. William Lyons, Jaguar's founder, intended to use the engine to power a new generation of fast luxury sedans. Luxury sedans had long been Jaguar's bread and butter, as indicated by their advertising slogan of "Grace, Space, Pace." Lyons knew that people expected something sexier than a sedan as a concept car, though, so he commissioned the XK 120 to get their juices flowing. He succeeded beyond his wildest dreams. When the car was first shown at the 1948 London Motor Show he was overwhelmed by people who wanted to buy the car. Always a shrewd businessman, he decided to delay the new sedans for a bit so his factory could put the XK 120 into production.

"You can have this one for $3,000." Jerry continued. "That way you'd have the two finest Jaguars ever built. The body and frame of this one have been completely restored. I've got the rest of it in a back room. All new upholstery, a rebuilt engine, and so many boxes of new parts I haven't even had time to go through them."

XK-120 Jaguar Roadster

Jerry went on to explain that he had acquired the car from a gentleman who, for whatever reason, had not finished the restoration. He didn't know who had done the body and paint, but in his expert opinion they'd done a good job. I thought the fact that Jerry hadn't done it was a point in its favor, but I diplomatically kept that thought to myself. If Jerry was telling the truth about having all the parts, all it would take to complete the restoration was time.

Unfortunately, time was a resource that I was sorely lacking in. I had to move to Indiana long before I would be able to finish the restoration. I had enough of a challenge just moving all the cars I already owned up to Indiana and I didn't want to take on the additional burden of moving a disassembled car – especially since once I got there I would be hard pressed to fit the car and all the spare parts into my one stall garage. It would take me months, if not years, to complete the restoration, and once it was completed I wouldn't want to park it outside in the rain and the snow. That meant my other cars would be condemned to suffer through the long Indiana winters. On top of everything else, there was the fact that I already had two sports cars, one of which was a Jaguar. As beautiful as this car was, I was hard pressed to think of any set of circumstances where I would need to drive an XK 120 instead of one of the cars I already owned. With great reluctance, I told Jerry I'd pass on this one.

A couple of weeks later I stopped by the shop and Jerry told me he'd dropped the price to $2,500. This time I actually looked in the back room at all the boxes Jerry said he had. He was right. Brand new carpeting. A new leather upholstery kit. A spotlessly clean engine, freshly painted, with new gaskets sparkling from every seam. I had another long, soul searching episode, but I came to the same conclusion. I simply didn't have either the time or the space to reassemble this car.

About a week later Jerry called me at work. "I need to sell that car, Steve" he said. "Will you give me 2 grand for it?"

I told Jerry I'd think about it. Even as I hung up the phone the Gods of Reason were battling the Demons of Lust in my brain. I absolutely did not need another car, even a drop-dead gorgeous XK 120 in brand new condition that I could sell for two or three times what Jerry was asking for it. The smart thing to do was to just let it go, and then kick myself for the rest of my life. The battle raged for days. Finally I drove to Florida Sports Cars, just to take another look at it. I still didn't intend to buy it, but maybe. . .

This time Jerry sauntered out of the shop into his tiny showroom. He didn't rush out the way he had the last few times I'd entered his domain. "Should have bought it while you had the chance" he crowed. My heart sank, but my brain rejoiced. "I was about ready to call you and ask you to name your price" he continued.

"I'd have offered you $1,500" I replied. During my agonizing internal debates I'd already established that as the price at which I would have to buy the car.

"I'd have taken it" Jerry said. "I was to the point where I had to sell the car to make payroll. Just as I was getting ready to call you, though, a man walked into the shop and fell in love with that car. 'How much do you want for it?' he asked. 'Do you know what it's worth?' I replied. He looked the car over and said 'It's got to be worth at least $3,500.' I pretended to think about it for a while, and then I said 'I can't put it together for that.' So we worked out a deal. He paid me $3,500 up front for the car, and he hired me to put it together for him. At my normal hourly shop rate, of course." Jerry smiled.

So I didn't get the car. Jerry got more for the car than he was originally asking, and he also got a guaranteed way to meet his payroll for the next several weeks, even longer if "problems" developed. Knowing Jerry, I suspect a few problems did arise.

Once school began, I had very little time to spend on my cars. I had expected a PhD program to be difficult. What I hadn't anticipated was how much I'd forgotten since I got my Master's degree, or how out of practice I was at being a student. From the time I started first grade until the time I completed my Master's program, school was an end in itself. My goal had been to pass the course, not to learn the material. Homework and tests were purely "academic" in that they bore no relation to my life outside of school. A wrong answer was bad because it could detract from my grade, but there were no other consequences to wrong answers. Now that I'd spent several years designing and building things in the real world, I saw things differently. I was studying subjects with a goal to understanding and applying them, not just passing the test. Wrong answers could be devastating because wrong answers could cause bridges to collapse, buildings to topple, or worse yet, projects to go over budget! I felt I was learning more from my classes now than I ever had before, but it was taking me much longer. I didn't just double-check my answers before turning in a test; I double-checked my answers before turning in a homework assignment.

Not only that, I was almost 10 years older than most of the other students in my classes, and a lot had changed during those 10 years. That point was driven home one day when a campus policeman came do the door of my Calculus class and announced there had been a bomb threat on the building. The policeman said he didn't think it was a real threat, but they were going to check it out and in the meantime the students were free to leave the classroom.

"What about me?" the professor asked.

"You can leave too," the policeman assured him. We all began to pack up our books and papers. There was a buzz of excitement in the room. A girl who sat beside me knew that I'd been to Purdue before, and she breathlessly asked me if I'd ever been in a bomb threat before.

"Oh sure." I answered. "Lots of times."

"Really?" she asked. "Did they ever blow anything up?"

"Nah. Somebody threw a smoke bomb in the Armory once, but that was about it."

"The Armory?" She looked confused. "Why would anyone want to throw a smoke bomb in the Armory?"

"They were protesting ROTC" I replied. The puzzled look remained on her face, so I added "This was during Vietnam."

"Oh." Was all she said, but from the look on her face I suddenly realized with sickening clarity that Vietnam was just something she'd read about in history books.

My being older than the rest of the students may or may not have had anything to do with the amount of time it took me to complete my homework, but the fact was I pretty much spent all the time between getting up in the morning to going to bed at night with my nose buried in a textbook. In addition to my regular coursework, I had to pass Area Exams on several engineering topics by the middle of my second year, and I spent many months studying for those exams. (Area Exams are intense tests you need to pass early in a PhD program to prove that you're worthy of enduring the advanced classes needed to finish your degree.) I did, however, take a break every Friday night to go out for pizza with Don and Desiree. I'd come home from class on Friday afternoon, give the house a quick cleaning, and then dive into my homework. As the hours ticked by I'd listen impatiently for the ringing of the doorbell, as that meant I could put my books away and relax for a few hours. Sometimes, if there were no major exams coming up, I could take off Saturday as well, but on Sunday I'd force myself to knuckle down and start studying again.

Desiree worked as an accountant, and from New Year until April 15'th she was pretty busy herself preparing taxes for her clients. She generally worked Saturdays during this period, and sometimes she and Don would spend Friday night at my house. This let her sleep in a touch longer on Saturday morning, as my house was closer to her office than their house in Attica, and it meant Don and I could bum around together on Saturday. One particularly cold winter day we spent a Saturday changing the rear springs on Don's MGB. When I say particularly cold, I mean it. The temperature dropped to 20 degrees below zero that night, which is extraordinarily cold for Indiana. I had a little kerosene space heater in the garage, but there was no way it could keep up with these temperatures. The job was going really slowly because we could only spend a half-hour or so in the garage before we had to come back into the house and thaw out. About 6:30 Desiree called to say that her car wouldn't start. Could we come pick her up?

Since Don's car was disassembled in my garage, we decided to take my Pinto. Sadly, for the first and only time in its life, it refused to start. Next I tried my MG. It wouldn't even turn over. I guess they don't get much 20 below weather in England, and when they do even the British aren't mad enough to try driving a sports car with side curtains. My next choice was the Jaguar. I was surprised that it actually turned over, as that car held 12 quarts of oil and at those low temperatures the oil was the consistency of refinery sludge. Turning over is not the same as starting, however, and although the engine gave a few tantalizing coughs it never quite caught before the battery died. That left the Model A.

The Model A refused to turn over when I pressed the starter pedal, but that wasn't unusual. The battery was pretty old and sometimes the electric starter wouldn't work even in the summer. I grabbed the hand crank and tried to start it by hand. The phrase "stirring peanut butter with a canoe paddle" accurately describes what it felt like to turn that engine over with the hand crank, but it did turn over. After a few cranks it turned over a little easier, and then suddenly it coughed, stumbled for a moment, and then roared to life. Don and I were bundled up so heavily we could barely squeeze into the front seat, but somehow we managed. We wrapped ourselves in the lap robe and started off to rescue Desiree. By this time it was pitch black and the roads were slick with ice. That really didn't matter, because we pretty much had the streets to ourselves. We saw a few people struggling unsuccessfully to start their cars, but everyone else had sense enough to stay indoors. Everyone, that is, except two fools who were challenging the coldest night of the century in a 50 year old car with no heater. (The manifold heater put out very little heat even in the best of times, so that year I hadn't even bothered to bolt it on.) We picked up a very surprised Desiree at her office, had her sit on Don's lap to add a little more heat in the front seat, and chugged our merry way back to the cozy warmth of my house.

A few months later, when it was considerably warmer, I lost an old friend. I was awakened from a sound sleep by what seemed to be the sound of crashing metal. The sound ended before I was fully awake, so I wasn't really certain if I had actually heard something or if it was just a dream. I looked at the clock and saw it was just past 3:00 AM. Everything was quiet, but I thought the noise that I thought I'd heard had come from outside. I sat up and looked out the window over my bed. The streetlights were shining brightly and I could clearly see my front lawn and the street in front of my house. Everything looked normal. There was a railroad track not far from my house, and sometimes I could hear the sound of the boxcars crashing together when a train stopped or started. I convinced myself that was probably what I'd heard and tried to go back to sleep, but something just didn't seem right. Then I realized I hadn't seen my Pinto parked in its normal spot in front of the house. I sat up and looked again. No Pinto. I put on my glasses. Still no Pinto. I looked at my driveway. The MG and the Model A were there, and the Jaguar was in the garage, but there was no sign of the Pinto. Could someone have stolen it? Who would steal a car like that? Even before the tin foil bodywork fell off the big rust hole in the fender this wasn't the type of car that made you think "I want that car so badly I think I'll commit a felony just so I can call it mine." I hurriedly put on a robe and slippers and stepped outside.

Outside everything was quiet and peaceful. The world was asleep. The street lights were shining onto an empty street. All was as it should have been, except my Pinto should have been parked on the side of that empty street. Suddenly, a man ran out the front door of the house across the street and headed for my neighbor's yard. "Is anyone hurt?" he yelled. I looked at my next door neighbor's lawn, and there was my Pinto. It was upside down, lying on its back with four tires pointed at the stars. Like a goldfish floating belly up. Or a dead cow with its hooves stretched toward the sky. Most of all, it looked like a dead blue cockroach, lying on its back with its now useless legs splayed forlornly in the air. A small crowd of neighbors were gathering around it, peering inside to see if anyone was there. I ran over to join them. The back end of the Pinto was mashed in and the skid marks on the curb told the story. Someone had run into the back of the Pinto as it was innocently parked in front of my house. The impact shoved it into the curb and the car that hit it kept moving forward, as the Pinto scraped along the curb for 20 or 30 feet before flipping end over end and landing in my neighbor's yard. There were no skid marks from the other car, so apparently the driver never touched his brakes. He also didn't hang around to leave his name and insurance info, as there was no sign of the other car or its driver. There were broken pieces of his headlight and turn signal lenses on the pavement and great swaths of light yellow paint on my Pinto, but the car itself had vanished.

I called the police and they quickly arrived and put out an "all-points bulletin" to look for a light yellow car with a smashed front end. They also helped arrange for a tow truck to remove my beloved Pinto from the neighbor's yard and haul it off to a junk yard. There was no sign of the other driver that night, but the next day the police received an anonymous tip that led them to a man with a terrible hangover and a smashed-up Oldsmobile. It didn't take them long to match the paint on my Pinto with his car, and his insurance company quickly offered to give me $500 for my car. The driver had an aunt who lived about a block and a half from my house, and the police theorized that after he hit my car he fled to his aunt's house and hid his car in her garage. The next day, when he'd sobered up enough to drive without smashing into parked cars, he drove back to his house. After he left, his aunt phoned in the anonymous tip.

As it happened, my Dad was about to trade in his 1975 Pinto for a new car. His Pinto was in great shape (he'd had it rust proofed when he bought it) but every day he had to make an hour's drive to and from work and he worried that the Pinto was getting a little too old to rely upon. He was more than willing to sell the car to me for the price the dealer was going to give him in trade. He got his new car, I got a dramatically improved winter car, but my old Pinto got a one-way ticket to the car crusher. It was a sad end for a car that had served me faithfully for several years.

That fall my brother Jack started his freshman year at Purdue. For some reason, Purdue had relaxed its policy on cars and freshmen were now allowed to have cars on campus. (Isn't that the way it always works? Younger brothers and sisters are allowed to do all kinds of things we could never get away with. My folks even bought Jack a motorbike, whereas I had gotten yelled at just for putting a baseball card on my bike to make it sound like a motorbike.) Anyway, Jack brought the '58 MGA with him so there were two virtually identical red MGAs running around campus. Jack sometimes joined Don, Desiree, and me for Friday night pizza. He joined a fraternity and soon had a very strange girlfriend with an even stranger ex-boyfriend. (He didn't think she was strange, of course. At least, not then.) Unfortunately, I didn't get to spend a whole lot of time hanging out with Jack because I was up to my neck in preparations for my Area Exams. Calculus, thermodynamics, vibrations – all the fun subjects I'd sweated over 10 years previously were now causing me to sweat at a higher level of abstraction. Finally, at the end of the fall semester, I passed my area exams. It was the best Christmas present imaginable. I still had more classes, a research project, and my dissertation to worry about, but at least I had those damn area exams out of the way. To celebrate I decided to finally fix the rust in the Model A fuel tank once and for all.

The Model A fuel tank sits over the driver's knees. What would be the dashboard on a modern car is the fuel tank on the Model A. It's securely bolted into place – I counted over 140 nuts, bolts, washers, and other miscellaneous hardware that I had to remove from the car and refurbish as part of this project. The steering column bolts to the underside of the fuel tank and needs to be removed to take the tank out. So, as long as I had it out, I rebuilt the steering box. The instrument cluster needed to come out too, so I polished it and had it re-plated in the original nickel finish. I also had to remove the gearshift lever, part of the firewall, and other miscellaneous braces before I could finally drop the tank down and slide it out the driver's door. Once I had it out I took it to a radiator shop to have it boiled out and thoroughly cleaned. I neutralized the remaining rust with phosphoric acid, and then coated the inside of the tank with a special rust preventive glop known as a "sloshing compound." This stuff is well named. You pour it into the tank, plug all the tank openings, and then slosh it around by twisting the tank every way imaginable until every square inch of the inside of the tank is coated with this compound. Once the inside of the tank was sealed, I painted the outside of the tank and began the laborious process of bolting everything back into place. All in all this project took several months (Hey, I had other things to do with my time too!) but the results were worth the effort. For the first time ever I could drive the Model A anywhere I wanted, for as long as I wanted, without ever having to stop and blow rust out of the gas line. The tank was perfect!

A couple of weeks later I was driving the MG home from class when the fuel pump died. This was not a totally new experience. MGs came with SU electric fuel pumps which would basically last forever as long as you put a new set of points in the pump every 12,000 miles or so. Replacing the points is a pain because you need to jack up the car to remove the pump, but it's not particularly difficult. Naturally my pump didn't die where it was convenient to do this. Normally you can just whack the pump a few times with a good solid object such as a hammer, a wrench, a shoe, or a roadside rock and it will chatter back into life long enough to get you home. For some reason that trick didn't work this time, and I wound up buying a gas siphon hose & hand pump from a local auto parts store along with a long piece of fuel line. I stuck the fuel line down into the gas tank through the filler cap, connected it to the siphon hose with the hand pump in the passenger seat, and ran the other end of the siphon hose through my hood vent into the engine compartment and connected it to my carburetors. It was a crude system, but I was able to pump gas by hand and drive the car back to my garage.

As I was jacking the car up to remove the pump I noticed a little bit of gas seeping out of a pinhole leak in the bottom of my gas tank. Another unwelcome development, but not particularly surprising in a car that was nearly 30 years old. I'd have to remove the tank to fix it (fortunately it was much easier to remove than the Model A tank!) but first I had to drain the gas and put it somewhere. I had two small gas cans for lawn mower gas in my garage, but they weren't nearly big enough to hold all the gas in the MG tank. So I siphoned the gas out of the MG into the lawn mower cans and dumped them into the Model A tank. In no time at all I transferred all the gas into the Model A, removed the MG tank, and took it to a repair shop to have the leak welded.

A few days later I decided to take the Model A for a drive. I barely made it half-way down the driveway before the car sputtered to a halt with a sound I knew all too well. The gas line was plugged. How could that be? I had just spent a couple of months fixing that problem! I pulled the gas line off the carburetor and blew back into the gas tank to clear the line. I had to blow much harder than usual, and when I finished my lips were burning. Not the normal tingle that comes from wrapping your lips around a fuel line, but a strong burning sensation. As I reconnected the fuel line a little gas dripped onto my hands and they started burning, too. I went inside and washed my hands and lips thoroughly, but even after I washed all the fuel off they looked red and inflamed. I went back out to the Model A, drained a little gas into a can, and sniffed it. It smelled like hydrochloric acid. I got some baking soda from the kitchen and sprinkled it into the can. It foamed up in a giant geyser – just as if I'd poured it into hydrochloric acid. In an instant I realized what had happened. That idiot ex-boyfriend of my brother's wacky girlfriend tried to sabotage my brother's MG by pouring acid into the fuel tank, only he sabotaged my MG instead because he couldn't tell them apart. That's why my fuel pump died, and that's why my gas tank started leaking. I then compounded the damage by pouring the tainted gas into my Model A, where it loosened the sloshing compound to the point where big hunks of the compound were breaking free and clogging my fuel system. It wasn't doing the gas tank any good, either.

In the end, I managed to clean out the MG and Model A fuel systems to the point where nothing was totally destroyed. I could see where the acid had etched the fuel pump and carburetors, but I was able to rebuild them. I had the MG tank repaired and I was able to flush the loose compound out of the Model A tank, but I didn't have the heart or the time to remove the Model A tank and reseal it. Occasional stops to blow out the fuel line once again became part of my normal driving procedure. The campus police tried very hard to prove that the ex-boyfriend was guilty of sabotaging my car, but they couldn't find any witnesses or definite proof that they could use in a court of law. They analyzed the acid, but it was plain old hydrochloric acid, available in hardware stores all over the city, and there was no way to trace it to him. I was disappointed they couldn't pin it on him, but not vindictive. I figured the guy was probably facing eternity plus two years in Hell anyway. I was pretty sure that anyone who was vile enough to pour acid into an antique car would have already done enough stupid stuff to earn eternal damnation, and I was hoping God would tack an extra two years onto this bastard's sentence for vandalizing my cars. Like I said, though, I wasn't vindictive.

Chapter 20 – True Love

Now that I finally had my area exams out of the way it was time to get serious about my research project. The only problem was, I didn't have a clue what I wanted to research. OK. I had some semblance of a clue because I knew I wanted to focus my research on Heating, Ventilating, and Air Conditioning (HVAC) controls, as that was what I would be teaching in the Air Force. The Air Force, along with most of the civilian world, was having major problems with their control systems. They didn't keep buildings comfortable, and they wasted a lot of energy. Surprisingly, most college courses only touched on this topic briefly, if at all. HVAC controls were pretty much a "black art," understood only by a few specialists who worked for the companies that manufactured control systems. Unfortunately, many of the contractors who sold and installed these systems were not privy to the secret calculations and incantations that actually made them work. That plus an abysmal lack of maintenance led to a bewildering abundance of screwed-up systems, and unlimited opportunities for anyone who actually understood controls. Abner Doble, who designed superb steam cars in the 1920's, once said "Any fool can design a boiler, and most fools can design a steam engine, but it takes a hell of a fool to design a control system." I wanted to be one of those fools.

I also knew that I wanted to focus my PhD research on a practical application. Normally, the terms "practical" and "PhD" don't appear together in the same sentence. Like matter and anti-matter, the two just can't coexist peacefully. There's a reason the phrase "piled higher and drier" is often used to describe a PhD program. PhD research is supposed to be cutting edge, boldly going where no geek has gone before. If a mere mortal can understand your dissertation, it's not worthy of a PhD program. In the after-hours soirees in the ivied halls of academia, where ice tinkles in crystal glasses and the pomposity meter goes off scale, noses wrinkle and lips curl at the mere suggestion of "applied research." I wasn't interested in abstract research, though, and I knew abstract research into HVAC wouldn't be of much benefit to the Air Force. The Air Force didn't need a new concept that might improve their HVAC systems in 20 years. They needed the damn things to work now! I was more than willing to step up to that challenge, but it meant I'd have to choose my faculty advisory committee very carefully. I needed professors who were truly interested in applied research and who didn't have any hang-ups about PhD research needing to be abstract and incomprehensible. Fortunately my major professor had such an attitude, and he helped steer me toward like-minded professors to serve on my committee. One gentleman in particular put my mind at ease that I'd made a correct choice. After I outlined the general idea of my research project he said "Sounds great! A research project that's actually useful. Whatever you do, don't study boiling water. We have shelves full of dissertations on boiling water in the library. Bubble formation, transient heat transfer at the boundary layer, the effects of induced convection currents. . . And you know what? Nobody cares!"

Once I had a committee, I had to start researching the scientific literature to find a problem that hadn't been solved yet and that, hopefully, I could tackle in a one year research project with no research funding. That meant many, many hours in the library pouring through obscure engineering journals. Today we take the Internet for granted. We type a few key words into a text box, click "search," and grumble if it takes more than three seconds to give us 70,000 hits. I wish I could have done that as part of my project. Instead, I haunted the dusty aisles of the Purdue Engineering Library looking for such exciting tomes as the "Transactions of the American Society of Heating, Ventilating, and Air Conditioning Engineers, Volume 87, part 2." Or the riveting "Journal of Heat and Mass Transfer, Volume 24, Issue 12." And then of course there was the ever popular "Proceedings of the 1981 ASME-JSME Joint Conference on Thermal Engineering." I would carry these books to an empty study table and leaf through them, looking for papers that were at least remotely connected to my area of interest. (For some reason there were always empty tables in this section of the library, and I almost never found that someone else had checked out a book I wanted.) When I found something of interest, I would carefully check the references for related articles and then search through the library's card catalog to see if they had that paper on file.

My search was made more difficult because at the time very few people were publishing scholarly works on HVAC controls. The entire field of HVAC had only recently come to the attention of academia. The science of HVAC had really been developed by technicians in coveralls and engineers with Coke-bottle glasses who worked within the HVAC industry. For years it wasn't considered scholarly enough to be worthy of study at the University level. That attitude began to change in the 1940's and 1950's, but the change was slow. At Purdue, for example, the main HVAC lab wasn't even on the Engineering campus. It was way out in left field, in a converted horse barn on the Agriculture campus. The reason it was out there was because back in the 1940's, when a few mechanical engineering professors began to take HVAC seriously, there were no air conditioning systems on the main campus. The university shared the opinion of my father and of nearly all men of his generation – you don't need air conditioning in Indiana. It's only hot for a few months out of the year, and you can always open a window. In particular, students didn't need air conditioning. They were young, they were tough, and they were prone to fall asleep if you made them too comfortable. On the Ag campus, however, things were different. They had pigs on the Ag campus, and pigs were important! Scientists had discovered that pigs were healthier, happier, and more productive (they put on weight faster) if they were kept in an air conditioned environment. So they had air conditioning for the pigs on the Ag campus, and that attracted the HVAC lab.

As I wore out the pavement between the horse barn and the Engineering Library a vague concept for my research began to take place. The microprocessor revolution was just beginning to affect HVAC controls. The vast majority of control systems were pneumatic, which meant they ran on compressed air. They weren't even electrical. A few of the newer controls were electric, but experiments with digital controls were just beginning. Efforts to connect massive mainframe computers to HVAC controls weren't showing much success, but a few researchers were having better luck with microprocessor based control systems. I was taking a course in microprocessor control, writing very simple algorithms in assembly language, and my professor was intrigued by the idea of applying this technology to an HVAC system. I began to focus my literature search on microprocessor control of HVAC. There were only a few books on the dusty shelves which dealt with microprocessor control, and I began scouring the "new arrival" technical journals and trade magazines for articles or references of interest. Sometimes I couldn't find a referenced article in the Purdue library, and I'd have to request it through inter-library loan. One day as I shuffled up to the reference desk to request yet more inter-library loans I looked up from the article I was reading and discovered there was a strikingly beautiful woman sitting at the reference desk. She had long dark hair, soft brown eyes, a flawless complexion, and a very professional looking blue dress that just hinted at the possibility that there might be a lovely figure underneath. She didn't look anything at all like the acne-faced students who normally worked at the library.

"May I help you?" she asked. Her voice was professional, yet feminine. She looked up from her desk and captivated me with those brown eyes. She was wearing just a little bit of makeup. Her dark eyebrows were perfectly shaped. Her lips glistened, exquisitely outlined with a natural colored lipstick. Now those brown eyes clouded with a trace of emotion. Petulance? Impatience? Ohmygod! She asked me a question, and now she's waiting for an answer.

"Oh, uh, here. I need to get this through inter-library loan." I set the journal I had been reading down on her desk. She looked at it quizzically. "Oh, not this one" I blurted out. "You've already got this one. I need the articles here in the references. The, um, third and fifth references. I wrote them down on this." I placed a 3" x 5" index card on her desk and immediately regretted it. When I was first starting my PhD research I had found a gray metal box filled with blank 3 x 5 cards at an old junk shop. It was dirt cheap so I bought it and always carried a stack of blank cards with me to the library. I'd write notes on them and file them away in the gray box when I got back home. I also used them as scratch paper, writing down things like the list of journals I wanted to get through inter-library loan. For the first time I noticed the cards were yellowed with age, dog-eared from being carried around, and water stained from the rain showers I occasionally carried them through. Actually, the appearance of the cards blended very nicely with the childish scrawl of my handwriting.

The lovely librarian squinted a bit as she deciphered my handwriting, but she figured it out and began to fill in a form. "What do you need these for?" she asked.

"I'm trying to narrow down my research topic" I replied. "You know, trying to find out what's already been done and what still needs to be researched." I relaxed a bit. This was the first coherent sentence I'd spoken since I walked up to the reference desk.

"Have you had a literature search done?" she asked.

This caught me by surprise. "Well, I, uh, I thought that's what I was doing. You mean I can get somebody else to do it for me?"

"We can go online and do a computer literature search" she answered. "You describe the subject and give me some key words, and I'll search an online database to see how many articles match your criteria. If there are too many, we'll add some more key words until we narrow it down to a reasonable number. Then we'll have them send us abstracts of all the articles that match your search. If we don't have the articles here, we can order copies of the articles through the same service. You only have to pay for the abstracts and articles they actually send you. Most research grants will pay for the search. What's your research topic?"

I didn't want to tell her I didn't have a research grant. Not having a research grant at a university is a little like telling your prom date she'll have to ride on the handle bars of your Schwinn. It simply screams "bush league." My major professor thought he could probably get some money from the Purdue Physical Plant once I actually had a research proposal. Until then, I figured I could pay for the literature search out of my own pocket. A bigger problem was the fact that I still only had a vague notion of what my research topic was going to be. "It's still pretty broad" I said.

"We can narrow it down during the online search" she replied. "That's one of the purposes of the search. We can add more key words until we've narrowed our search down to something with a reasonable number of hits."

"I'm not certain I'm ready for that" I said. "I think I still need to do some more research on my own before I can even come up with the right key words."

"We could try" she insisted. "Just tell me what your topic is."

"Well, I think it will have something to do with computer controlled heating and air conditioning."

"Oh," she replied, using the same tone of voice mothers use to hide their dismay when their toddler says they want one of Santa's reindeer for Christmas. "That's way too broad. You need to narrow it down." She turned away to deal with some paperwork that was obviously more important than an indecisive grad student. Feeling a little crushed, I walked away with my copies of the inter-library loan requests.

I wouldn't say that my encounter with this efficient librarian spurred me to redouble my efforts at finding a research topic because they were pretty thoroughly doubled to begin with, but it was a little extra incentive. Our conversation at the reference desk hadn't exactly been the stuff that dreams are made of, but I was hoping for a rematch. I spent a couple more weeks poring over dry journals and musty textbooks at the library, and eventually I came up with an idea for a research project. My major professor thought it was a good idea, my microcomputer professor thought it was feasible, and the Purdue Physical Plant was willing to fund the project and let me use one of their buildings as a test bed. Now all I needed to do was search the available literature to make certain no one else had ever done this.

Filled with new confidence, I returned to the reference desk. There was no one there when I arrived, so I waited with bated breath for the dark haired librarian to return. Only she wasn't the one who showed up. It was a skinny, middle-aged man with bad teeth.

"What can I do you for?" he asked as soon as he got to the desk.

"I need to have a literature search done." I tried not to sound disappointed.

"You'll have to talk to Miss Kelly about that" he replied. "She's the only one who does literature searches. She's at lunch now, but she'll be back at 1:00. You can catch her in her office." He nodded toward an office next to the reference desk.

Miss Kelly. That was certainly a good sign. And her office was easily the most impressive room in the library. A corner office next to the reference desk, with huge glass windows on two walls. I was surprised I'd never noticed this office before, or more to the point, the woman who obviously worked inside it. There was a sign next to the door: Elizabeth Kelly, Assistant Professor. Even more impressive.

I wasn't exactly a stranger to the library, so I had no problem finding things to do for the next half-hour. Precisely at 1:00 PM the punctual Miss Kelly returned from lunch and entered her office. I knocked at her door.

I don't remember what we said during that meeting, only that it was strictly a business conversation and I set up an appointment to do a literature search at 1:00 PM the following Friday. If I didn't get a chance to dazzle her with my wit and savoir-faire, at least I didn't drown her with more "ums" and "uhs."

The literature search was also strictly business. We spent the better part of an hour together in a small room off the main library, but all we talked about were key words and my research topic. In those days, an online literature search consisted of dialing into a mainframe computer at a commercial service using a terminal and a 4200 baud modem. Once we were connected, Miss Kelly typed in key words and connected them with "AND" and "OR" logic. The computer then spit back replies like "247 hits." Once we narrowed the number of hits to a number I could afford to pay for, Miss Kelly placed an order for the abstracts, which would be printed on a dot matrix printer at the search company and mailed to the library. She said I could pick up the list a week from Tuesday.

Tuesday. Tuesday was good. Tuesday was uniform day. The Air Force wanted to make certain their students didn't forget who was paying the bills and who owned their soul after graduation, so every Tuesday we had to wear our uniform to class. I hadn't been able to make much of an impression on Miss Kelly in my civvies, but maybe she'd fall for a man in uniform. Maybe the fact that I was a Captain in the United States Air Force would help me stand out from the other grad students, and just maybe I could find a crack in that professional shell she was always wearing.

On Tuesday I put on my best freshly starched class "B" blues and headed for the library. I debated wearing the full-blown class "A" blues – the formal blouse with ribbons and insignia like you see in the movies, but decided that would be overkill. The class "B" blues were a long sleeve dark blue shirt and tie with rank and a name tag, but no ribbons. Understated elegance. My shoes were freshly polished, I'd ironed a knife-edge crease in my trousers, and my belt buckle gleamed silver against a sea of dark blue. If this didn't do the trick, nothing would. I knocked on the door to her office and strode in confidently. As it turned out, she was a sucker for a guy in uniform! OK. Maybe that's overdoing it a bit. She didn't fall head over heels in love with me the moment I walked into her office, but the uniform did help break the ice. She had just finished doing her civic duty by serving as the foreman of a jury where the defendant was suffering from post-traumatic stress after having served in Vietnam. It had been a very difficult case and she needed to "decompress" by talking it over with somebody. By sheer coincidence, a "somebody" walked into her office wearing a military uniform. I'd never been in combat and I hadn't served in Vietnam, but I knew plenty of people who had and we talked about the mental stress of combat for a long time. When she finally put those demons to rest the conversation changed to nuclear weapons. Her father had been in an Army artillery unit providing support to the Marines during the Pacific island-hopping campaign in World War II, and he was slated to go ashore on the first day of the invasion of Japan. The atomic bomb had made that invasion unnecessary, which he figured that was the only reason he was still alive. He'd been involved in the planning for that invasion, he knew what the anticipated casualties were, and he knew how slim his chances were of surviving that battle. Since Miss Kelly wouldn't exist if he hadn't survived, she had an interesting perspective on nuclear weapons. As a uniformed member of the armed forces, she was interested in my views on the subject. Later the conversation turned to World War One. (I may have had a hand in that change of topics.) We discussed the von Schlieffen plan and I managed to guarantee a return visit to her office by promising to loan her a copy of The Zimmermann Telegram. Vietnam, post-traumatic stress, nuclear weapons, von Schlieffen – all in all it wasn't your typical first date conversation. Actually it wasn't a first date at all, but it was a beginning. On top of everything else, I'd learned her friends called her "Betsy" and I hoped to weasel my way onto her list of friends.

I waited several days before I "dropped by" to loan her the book, just so I wouldn't appear over-anxious. During that time I made several reconnaissance trips to the library to learn when she was most likely to be in her office. That way I could schedule my library research for times when she would be there. I'd wave to her through the window, and if I was lucky, she'd invite me in for a chat. Not until years later did I discover that she was paying attention to the days and times when I was most likely to visit the library, and she arranged her schedule so she would have some free time in her office when I passed by.

After several weeks of these happenstance encounters I figured it was time to ask her out on a date. I wanted to keep it low key and casual, something that didn't sound like a date so I could still keep visiting her office even if she turned down my invitation. After careful deliberation, I decided to ask her to join Don, Desiree, and me for our Friday night pizza. I knew this was risky because Don could sometimes be a bit, uh, bizarre, but on the other hand a night with those two was highly entertaining. I had my plans made, my logistics in place, and I was just looking for a good opportunity to pop the question when Betsy struck first. She collected oriental rugs and there was going to be an Oriental rug auction next Saturday. She thought if I was interested in rugs I might like to drop by. She'd probably be there around 11:00 AM, if I was interested. Then she hastened to add that this wouldn't be like a date or anything, as she was already dating a man in Michigan.

Already dating a man in Michigan? DAMN! I told her the rug auction sounded interesting and I didn't think I had anything else planned for Saturday morning so I just might stop by. I also said I understood perfectly that this wasn't a date, which was fine with me as I was already dating someone myself. OK. This last part was sort of true. I just didn't mention that the "someone" lived in the Florida town I'd left two years previously and our relationship wasn't exactly going anywhere.

Saturday morning I scrubbed my apartment until it could pass a boot camp white glove inspection. I didn't have any definite plan as to how I could lure her back to my place for dinner, but I wanted to be ready just in case an opportunity presented itself. Then I drove to the Oriental rug auction. Only it wasn't really an auction. It was a warehouse filled with rugs with a few people milling around. Apparently a traveling rug salesman came to Lafayette every once in a while and sometimes they held an auction, but if there weren't enough customers to make a good auction you just haggled with the salesman over any rugs you happened to be interested in. I'll have to admit, the only interest I had in the rugs themselves was a mild curiosity to find out just what an Oriental rug actually was. I'd read about them in books, but wasn't entirely sure I knew what they were. Once I saw one at the auction I thought "Oh, so that's what an Oriental rug is. I've seen those before." My main interest wasn't in the rugs but in one particular customer, who didn't seem to be at the auction. I wandered around the warehouse for about 15 minutes, looking listlessly at rugs and waving off the salesmen who wanted to tell me about them. I was about to give up and go home when I spotted her at the far end of the warehouse, looking at a deep red carpet. As casually as possible, I wandered over that way.

Betsy smiled and said hello when she saw me and the excitedly began pointing out details in the rug she was examining. She said it was a Bohari, or a Bogarti, or a Kilimanjaro, or something exotic like that. She was particularly impressed by the knotting. It was indeed a beautiful rug, but I had trouble keeping focused on the stitching. My attention kept wandering to her hands, her face, and her hair. We haggled with the salesman but he wouldn't come down to anywhere near what she considered to be a fair price so we said good-bye to the rug and walked to the parking lot. I was trying to find a way to invite her to my house when the rug salesman hunted us down. He said he hadn't sold a rug all day, and if we'd come back inside he was ready to make a deal on the rug we wanted. We followed him back inside and he lowered his price to a level Betsy was willing to pay. I carried the rug out to her car for her.

I was curious to see what kind of a car she had and I was a little surprised to find it was a dirt brown 1979 AMC Concord. Certainly a nice car, and an uncommon one as well, but not as beautiful or exotic as I expected someone like her to be driving. I pictured her behind the wheel of a Bugatti, or a Ferrari, or maybe something understated like an Aston-Martin. I probably didn't have a realistic view of what librarians earned. Much later I learned she had me pegged as a Chevy Citation driver, so I guess I didn't come across as being quite as debonair as I'd hoped.

As I was loading the rug into her car she asked me if I'd mind following her to her apartment and carrying it upstairs for her. That invitation caught me by surprise, and I began to suspect that maybe I'd cleaned my house for nothing. Somehow I wasn't disappointed at having wasted the effort. I followed her back to her apartment and carried the rug upstairs. (It wasn't heavy, I'm sure she could have carried it herself with no problem.) Then we sat around her apartment and talked, shared a bottle of wine, and then fixed dinner together. All in all it was a very pleasant afternoon.

Now that she'd fixed dinner for me at her apartment, I had a legitimate excuse to invite her to my house for dinner. The following Saturday I again gave my house a thorough cleaning, even going so far as to pick up the furniture and vacuum underneath it. Then I did something I'd never done before – I made homemade manicotti, starting with a bag of flour and making the pasta from scratch. I was following a recipe I'd read in the newspaper and, surprisingly, it came out great. Of course, it may have tasted better because it took much longer to cook than I'd expected. We didn't eat until late in the evening and by that time we were both starving. We'd also finished one bottle of wine and were well into the second bottle before the manicotti was done, so everything tasted great. While we were waiting for the manicotti to cook I showed her my collection of wind-up phonographs. (What can I say? I'm a geek. I have unusual hobbies.) At one point we were both kneeling on the floor, peering into the spring motor on an Edison Diamond Disc machine. Our arms were almost, but not quite touching and I felt a strange tingling which I can only describe as "electricity" between our bodies. This was a new, exciting, and somewhat unsettling feeling – something I'd never experienced before. I didn't dare say anything to her at the time, and it was years before I learned that she'd felt the same thing.

After that we saw each other regularly, but still only as friends. I stopped by her office regularly, we went out for Friday night pizza with Don and Desiree, and we even corresponded over the campus Unix computer network using a primitive form of e-mail. On Memorial Day Don and Desiree invited us to their house for a cookout. At one point Betsy and Desiree were in the back yard cooking hamburgers when Don took me into the front yard to show me a "spoon" (3 wood) golf club he'd just picked up at a local antique store. Don and I both enjoyed playing golf with vintage clubs (OK. We're both geeks.) and he was particularly proud of this club. He took a powerful swing to demonstrate the club and then stared in amazement at his empty hands. Meanwhile the golf club was sailing over the roof of his house, lazily spinning end over end. We both ran to the back yard, and as we rounded the corner we heard the club crashing through the trees by where the girls were standing.

"What was that?!!" Desiree demanded.

"My spoon! My spoon!" Don shouted.

"That was a spoon?" Desiree asked incredulously. "It sounded like a dinosaur!"

Don retrieved his spoon, which appeared to be none the worse for its aerial excursion. The rest of the afternoon passed without incident, although Desiree did ask a few pointed questions about why Don was pitching golf clubs over the roof of their house.

It was a lovely spring night for a drive in the MG as Betsy and I made our way back to Lafayette. She invited me up to her apartment for a glass of wine, and we talked until two in the morning. During this conversation she told me her relationship with her boyfriend in Michigan was going nowhere and they really had never been that close to begin with. I confessed that my relationship with the girl in Florida was in a similar state of torpor, and after an awkward pause we both admitted that we might actually have some romantic interest in each other. When I got up to leave we hugged, and it was the most wonderful hug of my life.

Now that we'd finally dropped the pretense of being "just friends" we got down to the serious business of falling in love. We did all the standard things that couples do when they're courting – dinners, movies, picnics, long walks, and attending a particularly atrocious performance of "Swan Lake." I'd never been happier. I remember one afternoon in particular, when we were having a picnic together in a city park. Betsy had excused herself for a moment, and as I watched her walk back to our picnic spot I marveled at how beautiful she was and how incredibly lucky I was that she was walking back to me and not to some other guy.

Betsy really wasn't much of a car person (this is supposed to be a book about cars, remember?) but she accepted the fact that I was interested in these strange decrepit machines and she never complained about them. She had grown up in New Jersey, and the only people she'd known who worked on cars were gas station mechanics and high school greasers. She found it odd that an Air Force Officer and PhD candidate would get some sort of pleasure out of crawling under a 50 year old jalopy and cramming antique grease under his fingernails, but since it made me happy she was perfectly willing to go along with it. She even found it possible to kiss me after one of my periodic stops to blow rust out of the Model A gas line, something no other woman had ever done.

As the summer faded into fall and fall gave way to winter we found ourselves spending more and more time together. My research was proceeding nicely and I began to believe I'd actually finish it on schedule the following spring. We talked about my upcoming teaching assignment in Ohio, but to my disappointment she told me she had no interest in being a camp follower and moving to Ohio on her own. I was perfectly happy with our current relationship and would have liked it to continue forever, but I slowly realized that wasn't going to happen. After many hours of deliberation, I gave her a ring for Christmas.

Christmas was especially exciting that year. We celebrated our engagement with her family and then drove to Yodersburg to celebrate with my family. We made plans, spun dreams, and plotted out our new life together. Part of me was extremely happy, and part of me was still in a state of shock. After 33 years of bachelorhood, I was about to get married. I called my friend Viktor in Chicago to tell him I'd gotten engaged. There was a long period of silence on the other end of the phone.

"Well," he said philosophically. "You've had a lot of good years."

As spring approached, things got hectic. I was scheduled to defend my dissertation, get married, and move to Ohio within a single week. I figured I'd be in such a state of shock over finishing my dissertation and moving that I could slide through the wedding without really knowing what was happening. We danced around the question of a honeymoon the way new couples do, each trying to figure out what the other one wanted without voicing an opinion that might upset the other. We collected brochures on romantic mountain resorts, Caribbean cruises, and other traditional honeymoon venues. When we finally managed to communicate our true feelings we discovered we were both viewing the honeymoon as "just one more damned thing we had to get through." We decided to postpone our honeymoon for a year or two, when we'd actually have time to enjoy it.

The blessed event occurred on a beautiful spring day in late May. We had a small family wedding in my home town church, followed by a reception at my folk's house. We talked Father Dupree into coming out of retirement to officiate, and he regaled us at the reception by playing ragtime music on my parent's piano. Don was my best man, and he drove us to the reception in the Model A. After the reception we drove back to Lafayette in the Jag, stopping in Berrytown for a wedding feast at Mr. Happy Burger. The next day we drove to Attica for a cookout at Don and Desiree's, celebrating the one year anniversary of our Memorial Day hug. I was supremely happy.

Just Married

There is a postscript to the "electricity" incident, when we were kneeling in front of the Edison phonograph and felt a tingling between our bodies. Although we'd both felt it at the time, we were much too unsure of our relationship to say anything about it. It was several years before I mentioned that sensation to Betsy. She was surprised that I'd felt the electricity too, and even more surprised that I remembered it.

"I'm really touched you remember that night we felt the electricity in front of the phonograph" she said. Betsy has for years harbored a misconception that engineers are not romantic, even though I've explained to her, with quantifiable data, that this is not so.

"Of course I remember it." I replied. "How could I forget anything so extraordinary? We were looking at an Edison LC-38 London Console, which was introduced in 1922. That's three years before Western Electric introduced the electrical recording process, and nearly seven years before it was perfected to the point that Edison adopted it. The phonograph itself had a wind-up spring motor, so where could the electricity have come from?"

She raised her eyebrows and gave me a quizzical look as she grasped the significance of what I was saying.

256

"I figure it was probably static electricity from the carpet" I continued. "Either that or St Elmo's Fire."

"St Elmo's Fire?" she said incredulously.

"It's an electrical phenomena most commonly seen on sailing ships" I replied. "The World War One Zeppelin crews ran into it, too. I'll admit it's a long shot. It was probably static electricity. The weather conditions weren't right for St Elmo's Fire."

She sighed the way she always does when I prove a point with unassailable logic. "Tell me again why I married you" she said as she turned back to her book.

I opened my mouth to reply, but then thought better of it. She didn't seem to be in the mood for more logic. It might have been a rhetorical question anyway.

Chapter 21 – Teaching HVAC

Betsy and I had made a house-hunting trip to Ohio before we got married, and we bought a three bedroom ranch house with a huge back yard. We liked everything about the house, but it was the back yard that really sold us. It stretched back 100 yards or more to a cow pasture, with a line of shade trees along one side and a quiet, shady neighbor's lawn along the other side. Our only reservation was that there was a new highway being constructed nearby. We worried that the highway would create a lot of noise and traffic, but finally decided it was far enough away that it wouldn't affect the neighborhood. Still, we weren't sure.

Moving day never goes as smoothly as you think it will, and it was late afternoon before the movers got everything packed up in Indiana. Once our stuff was gone we had to clean my house and Betsy's apartment and then drive to Ohio. It was late at night when we got to our new house. The utilities were supposed to have been transferred to our name, but apparently that hadn't happened because there was no power in the house. We stumbled around by flashlight, laying out sleeping bags on the living room floor. We started to explore the house with our flashlights, but quickly gave up because it got too depressing. An empty house always looks a little depressing, and the dim circles of light given off by our flashlights made everything look seedy. Worn carpeting, marks on the wall where pictures once hung, truly hideous wallpaper – all the flaws seemed magnified by flashlight. It took me a long time to fall asleep.

"Steve! Steve! Wake up!" Betsy was shaking my shoulder. "Now I know why they sold this place so cheap!" she gasped in my ear. I sat bolt upright. It was 6:00 AM and the morning sun was just beginning to light up the house. The morning air was deathly still, and in the distance I could hear diesel engines starting and the piercing "beep – beep – beep" of construction equipment backing up. I looked over at Betsy, but she had already lain back down and fallen asleep. I lay on my back and stared at the ceiling for a long time, listening to the construction crew get started on the new road. I didn't think we'd bought the house cheap. It was more money than I'd ever paid for anything in my life! A lot more money than I'd paid for my house in Indiana. And now I was going to be stuck with it forever. Nobody would ever buy a house this close to a major highway, not with all that noise! It had only been a few hours since we'd gone to bed so I eventually drifted back to sleep, but my sleep was tossed about on the rough seas of buyer's remorse.

Our next shock came a few days later. The movers had finally delivered our household goods, and we worked long into the night unpacking and putting things away, trying to at least get enough stuff unpacked so we would have a place to sleep and a few pots and pans to cook with. It was about 2:00 AM before we had a minimally functional bedroom, and we were exhausted when we finally fell into bed. Five hours later I awoke to the sound of our doorbell being rung furiously. We hadn't unpacked my robe yet, so I staggered around the bedroom looking for a pair of pants. Then I went to the door to see who could be visiting at this hour of the morning.

A workman was standing at the door, wearing a hard hat and carrying a chain saw. A big orange truck was parked behind him, and more men in hardhats were unloading chain saws from the truck. Then the man at my doorstep spoke. "Them trees has got to go."

It turned out the line of shade trees Betsy and I admired so much had grown up into a power line. We hadn't noticed the power line because it was hidden in the trees. That isn't a particularly safe place for a power line, though, and I knew enough about real estate to know the power company owned a right-of-way for the power lines. If they needed to cut down trees that were posing a safety hazard to their lines there wasn't much I could do about it. Fortunately the guy with the chainsaw was really quite nice, and I managed to convince him to just cut off the parts of the trees that were near enough to power lines to cause a problem. The trees were oddly shaped as a result, but you didn't notice that from our back yard. All you could see was a beautiful line of shade trees along edge of our property, and you didn't realize they were flat on the back side, like a Hollywood movie set.

Despite this rather shaky start, our house in Ohio turned out to be a wonderful place to live. We never again heard construction equipment in the morning, and when the road was finished it was totally undetectable from our property. Our backyard trees recovered from their mauling and made our back yard a nice quiet retreat. The only real deficiency was that it only had a two-car garage and we needed a place to park the Model A, the MGA, the Jag, my

Pinto, and Betsy's Nash. (We nicknamed her car "the Nash" in honor of the fact that it could trace its lineage back to the Nash-Kelvinator Refrigerator Company.) We were still operating in the super-polite newlywed "share and share alike" mode so one stall went to Betsy's Nash. That meant two of my good cars had to sit out in the weather. Not ideal, but they'd suffered the same fate with the one stall garage I'd had in Indiana.

We had a long driveway leading up to the house, and it ended in a short "T." One leg of the T led to the garage, and the other leg led to a gravel parking area where I parked the cars that wouldn't fit in the garage. They sat there, huddled under car covers. One morning I got a call at work from a tearful Betsy. She was sobbing that she'd just been in a car accident.

"Are you hurt?" I immediately asked. I could feel the adrenaline pounding through my veins as I waited for her answer. Still sobbing, she insisted she was all right and nobody was hurt but she'd damaged the car. I sat back with a tremendous feeling of relief and assured her that cars could always be fixed and the important thing was that she was OK. Then I asked her what had happened. It turned out the "car accident" consisted of her backing her Nash into the Jag as she was leaving the garage. The Nash was unscathed, but the corner of its bumper caught the Jag right in the middle of its oval "mouth." This left a nice big dent in a spot that was almost inaccessible from behind, so it would be extremely difficult to pound it out. This didn't really concern me at the time, though, as I was still feeling relieved that Betsy wasn't hurt. Not until years later did I discover that she'd planned that whole phone call out in advance, thinking it was the best way to tell me she'd dinged my Jag. It took her close to half an hour to work herself into the proper state of tearfulness before she called me.

I really loved teaching at AFIT. Academically, it was very challenging. I quickly discovered what generations of teachers before me have known, and that's that you never really learn a subject until you try to teach it. You can do something yourself if you sort of understand it, but you can't teach someone else to do it unless you understand it so well that you can explain it six different ways and answer any question they could conceivably ask. The courses we taught were pretty intensive. They were fully accredited as graduate level college courses, but instead of teaching a one hour class three days a week we taught eight-hour classes five days a week. A typical class would last three or four weeks, then if we were lucky we'd get a week to prepare for the next class. Sometimes we taught back-to-back classes. Occasionally a student would complain about the fact that we kept them in class for eight hours and then assigned homework to be done after class, but we had very little sympathy for those complaints. We had to spend several hours every night grading their homework and preparing for the next day's lectures. They only had to put up with this schedule for a few weeks, but when they left we'd start all over again with a new class.

I worked with some extremely sharp engineers at AFIT, and we'd often get caught up in exploring new ways to control HVAC systems as well as working out better ways to teach the subject. We also worked with other instructors at AFIT who were teaching electrical engineering, civil engineering, engineering management, and scores of other subjects. We were often called upon as consultants, usually by former students, and sometimes we traveled to Air Force bases around the world teaching classes and helping them solve engineering problems at that base.

One morning I got a call from a fellow instructor. His wife, who was a professional architect, had been having trouble with her BMW so she took it to the local BMW/Porsche dealer to have it fixed. The instructor had followed her there in his Porsche, but when they got ready to leave the Porsche wouldn't start. Now it was in the shop too, and they needed a ride to work. I told him I'd be more than happy to come get them. I think maybe I neglected to mention the fact that I'd driven the Model A to work that morning, as they looked surprised when I showed up in a 60 year old Ford. They weren't half as surprised as the dealer, though. I made certain he was within earshot when I offered my friend some advice about the importance of buying a reliable car.

Our first child was born while we were living in Ohio. When we told Don and Desiree that Betsy was expecting, they told us that Desiree was expecting their first child too. We called and visited them several times over the coming months, excitedly sharing tidbits we'd learned about how to care for a new baby. Viktor's reaction was a little different. Victor and his wife already had two children, so he was an experienced dad. When I called him to tell him Betsy was expecting, there was no hesitation like when I told him I was getting married. This time his reply was immediate, and from the heart.

"Welcome to the land of the living dead" said Viktor.

In due time, Betsy gave birth to a beautiful baby boy. (Actually, it was well past due time, from Betsy's perspective.) He was healthy, happy, and ravenously hungry. The nurses at the hospital suggested we buy a cow to keep up with his appetite. Betsy and I traded off the late night feedings, middle of the night feedings, early morning feedings, and all of the diaper changes that came in between. Soon we were both staggering through the day in a semi-comatose state, fulfilling Viktor's prophesy. But the rewards more than made up for the sleep deprivation. Just seeing that baby smile made the whole day worthwhile, and his giggles transformed an entire week. I learned patience, responsibility, and the joy of parenting from that kid. I also learned that, no matter what they teach you in the Lamaze classes, do not tell a woman in the throes of a contraction that she needs to focus. That will give her something to focus on, her focus will be on you, and you will not be seen in a positive light.

Babies have a way of bringing changes to your life, and this baby was no exception. The first casualty was Betsy's Nash. When he grew older I would find a way to strap his car seat into my sports cars, but as a newborn his transportation options were limited to the back seat of the Nash. The Nash was a two-door, and it was a royal pain to squeeze a baby seat and a newborn into the back seat and make certain everything was buckled up correctly. Betsy decided we needed a four-door car. (I reminded her that the Model A had four doors, but apparently that didn't count as a "car.") One of the unexpected bonuses I'd gotten when I picked Betsy for my wife was that she hated shopping. She said her idea of purgatory was going from store to store trying on shoes. That suited me fine, except there were a few things I felt required a bit of comparison shopping. Like cars, for example. I was shocked when Betsy looked around the first used car lot we stopped at, pointed to a dark brown Oldsmobile 88, and announced "I want that car."

"Don't you think we ought to take it for a test drive?" I asked.

"Why?" she replied. "I'm sure it runs or they wouldn't have it on the lot."

In the end, she grumpily agreed to go for a test drive. She also waited impatiently while I looked at the odometer reading, the tires, the suspension, the transmission fluid, compared the wear on the pedals to the claimed mileage, and did all the other checks I thought you were supposed to do before you bought a new car. (This was years before you could get a vehicle history report online.) Everything checked out fine, and we wound up buying the Oldsmobile.

"I don't know why you had to spend so much time fussing with it" she said as we drove away. "I told you I wanted this car." In the years since then we have bought several cars using the "Betsy method," and to my shock we have also applied the same technique to house hunting. We'll sort through the listings to find houses we think we might like. Betsy will pick one to look at, and if she likes it we buy it. "I don't like shopping" she explains. To her credit, we've never bought a bad car or a bad house.

For the most part, our time in Ohio was devoid of any noteworthy automotive experiences. The MG's rear axle locked up one day while I was driving to work, but I had a spare I'd bought from the traveling MGA parts salesman in Florida so that was relatively easy to fix. And the Jag U-joints started clunking one day. That would be trivial to fix in most cars, but thanks to Jaguar's design philosophy of wrapping the body around the mechanicals I had to remove the entire rear suspension to get to the driveshaft. (I'm told that at the Jaguar factory they began building the E-Type by placing a starter motor on a jack stand and then building the car around it, but that may be a slight exaggeration.) And then there was the infamous incident when the Jag's left front brake started dragging while I was driving on a divided highway. It wasn't dragging much, but by the time I got to the next exit and pulled over to look at it the brake disk was red hot and a little bit of excess grease had caught fire. It burned itself out almost immediately, but Betsy was following in her car and in her eyes the car was on fire. This grew in family lore over time to the point where I'm now sometimes reminded of the time there were "flames spurting out of the wheel as I drove down the I-75."

I was beginning to think my automotive adventures were over. Then one Sunday morning we were sipping our after-breakfast coffee and reading the paper. Betsy was skimming the classified ads and she casually said "Here's an MG TC for sale."

"Oh really?" I said, not taking my eyes from the section I was reading. "That's nice."

Betsy looked at me with a puzzled expression. "Didn't you say you'd always wanted one?" Suddenly I realized she was serious. I had told her about Viktor's TC, and in fact I had always wanted a TC. Of course, there were a lot of other cars I'd always wanted, too. A Stanley, a Bugatti, a Duesenberg, a Blower Bentley, an Invicta, a 289 Cobra . . . I could probably fill several pages with a list of cars I daydreamed about. Betsy wasn't a daydreamer, though. She was a doer. Those other cars were clearly out of our price range, but a TC just might be a possibility. She handed me the classified section.

1947 MG TC. Red. Less than 5,000 miles since restoration. Asking $15,000.

I whistled at the price. That was six times the price I'd paid for the Jag, and the Jag was far and away the most expensive car I'd ever bought. Not only that, the asking price was on the high end of the market, even for a restored TC. I'd never bought a car at market value before. I'd always bought rusted out wrecks, poured money and sweat equity into them, and wound up with a rusted-out wreck covered with shiny paint. Betsy had already deduced that this wasn't the best way to build an antique car collection.

We called and made an appointment to look at the car, but as soon as I saw it I knew it wasn't the car for me. It wasn't a bad car, but it was a long way from being a $15,000 car. The "restoration" had apparently consisted of bolting on some reproduction parts and giving it a quick paint job. I wasn't an expert on TCs, but even I could see that some of the reproduction parts were wrong. For example, the TC had what's known as a "chronometric" tachometer and speedometer. Horrendously complex, the instruments actually had a clockwork mechanism inside that caused the needle to "tick" from one position to the next as the speed changed. This car had a reproduction tachometer with a needle that sort of wandered back and forth as you revved the throttle – clearly not a chronometric tach. Not only that, the original tachometer included an electric clock. This tach just had a clock face painted onto the tachometer dial. (I have since seen ads for this reproduction tachometer. The ads claim their clock is more accurate than the original TC clock because theirs is guaranteed to be right twice a day.) This might be a nice car for somebody else, somebody with more money than sense, but not for me.

Betsy accepted the fact that I didn't want this car philosophically. She just put it down to the fact that for some strange reason I liked to shop around. She had, however, awakened me to the possibility that I might actually be able to buy a TC someday, and once I had the fever I started scouring the want ads. TC's are few and far between, but eventually I found an ad for one that was only located about 20 miles from our house. This time I fell in love with it as soon as I saw it. It was a 1948 model, British Racing Green, and it was all original. There were some period modifications, like 16-inch wire wheels and tires in place of the skinny 19-inch "bicycle wheels" that came from the factory, but essentially this was a car that had probably been owned by a sports car enthusiast through the 1950s, and had not been modified since. The current owner had owned it for about 15 years, and he just used it to take his grandkids for an occasional ride. He had bought it from a student who had driven it out from California. The car had no rust whatsoever (a shocking departure from my other cars) and had a fairly decent paint job that looked to be 20 or 30 years old. The price was on the high side for an unrestored TC, but not unreasonable for one in this shape. There was only one problem. Our situation had changed.

In between the time that I started looking for a TC and the time we found this green one, I had received orders to report to Alaska. I didn't know much about Alaska, but I was pretty sure it wasn't a good place to drive a 40 year old sports car. As a matter of fact, we were already in the process of selling my Pinto and finding storage for my other cars so we could drive the Oldsmobile to Alaska. We were also selling our house in Ohio and, in a surprise move, buying the lake cottage from my parents! On top of everything else, we knew we'd have to buy a car for me to drive once we got to Alaska, but we had no idea how much cars cost up there. All in all, this was a poor time to be spending thousands of dollars on a toy, particularly a toy that we'd have to put in storage as soon as we bought it.

The owner of the TC was a really nice guy, and he understood completely when we explained this to him. He wasn't all that gung-ho about selling the car himself. He'd put the car up for sale because his grandkids had outgrown the phase of begging to ride in grandpa's old car, but now he was having second thoughts. He said he was going to pull the car off the market, at least for now. We promised to keep in touch, and he said he'd let us know before he sold the car to anyone else. Then he did something that was fiendishly diabolical. He gave me a photograph of the car. For the next three years that photograph would sit on my desk at work, calling to me as the Alaskan winters piled snow against the windows.

1948 MG Midget Series TC

Chapter 22 – North to Alaska!

The drive to Alaska was the trip of a lifetime, and I mean that in a very positive way. Some people might have hesitated to take a 14-day car trip with a 2-year old, but Betsy and I enjoyed the trip immensely. Our son sat in his car seat, surrounded by a mountain of crayons, magic markers, paper, coloring books, picture books, and – Betsy's stroke of genius – a portable cassette player with a stack of children's books and songs on tape. In hindsight, the only thing I wish we'd done differently is buy him a set of headphones so he could have listened to them in private. He loved those tapes, so we heard the same songs over and over. Sometimes at night, when it's very quiet, I can still hear strains of "Here come the busy bees! Buzz, Buzz, Buzz, Buzz!"

We drove leisurely, seven or eight hours of driving each day, with occasional lunch and rest stops. We also took time to stop at interesting spots like Mt Rushmore, Yellowstone, and Sheridan Wyoming. OK, Sheridan wasn't part of the plan, but the master cylinder went out on the Olds and it was either spend a day in Sheridan or cross the Rockies without brakes. Fortunately Sheridan proved to be a delightful place to take an unplanned holiday.

The drive to Alaska was an eye-opener for Betsy, as except for one trip to North Dakota as a child she'd never been west of the Mississippi. She found the long stretches of dirt road in the Yukon unsettling because we wouldn't see another car for hours. She would scan the radio dial from end to end, AM and FM, without finding a single station. At times we were above the tree line, surrounded by nothing but rocks and lichen with a thin layer of fog hovering just off the ground. The landscape couldn't have looked any more unfamiliar if we'd been on a different planet.

Eventually we arrived at Eielson AFB Alaska, about 30 miles north of Fairbanks, and I began looking for a car to drive to work. I was correct when I assumed Alaska wouldn't be a good place for sports cars. The only sports car I saw was an MGA coupe which, for reasons that must have once made sense to somebody, was perched on top of a 30 foot pole in front of a salvage yard in the town of North Pole. Since it was apparent I wasn't going to be driving a fun car I immediately started looking at junkers. Force of habit I guess, but I soon found a beat up Toyota Land Cruiser with a broken windshield and an attractive price. This wasn't quite to Betsy's liking, and she found a 1985 Jeep Cherokee in brand new condition with 6 months left on the 3-year warranty. This was the closest I'd ever come to buying a new car. I choked a bit at the price, but Betsy didn't think it was "seemly" for me to drive around in a clunker. I guess that's one of the advantages to getting married. I'd bought a lot of used cars over the years and I thought I had a pretty good idea of how to check them out, but somehow I'd always overlooked "seemliness."

It turned out to be a good thing that we bought a fairly new car, as the winters we spent in Fairbanks were unusually harsh, even by Alaskan standards. The town of Fairbanks was founded by gold miners who picked the location because it was as far north on the Chena river as riverboats could go, not because it looked like a particularly good place to build a town. During World War II, the Army built an air base there because it was as close to Russia as they could get and still have some semblance of a supply chain. It was the last American stopping point for the lend-lease planes that were being flown to Russia. The terrain was flat and was covered with scrub pine, birch, and mosquitoes. There was almost never any wind, which allowed high pressure cells to sit still and build extreme temperatures summer and winter. It was not unusual for temperatures to soar into the 90's in July, and plunge to -60 °F or colder during the winter. In the winter the lack of wind meant powdery snow would pile up 3 or 4 inches deep on top of the power lines and sit there for days without falling off. In the summer it meant the mosquitoes could pile up 3 or 4 inches deep on your arm without falling off. We once had a group of archaeologists study the base to make certain our planned construction wouldn't disturb any valuable archaeological sites. They reported they could find no evidence of any prior human habitation on the site. I told them that didn't surprise me, as no one but a gold miner or a military planner would say "this looks like a good place to winter over."

The first winter we were there the weather almost set a record for the longest consecutive period where the thermometer never topped -40 °F. The temperature stayed that cold for several weeks on end, and just when we were about to break the record, a warm front passed through and the temperature climbed into the -30's. Then after a day or two of this balmy weather, the temperature again dropped down below -40 and stayed there for several more weeks. I believe the coldest official temperature during that spell was -62

°F, but unofficial temperature records taken near the runway showed -75 °F. I know, because I was standing out there in my parka and bunny boots playing war games while a sergeant was taking those readings. The stalled high pressure cell eventually raised the barometric pressure to the point they closed the civilian airport because pilots couldn't adjust their altimeters to compensate for the high pressure.

Funny things happen to cars when it gets this cold, and this time I don't mean funny in a positive way. To begin with, you need to plug in an electric block heater and a battery heater before you turn off your engine or it won't start again until spring. Diesel engines need special cold weather additives to keep their fuel from turning to jelly. Even propane turns to jelly at these temperatures. Fork lifts and other propane powered vehicles need electric heaters in the propane tank to turn it back into a gas.

Getting your car to start is only the first step. Moving the gearshift in a manual transmission car is like stirring peanut butter with a canoe paddle. Automatics tend to just sit still and complain for a while, until the transmission warms up enough to actually move the car. If it hasn't moved after 5 minutes, it's time to get your transmission rebuilt, which is what we had to do to the Olds the first winter we were there. When your car finally does begin to move, you experience a phenomenon known as "square tires." When you park a car with warm tires the tire naturally flattens out a bit on the bottom, where the weight of the car is pressing it against the pavement. Then when the tires cool off, say to -30 or -40°F, they freeze in this shape. The next time you drive the car drops noticeably with a "ka-Whump, ka-Whump, ka-Whump" every time the tires roll around to the flat spot again. Go around a turn, and the tires on the outside of the turn get out of sync with the tires on the inside. Now the car goes "Whump Whump Whump" and rocks side to side as you drive. Eventually the tires warm up enough to roll smoothly, but your troubles aren't over yet.

Rubber and plastic do not like cold weather. The rubber floor mats in my Jeep shattered when I stepped on them. When I picked the pieces up in the spring, it looked like someone had hacked them to pieces with a razor blade. Even the paint doesn't like cold weather. On one particularly cold day I slammed the door shut on my Jeep (door latches get recalcitrant at -60 °F too) and a big patch

269

of paint fell off the center of the door into the snow. Apparently the metal shrank more than the paint did, and the resulting stress caused the paint to pop loose.

My Jeep had plastic seats, which were not especially comfortable in cold weather. In fact, even when I was wearing insulated long underwear the seats were literally a pain in the ass. When the first cold snap hit, my nether regions became badly chapped. Since Chap-Stick didn't sell an applicator big enough to take care of my problem, I bought thick fake wool seat covers. That made things much better, at least in the front seats. I hadn't bought covers for the back seat. I forgot about that detail one time when we had a Colonel visiting from the Alaskan Air Command headquarters, which was located on the tropical coast of Alaska. (Anchorage) We had planned to take him to a fancy restaurant in Fairbanks, but the extreme cold weather made driving dangerous so we settled for a pizza parlor in the town of Moose Creek, which was just outside the base gates. The Colonel insisted on riding in the back seat, as he was the shortest one in the group I was taking to the restaurant. I didn't think anything about it until I noticed he was starting to squirm. He was walking a little funny the next day, and he didn't sit down much during our meetings.

One other aspect you had to worry about when driving in cold weather was ice fog. When the temperature drops below -40 °F the water vapor in the exhaust freezes as soon as it leaves the tailpipe, and it freezes into ice crystals that are so tiny they stay suspended in the air. If I remember my high school chemistry correctly, that's called a "colloidal dispersion." (You should have seen how surprised my brain was when I asked it to regurgitate that fragment of memory!) In any event, the net result is that every passing car lays down a layer of fog that doesn't go away, and the longer the temperature stays below -40 °F the thicker the fog becomes. During our months-long cold snap, it became very thick indeed! Combine that with the long hours of darkness and driving could be extremely hazardous. Eielson is below the Arctic Circle so we never had 24 hours of total darkness, but the winter days were very short. The sun would sleep in until around 10:00 AM, and then it would just barely peek above the horizon. When I drove home for lunch I had to flip down the sun visor to shield my eyes from the low hanging sun. By 3:00 PM it was dark again.

Fortunately winter doesn't last forever. "Break up," the season when the ice broke on the Chena river, would begin in late March or early April, and by the middle of May most of the snow was melted. (Historically, break-up was a big event as all major supplies came by riverboat. Occasionally a really intrepid soul would journey to Fairbanks by dogsled, but for the most part the town was cut off from civilization from the time the river froze in the fall until break up.) A few patches of snow would linger in the shadows until June, but overall the summer weather was great and we wouldn't see snow again until September. Alaska really is a beautiful state. Rugged mountains, raging rivers, vast forests, and seemingly endless stretches of uninhabited wilderness. The land almost seems to be alive, and you have the feeling that if you just listened closely enough you could hear it talking to you. I had a few occasions to fly in a private plane from Fairbanks to Anchorage, and in the early morning darkness we would see an occasional light along the highway connecting the two cities, and no other lights for as far as we could see in any other direction.

We were blessed by the arrival of a baby girl during our first full summer in Alaska. She was born in the military hospital at Ft Wainwright, the nearest full-service hospital to Eielson, on a sunny night in June. (Technically the sun does set during a Fairbanks summer, but it never dips far below the horizon and in June you can easily read a newspaper at midnight.) She came much more willingly than my son, and as I held her in my arms I could look out the window and see Mt McKinley far to the south.

Alaska is an outdoorsman's paradise, but you need to act fast to take advantage of the summer weather because it doesn't last long. I've never been much of a hunter, but I do enjoy fishing and the salmon fishing was great. The entire family enjoyed camping, and the Jeep proved to be a pretty good vehicle for the "civilized" camping you can do with a three-year old and a newborn. We rented a pop-up camper and limited our trips to campgrounds with utilities so we could run a small electric heater in the camper. That still provided us with lots of beautiful sites to visit. Homer, Valdez, Circle Hot Springs, Kenai, Portage Glacier, Denali, a trip to the Arctic Circle, and many other beautiful spots provided us with memories to last a lifetime. The National Park Service used to open Denali National Park to private vehicles one day a year, and we were fortunate enough to drive past Mt McKinley on one of the most beautifully clear days we'd ever seen. The road seemed to stretch forever, and long after Betsy was ready to turn back I insisted on pushing on "just a little bit further." The paved road gave way to gravel, the gravel gave way to two tracks in the grass, and eventually we were following a narrow trail and fording small streams in the forest. The map showed the road led to something called the "Kantishna Air Strip," which I judged to be just around the next bend. We rounded the bend, the rutted trail opened into a wide grassy field, and a Cessna was taxiing straight toward us. "This is far enough" I announced, turning the Jeep around and heading back into the forest.

The only drawback to the Jeep was that it was slightly underpowered. OK, it was a lot underpowered. It had a 2.5 liter 4-cylinder engine which was huge compared to my MG's engine, but the vehicle itself was even huger. Between the weight and the total lack of streamlining, that 4-banger would just barely get the Jeep up to highway speeds under normal circumstances. Pack a family of four and all their camping gear into it, hang a pop-up camper off the back, and drive into the mountains and you're talking serious dogginess. Fortunately there was very little traffic in Alaska, so I had no one riding my bumper when I dropped down into 2'nd gear on the long uphill stretches.

The air fare from Alaska to Indiana was horrendous and it took nearly 24 hours to make the trip, but we couldn't resist the temptation to make the trip for my daughter's baptism. After all, we had just bought the lake cottage so it seemed like we ought to get some use out of it. The only drawback was that it cost a lot to rent a car for the duration of our visit. Fortunately I already knew how to solve that problem - the same way I solved the problem of needing a tow vehicle to take the Model A to Florida. Never rent a car if it costs less to buy one! I had to spend a little more than $500 to get something Betsy was happy with, but we picked up a fairly decent '83 Buick Skylark for our lake car. That got us around quite nicely during the two weeks we spent at the lake, and when we were ready to head back to Alaska we just parked it in the garage at the cottage so it would be ready for our next vacation.

While I didn't have a lot of car adventures in Alaska there were plenty of engineering challenges. A few of these proved to be, if not exactly life lessons, at least the source of some memorable quotes. The first incident occurred around 6:00 PM on a Friday, when I was trying to finish the week's paperwork before heading home. Most of the other people in the office had already gone home and things were pretty quiet until the phone rang.

"Major Tom" I answered, still skimming through some paperwork.

"What kind of a @*&%# operation are you folks running?!!" demanded the voice on the other end. I immediately recognized the voice as belonging to Colonel Buck, the director of all aircraft maintenance operations. Col Buck was short, gruff, and profane. He was also extremely smart, and a reasonable man when he was in a good mood. Full Colonels don't have to be reasonable, and I appreciated the fact that Col Buck usually extended me that courtesy. At the moment, however, I somehow sensed that he was upset so I had to tread carefully. I realized his query was actually a trick question, as I could either try to answer it and admit I was running a @*&%# operation or I could feign ignorance and admit I didn't have a clue as to what kind of an operation I was running. I decided to sidestep the question.

"Is there a problem, sir?" I asked as politely as possible.

"Is there a problem?!!" he bellowed into the phone. "Of course there's a @*&%# problem! I wouldn't be calling you at six o'clock on a @*&%# Friday if there wasn't a problem! It's your @*&%# Saber contractor and their @*&%# kitchen cabinets!"

The problem just got a lot thornier. First of all it involved the Saber contractor. Saber was an experimental method of expediting small maintenance and repair work. The Saber contractor didn't actually work for me, he worked for a special branch of the Civil Engineering Squadron, but I knew Col Buck would only get madder if I tried to tell him it wasn't my problem. Secondly, it involved a contract to replace kitchen cabinets in base housing, and more particularly in Col Buck's house, so the problem wasn't just professional, it was personal.

To understand why replacing kitchen cabinets could be such a problem, you have to know a little bit about how the government does business. If you were going to replace the cabinets in your own house, you'd call a carpenter you trusted and get an estimate. If the estimate didn't seem reasonable you might call another carpenter and get a second estimate, but basically you and the carpenter would quickly come to an agreement as to what he was going to do and how much you were going to pay. If you owned a lot of rental properties, which is essentially what base housing is, you'd make arrangements to call the carpenter whenever someone moved out and replace the cabinets while the house was empty.

Things aren't that simple when you're spending the taxpayer's money. To prevent graft and corruption, there are volumes of rules and regulations that specify exactly how you need to go about asking for estimates, which requires doing a full engineering design before you ever talk to a carpenter. This design has to be written out in great detail because you're not actually allowed to talk to the carpenter yourself. You have to give the design to a separate government agency that advertises for bids. They give copies of your design to any interested carpenter so they can see exactly what needs to be done without actually talking to you. (If the contractor was allowed to talk to the designer, they might agree to a kickback deal.) Of course, this separate contracting agency has its own volumes of rules and regulations that they need to follow, many of which require them to tell you that your design can't be put out for bid the way you prepared it but needs to be redone in a different format. If it's a large contract there is a great deal of money involved, which means a big scandal if anyone screws up either through greed or incompetence. When this happens, it's not enough to simply hang the person who was caught screwing up, bureaucrats and politicians need to create several new volumes of rules and regulation to make certain this particular screw-up never happens again. Since none of those rules ever gets repealed, as the years go by it gets tougher and tougher to actually get anything done.

The net result of this process is that you can't afford to do all the design and contract preparation just to replace the cabinets in one single house. You need to wait until you have hundreds of houses that need new cabinets, and then you write a contract to replace the cabinets in all of them. The price of this contract is large enough that it may take you several years to push it through the budget process, and once you succeed, you get approval to spend money in a single year only. If you don't spend it by the end of the year the money goes away, so you can't wait until the house is vacant to replace the cabinets. You need to tell everyone to empty everything out of the cabinets because you're going to replace them right now, whether they want new cabinets or not.

The Saber process was designed to reduce the design and paperwork required for small contracts, but even so it was subject to the same basic rules as any other contract. I had been in meetings where the contract to replace kitchen cabinets was discussed and I suspected that Col Buck was unhappy with the fact that contractors were going to come into his house and replace the cabinets.

"Is there a problem with that Saber contract, Colonel?" I asked as innocently as possible.

"I'll tell you what the @*&%# problem is! They shoved a note in my mailbox that said they could replace my cabinets on Tuesday, Wednesday, or Thursday of next week. I needed to pick one day and empty everything out of the cabinets the night before. I wrote back and said none of those days would work for me. I'm going on vacation the week after next and they can replace the cabinets while I'm gone. So today I get this letter that says '@*&%# you! We're coming Tuesday!!'"

I knew at this point that there was nothing I could say that would make him happy, and my only chance for survival was to stay out of the line of fire until he finished ranting. I believe I said something innocuous like "Oh, my" but it really didn't matter what I said. He was on a roll and he proceeded to turn the air blue for the next 15 minutes while he told me about everything Saber had done wrong since he came to this base, everything the Civil Engineering Squadron had done wrong, everything the Civil Engineering Squadron at his last base had done wrong, and numerous other sins of omission and commission dating back to his high school basketball coach. Sometimes people just need to vent. When his fury was spent, he calmed down and was actually quite civil. Even so, I was surprised by his parting line.

"Thanks for listening, Steve. I know Saber doesn't work for you, but when I tried to call them they didn't answer their phone. I had to yell at someone, and I figured you'd be working late."

To this day, Betsy and I still use the line "@*&%# you! We're coming Tuesday!" to describe particularly bad customer service.

The other memorable line came from Bud, one of my contract management inspectors. Bud was a tall, lanky first lieutenant, born and raised in Oklahoma. I don't know if he'd ever actually worked as cowboy, but he looked the part. Bud was a "maverick," an officer who had started his career as an enlisted man and come up through the ranks. I never knew what job Bud had performed while he was enlisted, but I wouldn't have been surprised to learn it involved killing people with his bare hands. He was much older than any other lieutenant in the squadron, with a weathered face and a physique that just looked like it had been toughened by years of hard work. I don't think he ever actually chewed tobacco, but somehow he just looked like he had a wad tucked into his cheek. He spoke with a slow, comfortable drawl and was always pleasant, but there was something about him that made you not want to ever get him riled. Some Alaskans weren't particularly thrilled by the large number of "outsiders" who had come from Texas and Oklahoma to work on the oil pipeline. They joked that the sweetest sight in the world was a Texan headed south with an Okie under each arm, but I don't think they ever told that joke to Bud.

Along with several other projects, Bud was the Air Force inspector for a new F-16 Flight Operations building that was being built by the Corps of Engineers. Officially the Corps was in charge of the design and construction, since Congress didn't authorize the Air Force to have its own engineering corps when the Air Force became a separate service. We could make suggestions that related to whether or not the building would meet our functional needs, but we weren't supposed to have any technical input on the design and construction. However, since we would have to maintain the building and take flak from any general or colonel who was unhappy with anything from the floor plan to the bathroom paint color, our inspectors kept close tabs on every aspect of construction. Sometimes this led to turf battles with the Corps, but they never argued with Bud.

One day Bud stuck his head through the door to my office and said "Major, have you got time to look at the Squad Ops briefing room? It just don't look right to me."

"What's the matter with it?" I asked.

"I dunno. Maybe it's the paint or sumpin. It just don't look right."

"Let's see if Lt. Winfrey can come with us." Lt Winfrey was an architect from New York City. Small and excitable, he was almost the exact opposite of Bud. This was his first assignment out of college, but he had an excellent eye for design and color – a talent in which I was seriously deficient. We drove to the construction site and walked into the briefing room, which was basically a small theater where the pilots would be briefed on upcoming missions.

"What do you think?" Bud asked as we walked into the room. It didn't look that bad to me. Mostly gray, there was a patterned carpet on the floor and the theater seats were upholstered in a grayish fabric. The paint on the walls had a hint of purple mixed in with the gray which I didn't particularly care for, but I probably wouldn't have even noticed that if Bud hadn't asked for my opinion. I guess it says a lot about my sense of style that Bud could see problems that eluded me. Fortunately I never had to voice my opinion, because Lt Winfrey cut me off.

"Oh my God!" he moaned, clasping his hands to his head. "The dissonance is excruciating! The pattern in the carpet is fighting with the pattern on the upholstery, and the colors aren't even in the same registry. There is absolutely nothing on the walls to tie it to the room so the walls are just flying off into space, leaving the occupants abandoned in a cacophony of disparate themes!"

Bud stared at Lt Winfrey for a long time. "Right," he finally drawled. "I just knew it sucked. I didn't know why."

The last winter we spent in Alaska set a record for snowfall. That was a particularly serious problem, since the snow didn't melt between October and April. It just piled up deeper and deeper. I had to constantly tell my 4-year old son to stay off the roof of our house, as the snow which had slid off the roof had piled up to the point where he could walk from our yard onto the roof. The snow didn't slide off of most of our buildings, however, it just continued to pile up and add more weight to the roof. One of the maintenance hangars on the flightline was the first to show the strain this snow was putting on our buildings. One Sunday I got a call that the hangar was making "strange creaking noises." I'm not a structural engineer, but I only had to take one look at the twisting roof trusses before I ordered the building evacuated. I called in a true structural engineer and he confirmed my worst fears. We didn't even dare open the hangar doors to tow the airplanes outside, for fear that opening the doors would cause the building to collapse. Fortunately we had some very ingenious craftsmen at the base, and in no time at all they had punched holes in some old fire hoses, used cranes to drape them over the roof, and connected them to the base steam system so they could start melting the snow off the roof. Once the roof was relieved of the snow load, we could go back inside the building and make emergency repairs to the roof trusses.

We immediately set up a team of structural engineers to start examining the roof of every building on base. If they declared the roof to be safe, we'd put a crew of men on top of it to shovel off all the excess snow. Not exactly a fun job, especially when the temperature dropped below -40 °F, but we didn't lose a single building. We did have to evacuate a few buildings and make emergency repairs when the structural engineers found problems. One wooden maintenance building had survived over 40 winters in Alaska with no problems, but that winter it nearly came down. I had just returned to my office after ordering the evacuation of that building when I saw a hushed crowd gathered in the squadron orderly room. They were staring at a portable TV which was showing scenes of the first air attacks on Baghdad. The President had given the final go-ahead for Operation Desert Storm, and our fellow Air Force members were risking their lives over Iraq. Suddenly our worries about too much snow on the roof seemed insignificant.

There were two reasons my squadron didn't get called to Iraq: geography and politics. When I first got stationed in Alaska we were part of the Alaskan Air Command, providing "top cover for America" by guarding against Soviet bombers flying over the pole. With the fall of the Soviet Union that threat was gone, so the Alaskan Air Command was dissolved and we were assigned to the Pacific Air Force (PACAF). One of the biggest threats facing PACAF was North Korea, with their unpredictable President for Life Kim Il Sung. Kim refused to sign a peace treaty with South Korea at the end of the Korean War, and he had a huge army poised to roll south on a moment's notice. Many strategic experts were concerned that if the US stripped forces from the Pacific and sent them to Iraq, Kim would take advantage of the situation and launch his invasion. The US decided to keep its Pacific forces intact during Desert Storm, just so Kim wouldn't get any rash ideas. So, while other servicemen were risking their lives in the desert heat, I was freezing my ass in Alaska.

This realignment was also responsible for my next assignment. The Pacific Air Force was headquartered in Hawaii, and they suddenly found themselves responsible for operations in Alaska. No one on their staff had any arctic experience. One day after checking on several crews who were shoveling snow off roofs I went back to my office to thaw out and get a little paperwork done. The temperature was hovering around -30 °F. Not extraordinarily cold by Alaskan standards, but still on the chilly side. The phone rang, and it was a colonel at HQ PACAF. "How'd you like to move to Honolulu?" he asked. As I recall, I gave a favorable reply. Betsy's reaction was a little less restrained. "Is there a toll free number I could call to beg?" she asked.

We faced one unexpected hurdle before our orders could be finalized. Hawaii was considered an overseas assignment, and the Air Force recognized the fact that overseas assignments sometimes placed extra strains on family relationships. Ever concerned about the mental health of its families, Betsy and I had to be interviewed by the base psychiatrist to make certain our marriage could withstand the rigors of an overseas assignment. Betsy was incredulous. "Do you mean" she asked the psychiatrist, "that if our marriage isn't strong enough to take the strain of sitting under a palm tree on a tropical beach, you're going to keep us in this Godforsaken deep freeze?" I don't think Betsy enjoyed Alaska as much as I did.

As always, moving meant car hassles but they weren't the kind of hassles I'd had on every other move. I'd put those "hassles" in storage before we moved to Alaska. We did, however, have two cars in Alaska, and the Air Force would only move one to Hawaii. The question was, which one? Initially, it seemed like the Jeep would be the obvious choice. It was much newer than the Olds, and in better shape. On the other hand, it didn't have air conditioning. For my entire life I'd gotten along fine without air conditioning, but not cooped up in a "tintop" car on a tropical island. Besides, if we moved the Jeep it wouldn't be "my" car. It would be the family car. I couldn't really expect Betsy to strap two little kids into a sweatbox every time we needed groceries. The Olds had air conditioning, but it also had close to 100,000 miles on it. It's really amazing how much more durable cars have become. When people say "they don't build them like they used to" they're right, but not in the way they think. It used to be unusual for a car to make it to 100,000 miles. Few cars survived past the 10 year point. (And I bought most of the ones that did.) There didn't seem to be much point to having the Air Force ship the Olds to Hawaii, only to have it die once it got there. Faced with the dilemma of which car to ship, we changed the ground rules. OK, we cheated. For the first time in my life, I bought a new car. Technically it was Betsy's car. My record was still unblemished, but in any event we bought a brand new 1991 Ford Taurus. We drove that for our last few months in Alaska and then shipped it to Hawaii, where it was one of the few cars on the island with a block heater and a battery blanket.

The long-awaited Alaskan spring was changing to a short but glorious arctic summer when we left Alaska. Our Taurus was on its way to Hawaii, so we drove a rental car down the 23 mile stretch of the Richardson Highway that separated the air base from Fairbanks. We were catching the "redeye," the late night flight to the lower 48, though at that time of the year there really wasn't much difference between day and night. Alaska had truly been an interesting assignment. We would spend a few weeks leave in Michigan before flying to Hawaii. A tropical assignment sounded marvelous, but there was still a touch of sorrow as we said good-bye to the land of the midnight sun.

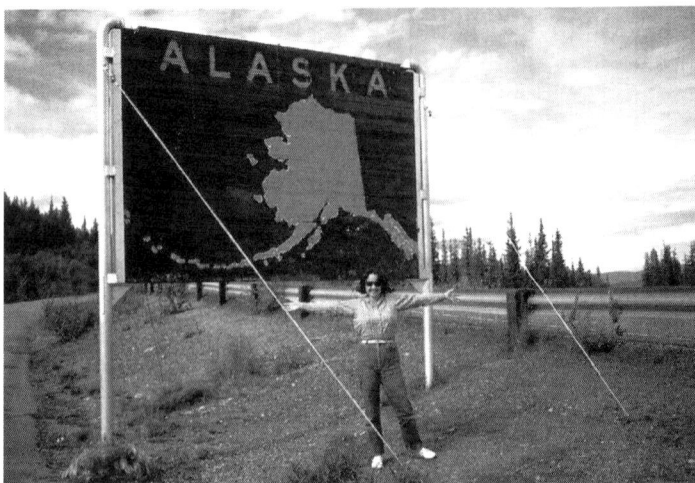

Alaska!

280

Chapter 23 – Home Before Dark

It was a warm summer day. I sat behind the massive wood-rimmed steering wheel of my newly purchased MG TC and listened to the engine ticking over ahead of me. I drank deeply of the fresh country air flowing off the corn fields, and scanned the saucer-sized gauges to make certain that all was well. Except all was not well. And the engine wasn't ticking over, it was simply ticking. That peculiar "tick. . . tick. . .tick" noise that a hot engine makes when it refuses to run and is slowly cooling off. And the fresh country air was filled with the pungent aroma of petrol, thanks to a guy filling his pickup truck at a nearby pump. And the weather had long since changed from "warm summer day" to "stinking hot." This was the third time that day that my fuel pump had died.

The day had begun pleasantly enough. After the previous owner gave me a quick rundown on the things he thought I should know about the car I gave him some cash and he signed the title over to me. Then I headed north out of Dayton Ohio, bound for our cottage in Michigan. Betsy and the kids were following in the Buick. It seemed silly to buy a car just so we could put it into storage, but we realized the car wasn't going to be available forever so we used a few of our precious vacation days between Alaska and Hawaii to drive to Ohio and buy the TC. The TC hadn't been on a long road trip for many, many years, but it stormed out of Dayton in great style. After driving for the better part of an hour I was beginning to relax and enjoy the sensation of driving a true vintage sports car. Then I smelled wood smoke. Since this was definitely not the time of year for people to be burning logs in a fireplace, I had a pretty good idea what the problem was. I pulled off to the side of the road and peered under the car. Sure enough, the exhaust system was touching the floorboards and the floorboards were beginning to char. Fortunately I had stowed a gallon of water behind the seat. I brought it in case the radiator overheated, but it worked just as well to soak the floorboards. Throughout the rest of the trip I would re-soak them periodically, just to keep the flames at bay.

Having successfully dealt with the burning floorboards I hopped back into the car, turned the key and. . . nothing. Turning the key should have activated the fuel pump, which would have given a reassuring "tick, tick, tick" as it pumped up pressure. When it stopped ticking, it would have been time to hit the starter. Since it wasn't ticking, it wasn't pumping. This meant I had no fuel going to the carburetors so there was no point in even trying the starter. With a sigh I grabbed my tool box from behind the seat, threw open the hood, and began working on the fuel pump.

SU fuel pumps have a reputation for never wearing out completely, but always needing to be fussed with. The most common problem is that there is a set of electrical contact points inside them that eventually burn up and don't make good contact. Sometimes you can file the burned part off the points and get it going again, at least for a little while. The good news was that the TC fuel pump was up front, under the hood, where it was easy to get to, not lurking beside the right rear wheel where MG fuel pumps usually live. So it was relatively easy for me to file the points. Unfortunately, that didn't fix it. So the next step was to remove the pump and disassemble it by the side of the road, being careful not to lose any of the eleven "spherical edged" spacing washers which for some mysterious reason lived underneath the diaphragm. Once it was disassembled, I could adjust something the owner's manual called the "contact breaker throw-over." It took me a little while to figure out how to set that (there really didn't seem to be anything wrong with the existing setting) but once I'd finished the pump eagerly chattered back to life. Flushed with the satisfaction of a successful repair, I closed the hood, tossed the toolbox behind the seat, and happily continued on my way.

About an hour later Betsy flashed her lights as we approached a gas station. Neither of us needed gas, but the kids needed a potty break and a soda. That only took a few minutes, then I hopped back into the MG, turned the key and. . . nothing. Had I not set the throw-over correctly? Reluctantly I got out my tool box and again disassembled the pump. The job went a little faster this time, as I was now an experienced fuel pump repairman, but I still didn't find anything wrong with it. As near as I could tell, the throw-over was set correctly, as was every other adjustment the manual mentioned. I put the pump back together and was a little surprised that it sprang to life as soon as I turned the key.

Now it was mid-afternoon, and the pump had died for the third time. This time I had stopped to fill the TC with gas, after which the pump refused to run. I pushed the car away from the pump and into a nearby parking spot. At least the TC pushed easily. For some reason, MG had never seen fit to highlight that attribute in their advertising. ("The best car you'll ever push!" would have been an appropriate company motto.) I opened the hood and began to fiddle with the fuel pump. Everything looked fine. Did I need to disassemble it yet again to adjust the throw-over? That hardly seemed likely, since I hadn't found anything wrong the first two times I'd disassembled it. I mentally reviewed the symptoms. It died when I turned the car off because the floorboards caught fire. I spent about a half-hour fiddling with it, and then it worked again. I hadn't found any problems with it. Then it died when I turned the car off so the kids could go potty. This time it only took me about twenty minutes to fiddle with it. I didn't find any problems that time either, but it started back up. I turned off the car when we stopped for lunch, but the pump started afterward with no problems. Of course, while we were eating lunch the car had cooled off. Then I drove for a couple of hours, stopped to get gas, and now it wouldn't start. Maybe my repairs hadn't fixed anything. Maybe the damn thing just got hot when I stopped the car and it needed time to cool off.

I walked over to the passenger door of the Buick and Betsy rolled down the window. I could feel an icy, air-conditioned breeze tumble out through the opening.

"What's wrong?" she asked.

"I think the fuel pump gets hot when I turn the car off. I think if we just wait a while it will start back up."

"You mean we scrimped and saved for three years to buy a car that needs to rest every time you turn it off?" She looked at me with suspicion.

"Look on the bright side," I suggested. "It encourages us to relax and take time to enjoy our surroundings. Like now, for example. Why don't we walk across the street and see what's in that antique store? Maybe they've got something really cool!"

Betsy gave me a look that made it clear she wasn't buying any of this, but she turned off the Buick. "Come on kids," she said. "Let's go wander through that antique shop." Betsy has many virtues, but patience is not always one of them.

We didn't find anything in the antique store that we couldn't live without, but by the time we finished the TC started right up. With a full tank of gas, I shouldn't have to stop for a long time. The miles flew by quickly now, and the late afternoon shadows began to shade the road. We were driving through what passes for hill country in northern Indiana. The hot summer day was now softening into a warm summer evening. It was a beautiful time for a drive. The road wound between cornfields and farmyards, now descending into a forested valley beside a small stream, now cresting a hill overlooking lush green fields. The road was lined on both sides by maple trees. Every now and then the leafy treetops met over the center of the road and we drove through a green archway. From the right-hand driver's seat I looked at the world over a long stretch of hood that ended in a chrome radiator shell flanked by twin chrome headlights. The trees beside the road were reflected in the headlights. I was thinking about how lucky I was to own a car like this when I heard the unmistakable "tink" of something metal hitting the pavement. Betsy immediately started honking her horn and flashing her lights behind me. I pulled onto the shoulder and walked back along the road until I found a strangely shaped piece of metal lying on the pavement.

It was a heavy metal rod with two right angle bends. I felt like an archaeologist examining a bone he's just unearthed. The materials and workmanship looked correct for a car of the TC's vintage, and the fresh scratches from the pavement made me pretty certain this item had just fallen off my car. I didn't have a clue what it was, though. It wasn't oily so I didn't think it came from the engine. There was a thin layer of heavy black grease on it. That would be consistent with a suspension part. It sort of looked like a suspension part too, but I didn't know what part it might be. More importantly, was it a critical part? I walked back to the TC and began inspecting the suspension very carefully. Eventually I found a part that looked just like it on the left front – a link that connected the shock absorber to the front axle. I checked the right front, and sure enough there was no corresponding link on that side. There were, however, holes in the shock absorber and the axle where this part had once resided. Amazingly, it appeared that this link just pressed into rubber bushings and was held in place by friction. I struggled for a few minutes to push it back into place, and then decided maybe I'd underestimated the value of friction. This was clearly a job that required tools I didn't have with me, but fortunately this part wasn't critical to the operation of the car. The handling wouldn't be the absolute apex with nothing connecting the shock absorber to the right front wheel, but the car would drive and steer OK without it. I tossed the part onto the passenger's floor and walked back to the Buick to tell Betsy the good news.

"It's just a shock link" I announced. "Nothing critical. The car will run fine without it."

Betsy eyed me suspiciously. "If the car runs fine without it, why did they put it on in the first place?"

"To help fight unemployment?" I suggested. Betsy wasn't entirely satisfied with that answer, but she let it ride. The rest of the trip passed without incident. I pulled the TC into the garage at the lake just as the gathering dusk was about to require headlights. Home before dark. The goal of every British sports car driver. In the years to come I would have many opportunities to reach for the giant "Off – Side – Head" light switch in the center of the TC dash, but on this trip I had made it safely home without needing the lights. It was a satisfying end to a memorable drive in a wonderful car, and as good a place as any to bring this story to a close.

Not that this was the end of my car adventures, of course. I eventually fixed the fuel pump, but in the years to come the TC's starter would fall off, taking pieces of the block and the transmission with it. And the differential would break. Twice. And a stub axle would break, allowing my left front wheel to chart its own course, independent of the trajectory the rest of the car followed.

Broken TC

285

While we were in Hawaii I bought a 1971 MGB. It was a terrific car for a tropical island and it's provided good, dependable transportation ever since (with a few minor exceptions), but let's face it. A '71 MGB is hardly a car to write a book about. It's practically brand new. It has a day/night mirror, radial tires, and an AM/FM radio. What more could one ask for in the way of modern conveniences?

Writing this book has given me new insight into myself and others. Among other things, I discovered that different people remember things differently. The drive home in the TC provides a perfect example. I remember it as a beautiful drive through the country, and a chance to bond with a terrific car that needed only minor tinkering to become roadworthy after years of idleness. Betsy remembers it as the road trip from hell, when my car caught fire, broke down at every gas station, and rained parts onto the highway.

Writing has also caused me to stop and think about why I like working on my cars. Partly I just like doing things with my hands. It gives me a sense of accomplishment to tear into something that was made more than half a century ago, figure out how it's supposed to work, figure out why it's not working now, and make it right. In some ways it's almost like a form of archaeology. You get a sense of the engineering that went into it, why people designed it the way they did, and how they made use of the materials and technology available to them at the time. That's probably why I prefer rebuilding existing parts to buying new parts whenever possible. I also like to rebuild cars to stock specifications, or to use period-correct accessories. I have no interest in modifying cars with new engines, air conditioning, and other modern accessories. At times I may be forced to use MGB parts on my MGA or to make reversible updates to improve safety and reliability, but I try to keep those modifications to a minimum. I also tend to view old cars as being historically significant, almost like an endangered species, and I like to preserve them. I know the "hot rods" of the 50's are of historical significance too, but you have to remember that the people who built those souped up Model T's and Model A's were modifying cars that were 20 or 30 years old at the time. They were commonplace cars back then, not historical artifacts. They were headed for the scrap heap until someone "rescued" them to turn them into a hot rod. It would be the equivalent of someone today modifying a 1980's Ford Taurus or a 1990's Honda. In my mind, cutting up a Model A today to drop in a modern V-8 engine is an entirely different proposition. That's like hunting an endangered species. It's not the hunting itself that I'm opposed to, it's what gets destroyed in the process.

It's also interesting to me that, as much as I enjoy fooling around with cars, they don't seem to be an integral part of my self-esteem, the way they are for some people. Or maybe I just have different tastes. I'd rather drive a battered MG than a brand-new Lexus just because to me the MG is more fun, regardless of what kind of a social statement it makes. I get amused when people look at a beat-up car and say "I wouldn't be caught dead in a car like that." I've driven many cars in my day that I'm sure those people wouldn't be caught dead in, and it never bothered me. (Looking back, I'm probably very lucky that I wasn't caught dead in a few of them, although I've always been careful to keep the brakes, steering, and other critical safety items were in good working order.)

While writing this book I've had a lot of fun remembering the cars I've owned over the years, but more than that, I've had a lot of fun remembering the people who were associated with those cars. People are much more memorable than cars. I've lost touch with some of the people in this book, but most are still good friends. I haven't heard from Chris in years. He worked as an aircraft mechanic for a while, then as a truck driver, and when last I heard he was doing missionary work. He had a 1961 Jaguar convertible, but he was looking for a 61 coupe, like his Dad's. I've also lost touch with Al. He did a stint in the Navy and when last I heard he was driving a truck. He'd sold his Model A, but bought a much more desirable Model 810 Cord.

I still see Cory every few years at high school reunions. He's a successful entrepreneur in California, married, and living a life style that's far removed from the farm commune. On the other hand, every once in a while he'll get that look in his eye that makes you realize he's still fully capable of doing something outlandish, like buying a DUKW. Marianne Kressler also lives in California, where she works as an actress, artist, and writer. I lost touch with her for many years, but we met again at our 40'th high school reunion and we now keep in touch by e-mail.

I keep in sporadic touch with Nick, who now lives in South Carolina. He rolled his Fiat Abarth in a racing accident years ago, but the last time I asked him about it he still had it in storage and was intending to rebuild it. He'd also acquired an extremely rare Bandini race car from the 1950's that he was trying to restore for vintage racing. I keep in closer touch with Viktor, who now lives in Chicago. He sold his Model A truck and his MG TC years ago, but he replaced them with a Model T touring car, an MG Midget, and a Triumph TR-4. He has also acquired a Stearman Biplane, which puts all my cars to shame. Then, roughly 30 years after he sold it, he bought his MG TC back from the guy he'd sold it to. That guy had restored it but, not surprisingly, not to Viktor's standards. Viktor immediately ripped it apart and is in the process of rebuilding it the way he wants it.

Sadly, Luis Riccotto died a few years ago while vacationing in Florida. Leto just died recently. Their son Mario, who is the spitting image of Luis, now runs the shop. They no longer sell new MGs, of course, but they still service an occasional MG and Mario races an MG Midget. They also still service Triumphs, Fiats, Renaults, and once in a while an American Motors vehicle – all cars which they once sold new. They lost the Jaguar distributorship when Jaguar was bought by Ford, but Mario built a flourishing business as a Chrysler/Jeep dealer. Then, when Chrysler went into bankruptcy, they lost their franchise as part of the reorganization. Almost exactly 50 years after Luis became the youngest new car dealer in the state of Indiana, Riccotto and Sons was left without a new car to sell. Mario is actively working to pick up a new line of cars, and I have the utmost confidence that he will succeed.

Andy, Don, and I are still good friends and we get together every summer. Don and Desiree still live in Lafayette, and Don's fleet of cars is almost as out of control as mine. In addition to an indeterminate number of Saabs, he has a Model T Ford, an MGB, a TR-6, and a VW Microbus. Like me, Don has no problem driving cars other people wouldn't be caught dead in. When "Car Talk" published their list of the worst 10 cars of the last millennium, Don was proud of the fact that he'd owned 3 of the 10 winners, but he was surprised that none of his Fiat's made the list. (My Pinto was the only car I'd owned that made the list.)

My son is in college. He has earned his private pilot's license, and hopes someday to become a commercial pilot. He loves driving the Model A (I went out of my way to make certain that was the first car each of my kids ever drove, just because I thought that would make a good story for them to tell to their kids) and he drove my MGA all through high school. Automotive-wise he crossed over to the dark side and is infatuated with the muscle cars which I thought were silly when I was in high school, but even I have to admit his 1968 Mustang is pretty cool.

My older daughter drives a 1971 MGB which we rebuilt together. It's just a coincidence that it happens to be the same year as my MGB, but that's a coincidence that sometimes confuses our insurance company. I'm sure it's not very often that they get a call from a customer who wants to make a change to his policy, and when they look up the policy they have to ask "Which 1971 MGB are you talking about?"

Me working on my first car (left) and my daughter working on her first car. (right) Some people say there's a family resemblance.

Betsy and I were blessed with another daughter after we left Alaska. Not surprisingly, she is interested in cars too. After all, she is growing up amidst a fleet of old cars that her father and her older siblings are constantly working on. (Betsy sometimes bewails the fact that all of her children share "the car gene." "Couldn't I have had at least had one normal kid?" she moans?) When my daughter was two years old and just beginning to understand the concept of Santa Claus she asked Santa to bring her "A pink MG and a buzzard." He granted her wish, although admittedly the MG was a matchbox toy car and the buzzard was a beanie-baby stuffed animal. As she grew older her tastes became a little more refined, and she's currently nuts about Ferraris. She's not old enough to drive yet, which is just as well because her father is not about to buy her a

Ferrari. Not even an old, beat-up model. (Is there such a thing as a beat-up Ferrari?)

As for me, I still enjoy driving my cars. The three MGs pretty much fill our garage, so I have to keep the Model A and the Jaguar in storage near our cottage in Michigan. I get them out and drive them every year when I'm up there on vacation. The rest of the year I drive the MGs. We now live in Georgia, which has sports car weather almost year round. The TC makes a great summer car, as with the windshield folded flat I get plenty of air to stay cool even during a hot Georgia summer. I use the MGB when the weather is unsettled, summer or winter, as I must admit I appreciate the value of roll-up windows when the weather turns nasty. If the weather is really nasty I have a 14-year old Toyota van which makes an even better rain car, but it ranks pretty close to zero on the fun meter. The MGA is in the middle of a frame-up restoration. A drunk in an SUV started that project for me when, for reasons that only make sense to a drunk, he threw his car into reverse and shot backwards into the MGA at a stoplight. My son was driving the MGA at the time and I thank God he wasn't injured. As much fun as old cars are, they have none of the safety features which have dramatically improved the crashworthiness of modern cars. Good maintenance and defensive driving can reduce the risk of getting into an accident, but there's no way to eliminate the danger posed by idiots (and drunks) behind the wheel of the two and three-ton behemoths that fill today's highways.

As much as I enjoy driving my MGs, I do feel a sense of restlessness. It seems like it's been years since I've had a true automotive adventure. I recently took up golf as a hobby, and I realize that's probably a sign than I'm not getting my minimum daily requirement of frustration. I play with 80 year old hickory shafted clubs, but even that doesn't fully fill the void left by a lack of broken axles and flaming floorboards. I think it's time for something new. I think maybe it's time to buy a Stanley.

Happy Motoring!

Illustrations and Credits

Note: The illustrations in this printed book are black and white. Full color illustrations may be seen at www.random-writings.com.

Stanley "Gentleman's Speedy Roadster"   Jeff Theobald www.steamcar.net

1941 Buick Coupe   excard1970 on Flickr.com

Chief Pontiac Hood Ornament   Carl@TrainWeb.com

Jaguar E-Type Coupe   www.borrani.co.uk/

Jaguar E-Type Engine   www.fotos247.com

First Love – My 1928 Model A Ford   Author's collection

Don with the Thompson   Author's collection

Snow-covered Model A   Author's collection

Don and Andy with the "A"   Author's collection

Canoe Camping with Dad   Author's collection

Viktor's 1949 MG TC   Author's collection

1929 Duesenberg Town Car   Owls Head Transportation Museum www.ohtm.org

Triumph Herald   Photo Courtesy of WendyLou

New Love - A 1957 MGA   Author's collection

MGA From Above   Author's collection

The MG Mechanics   Author's collection

Senior Beard   Author's collection

A World War II DUKW   US Government Photo

Delivering a Blood Chest   Author's collection

Scuderia Banca Rotta   Author's collection

Don's Bumper   Author's collection

XK-150 Drop Head Coupe   www.heritageclassics.com

New Cars on the Lot at Riccotto's   Author's collection

The TR-3 next to Don's MGB   Author's collection

About the Author

Steve Tom has published many technical articles in engineering journals and is a contributing author to several books on energy and controls. Of more interest to general readers, he has published articles, humor, and short stories in publications such as *British Motoring, Stymie, The Steam Car,* and *A Wee Nip.* Many of his stories are available at www.random-writings.com. This is his first non-technical book. He is a registered Professional Engineer and has a PhD in Mechanical Engineering from Purdue University. He lives with his wife and three children near Atlanta GA, where he drives old cars, annoys his family by playing ancient records on wind-up phonographs, and flails at golf balls with hickory-shafted clubs.

.

13153910R00167

Printed in Great Britain
by Amazon.co.uk, Ltd.,
Marston Gate.